# African Socialism

HOOVER INSTITUTION PUBLICATIONS

# African Socialism

*Edited by*

William H. Friedland

Carl G. Rosberg, Jr.

*Published for the*
Hoover Institution on War, Revolution, and Peace
*by Stanford University Press, Stanford, California*

The Hoover Institution on War, Revolution, and Peace,
founded at Stanford University in 1919 by Herbert
Hoover, is a center for advanced study and research on
public and international affairs in the twentieth century.
The views expressed in its publications are entirely
those of the authors and do not necessarily reflect the views of the Hoover Institution.

Stanford University Press
Stanford, California
© 1964 by the Board of Trustees of the
Leland Stanford Junior University
Printed in the United States of America
Original edition 1964
Reprinted 1965

# Preface

African Socialism is a doctrine of growing significance. To increasing numbers of African political leaders, African Socialism is viewed as a communicable ideology which gives a perspective for the exigencies of present rapid development and change in society. It is not a unitary doctrine; neither is it totally amorphous. This volume concentrates on an examination of the similarities or common themes in African Socialism. It seeks to understand the meaning of the current intellectual trends in Africa as well as particular processes of development as means are sought to translate socialist ideologies into action.

African Socialism represents a broad field for students of social and ideological change, and provides an opportunity to study why and how ideas are generated. Social scientists have long been interested in the history and social function of ideas. Ever since Marx argued that ideas represented the justification and rationalization by economic groups of their position in society, a major dilemma has been posed for social scientists. The classic studies by Weber (*The Protestant Ethic and the Spirit of Capitalism*) and Tawney (*Religion and the Rise of Capitalism*) display this unresolved conflict.

Whether ideas are shaped by economic and social interests or vice versa, the study of African Socialism specifically permits the analysis of the effect of ideas upon action. Africa is undergoing a vast process of modernization, and if this process is not as rapid as some would desire, new and modern institutions are nevertheless developing with considerable speed. In these circumstances the study of ideas and their impact on the development of modern institutions is extremely valuable. It may well be that African Socialism, like ideologies the world over, contains a large element of pure rhetoric, and that Africa's leaders, like other politicians, use the ideology to justify their authority and mobilize their people. However, the impact of this ideology upon the people should not be underestimated.

Accordingly, the study of African Socialism presents the opportunity for social scientists to examine the interplay of ideas and action, and in this respect it goes far beyond the parochial concerns of the continent.

This volume should be regarded as exploratory: the newness and freshness of African Socialism, the lack of definition of the ideology, the considerable pragmatism of African leaders and thinkers, all contribute to making specific definitions of African Socialism difficult. Nevertheless, we feel that the proliferation of the ideology of African Socialism has been so significant in the past five years that an attempt must be made to define its parameters. This volume represents the first multi-disciplinary approach to such a definition.

We wish to acknowledge and express our appreciation for the assistance we have received from the New York State School of Industrial and Labor Relations, Cornell University, and the Institute of International Studies, University of California, Berkeley. Naturally, none of these institutions is in any way responsible for the views or judgments expressed in this symposium.

A symposium of this nature is a major operation involving the activities of a great many people. We have placed many demands upon our contributors during the preparation of this book, and we would like to express our thanks to them for bearing with us with fortitude. Naturally, the responsibility for the views and opinions which appear in the individual chapters is that of their authors. We are grateful to President Nyerere, President Nkrumah, President Senghor, and the Honorable Tom Mboya, and to the journals *Transition, Pan Africa,* and *West Africa* for permission to reprint their statements on African Socialism. We would like especially to extend our thanks to Mrs. Dorothy Padmore for permission to use the material prepared by the late George Padmore.

We would also like to acknowledge editorial and bibliographical assistance rendered by Mr. David Boesel, Mr. Charles S. Green III, and Miss Audrey Wipper. Mrs. Ann Albertsman spent a great deal of time in the past year in typing manuscripts.

Finally, we are particularly grateful to Dr. Peter Duignan of the Hoover Institution and Mr. J. G. Bell of the Stanford University Press for their encouragement, patience, and guidance.

W. H. F.

C. G. R.

# Contents

## Part I

# Definition and Exploration

## Part II

# National Programs

# Appendixes

# Contributors

CHARLES F. ANDRAIN is a doctoral candidate in political science at the University of California, Berkeley. He has held a National Defense Education Act fellowship in African Studies, 1960–63. His publications include "The Pan-African Movement," *Phylon*, Spring/1962; "A Scale Analysis of Senators' Attitudes toward Civil Rights," *The Western Political Quarterly*, forthcoming 1964.

FRED G. BURKE is Professor of Political Science and Chairman of the Program of East African Studies at Syracuse University. He has completed two lengthy research periods in Uganda and Tanganyika. In addition to numerous publications in various journals, he is author of *Africa's Quest for Order* and *Local Government and Politics in Uganda: Grass Roots to Nation Building*.

WILLIAM H. FRIEDLAND is Associate Professor, New York State School of Industrial and Labor Relations, Cornell University. Author of *Unions and Industrial Relations in Underdeveloped Areas,* he is a sociologist currently conducting research on social change and is completing a study of trade unions in Tanganyika conducted under a Ford Foundation fellowship.

KENNETH W. GRUNDY is Assistant Professor of Political Science at San Fernando Valley State College in California. From 1959 to 1962 he was a National Defense Education Act Fellow at the Pennsylvania State University, where he received the Doctor of Philosophy degree in 1963. He has published articles dealing with African politics in the *International Journal* and *World Politics*.

IGOR KOPYTOFF is Assistant Professor of Anthropology at the University of Pennsylvania. His main interest is cultural anthropology, with emphasis on ethnographic analysis and African ethnology. In 1958 and 1959, he spent twenty months in southwestern Congo (Leopoldville) doing ethnographic research among the Suku, under a Ford Foundation fellowship. He has contributed articles to several journals and volumes.

COLIN LEGUM is the African and Commonwealth correspondent of *The Observer* in London. Born in South Africa, he has served as editor of a labor paper, the newspaper of the South African Mineworkers' Union, and the bulletin of the South African Labour Party. He has also been leader of the Labour Party majority in the Johannesburg City Council. He is author of *Must We Lose Africa?; Bandung, Cairo and Accra; Congo Disaster;* and *Pan-Africanism: A Short History.* He has edited *African Handbook* and the volume by Patrice Lumumba, *Congo My Country.*

CHANDLER MORSE is Professor of Economics at Cornell University. He led a survey mission to Britain's High Commission Territories, which produced the volume *Basutoland, Bechuanaland Protectorate, and Swaziland: Report of an Economic Survey Mission.* He is co-author with H. J. Barnett of *Scarcity and Growth: The Economics of Natural Resources Availability* and has contributed to various economic journals. Professor Morse devoted the past academic year to research in economic development in Africa and visited Tanganyika, Nigeria, Ghana, Guinea, Senegal, and Mali.

DOROTHY NELKIN is a Research Associate at the New York State School of Industrial and Labor Relations, Cornell University. She is currently undertaking research in the modernization process in developing countries.

I. I. POTEKHIN is Director of the African Institute of the Academy of Sciences of the USSR and a leading Soviet Africanist. He has traveled widely in Africa and published extensively in Russian on Africa. Many of his publications have been translated into German, French, and English. Professor Potekhin was active in the creation of the International Congress of Africanists and is a member of its Permanent Council. In 1962 he discussed African studies in the Soviet Union at the annual meeting of the African Studies Association of the United States.

MARGARET ROBERTS is Secretary of the Commonwealth Bureau of the Fabian Society. She is also editor of the monthly journal *Venture* and, in private life, Mrs. Colin Legum. She has lectured in economics and politics at Rhodes University and conducted research on farm labor in South Africa. She contributed the chapter "Africa's Divided Workers" to her husband's volume *Pan-Africanism,* and her article "Trade Unions in Africa" was published in *The World Today* (Royal Institute of International Affairs, 1961).

CARL G. ROSBERG, JR., is Associate Professor of Political Science and Chairman of the Committee for African Studies of the Institute of International Studies at the University of California, Berkeley. His main professional interest is in comparative politics, with a special concern with African political studies. His publications include *Africa and the World Today* and, as co-author, *The Kenyatta Election: Kenya 1960–61* and *An East African Federation*.

ARISTIDE R. ZOLBERG, Assistant Professor of Political Science, is a member of the Committee for the Comparative Study of New Nations and of the Committee on African Studies at the University of Chicago. His major interest is in comparative politics and political sociology, with a special interest in French-speaking Africa. His publications include *One-Party Government in the Ivory Coast* and contributions to journals in the United States, France, and Great Britain.

# African Socialism

Introduction

# The Anatomy of African Socialism

William H. Friedland and Carl G. Rosberg, Jr.

The present decade has seen the mushrooming of a new doctrine, largely unknown only five years ago, which African leaders call "African Socialism."* The expansion of writings on this subject surely marks one of the most rapid developments of an ideological orientation in recent times. The speeches of a great many of Africa's political leaders, their articles, their books, and in many cases their programs of economic development, have contributed to the development of African Socialism. Indeed, the growth of African Socialism has been so marked that the African nations, at the invitation of the Senegalese government, gathered in Dakar in December 1962 to examine its character.

As will be shown in succeeding chapters, there was a marked failure by Africans themselves at the Dakar conference and elsewhere to present a precise definition of African Socialism. This was to be expected, considering the youthfulness of the ideology of African Socialism. While time has not permitted the formulation of a coherent ideological orientation, African Socialism, in contrast to most other movements of socialism, has not been the product of a single thinker. The history of socialist thought is marked by clear relationships between individual thinkers and the ideological movements to which they gave birth. African Socialism differs in that no single leader has been distinctively and uniquely associated with the ideology. Rather, the ideology of African Socialism has been the product of diverse leaders operating within a variety of exigencies in their own countries, which helps to account for the lack of development of a unified theory.

## Search for Definition

For those students who look for a hard, residual core in African Socialism, the search is difficult and somewhat frustrating. Years ago,

---

* A note on style: We shall distinguish between African Socialism and other forms of socialism by capitalizing the former and using lower-case type for the latter.

in quite a different context, Philip Selznick characterized the situation within which the Tennessee Valley Authority was created as one of "unanalyzed abstractions."[1] He argued essentially that TVA was organized in response to generalized political and social needs. In the process, only the most general guidelines were laid down in the form of legislation. For those placed in charge of TVA, these guidelines were only "unanalyzed abstractions" that had to find concrete meaning in day-to-day behavior.

In a sense, African Socialism represents much the same kind of "unanalyzed abstractions," except that the relative concreteness of legislative language is not present. Though African Socialism is neither a precise ideology nor a specific guide to action, it is nonetheless a set of dimensions to which Africans will give specific content as they work out their problems on a day-to-day basis. Just as the administrators who directed TVA worked out a "grass roots" ideology which contrasted sharply with the general orientations of the New Deal, so African leaders seek to develop an ideology that will support their long-range generalized goals.

This does not mean that as Africans add content to the dimensions of African Socialism they are engaged in some sort of ideological deception. African Socialism must be seen in its proper context as an attempt to find an ideology that will satisfy the often divergent needs of the times. In this respect, a great deal of experimentation is taking place as the new nations of Africa pass through different stages of development and as ideology is shaped to meet different situational demands. At first the ideology tends to be a highly flexible, amorphous set of ideas that fails to meet the criteria of sophisticated thinking, but in time it will probably crystallize as consensus is reached upon a general direction and the theoreticians have time to systematize its tenets. The many tendencies that exist today in African Socialism make it appear as a potpourri of ideas having little coherence. However, it must be seen in the light of an ideology struggling to meet a vast and formidable range of problems. In time, as some tendencies prove more viable than others, their acceptance, and the discarding of the nonsuccessful, will give to the ideology a clearer direction.

### African Socialists

Not all of Africa's leaders regard themselves as "socialist." While African Socialism is currently popular among most of the politicians, a great many of them abhor and avoid the term. Just as Nkrumah, Senghor, Touré, and Nyerere are African Socialists of conviction, Houphouët-Boigny of the Ivory Coast, Tubman of Liberia, and M'ba of Gabon ignore the concept. Similarly, while His Imperial Majesty, Emperor Haile Selassie of Ethiopia, is not what one would consider an active socialist, it is interesting to note that his country was represented at the Dakar colloquium on African Socialism. Thus, there are important distinctions between those leaders who consider themselves to be African Socialists and those who do not.

As important as the previous distinction are the differences to be noted among those leaders who consider themselves to be African Socialists. An examination of the approaches of various leaders indicates just how significant these are. Chapter 9 in the present volume illustrates the difference in orientation between the Senegalese socialists—Senghor and Dia—and the Guinean—Sékou Touré. Similarly, a comparison of Nyerere and Nkrumah indicates sharply varying interests.

And just as there are differences in language, there are differences in primary goals. Nyerere's socialism, which stresses projects that operate mainly at the village level for community development, has been a major preoccupation in Tanganyika. Although community development has not been ignored by Nkrumah, much heavier emphasis has been laid in Ghana on the creation of modern economic institutions in which the state plays a pre-eminent role.

Even though there are differences between the socialists and the nonsocialists on the one hand, and between the different socialists on the other, it is important to note that there are significant similarities. President Tubman of Liberia may shun the word "socialist," but the fact is that Liberian economic development is similar to that of Guinea, an avowedly socialist country. As the late D. K. Chisiza pointed out in his perceptive *Africa—What Lies Ahead,*[2] a pragmatic pattern of development will probably be followed by most African nations. This will entail substantial involvement by the state in economic activities, and thus all African nations, whether avowedly "socialist" or "capitalist," will follow a basic pattern. This point, emphasized in Chapter 2, should be underlined.

## Themes of African Socialism

Despite the fact that little homogeneity as yet exists in the considerable volume of ideas on African Socialism, at least three main themes may be discerned: (1) the problem of continental identity,

(2) the crisis of economic development, and (3) the dilemmas of control and class formation. In the chapters that follow, these themes will be explored from different perspectives. Here we will seek to summarize some of the main arguments.

*The problem of continental identity.* What immediately strikes the observer of African Socialism is the fact that this doctrine represents a way of differentiating the socialism of Africa from other kinds of socialism. The ideology thus embodies a cluster of ideas through which African leaders are searching for some common identity. Socialists in Africa did not originally regard their position as particularly distinctive: early socialists held the orthodox view that socialism is a doctrine representing the interests of the proletariat against an exploiting bourgeoisie. It did not occur to them that socialism might have a unique African character. But that was soon to change, and the rejection of all things originating from the metropolitan powers resulted in the growth of African Socialism. African Socialism has thus become both a reaction against Europe and a search for a unifying doctrine. In the eyes of African leaders the British Labour Party and the French Socialist Party were compromised by the colonialism of their governments. Understandably, African parties of socialist orientation sought doctrines that would distinguish them from their European counterparts.

In the ferment of nationalist struggle in the 1950's many African leaders found themselves saying identical things in varying ways. Léopold Senghor's *Negritude* and Kwame Nkrumah's *African Personality* are indications of this search for continental identity. It was in these circumstances that an African form of socialism began to emerge. The mythos of an African Socialism developed as political leaders sought a doctrine to replace the outmoded unifying influence of anticolonialism. Anticolonialism had been a powerful force for organizing the African peoples during the pre-independence era. With independence there was the need to find new doctrines that would continue to unify the African population. A number of approaches were attempted, such as nationalism and neocolonialism, but none has been found wholly adequate.

Instead, the form of consciousness that has emerged with enormous significance (albeit with little organizational power for the moment) has been that of *African-ness*. If there is little consciousness of being a Ghanaian, a Togolese, or a Nyasalander, Africans are nonetheless conscious of being African, and it is this sentiment that political leaders have sought to mobilize. Underlying the proliferation of ideas on African Socialism is the formulation of an ideology that stresses the identity of the people of the continent while rejecting the influence of the outside world. As consciousness of Africa has developed, those Africans who were socialists and believed socialism to be a universalistic doctrine found themselves inundated by the growing consciousness of the continent. With the achievement of independence, Africans who had been socialists disappeared, to re-emerge as African Socialists.

Part of the search for identity consists of discovering ostensible roots of African Socialism in indigenous society. This theme is so prevalent that most of our contributors have emphasized it. The essential contention is that Africa has always contained much indigenous socialism. Among the various elements of traditional socialism cited are the communal ownership of land (or the nonownership of land by individuals on a private basis), the egalitarian character of society (or the low degree of stratification), and the extensive network of social obligations that led to considerable cooperation. The existence of these traditional elements is held to represent indigenous socialism. Not only do they represent a set of roots for African Socialists, but it is believed that their existence will facilitate the creation of modern economic institutions on a socialist basis. It is thus held that capitalism is not an appropriate economic form because it is "unnatural" to Africa.

*The crisis of economic development.** One of the most significant features of African Socialism is its identification with economic development. In equating African Socialism with economic development, one important connection is clearly evident, that African economic development will be largely in the public sector. There is, of course, great fluidity in the policies that African governments adopt in undertaking economic growth. Several of the articles in this symposium illustrate the shifts that have taken place in government policies with respect to public and private investment. In spite of this fluidity and the search for private capital, there can be little doubt that the role of African governments in economic development will be far greater than that of earlier industrializers.

In stressing the role of government in "planning," in providing capital, and in guiding the economy, not much encouragement has been given to the growth of a class of African entrepreneurs. Among those espousing African Socialism, African entrepreneurs

---

* We are indebted to Aaron Siegel for a number of points in this section.

tend to be regarded as self-interested rather than as contributors to the general welfare. The growth of an entrepreneurial African class is therefore not looked upon with favor. As will be shown, there appear to be many advantages in permitting and encouraging foreign private investment while inhibiting the development of indigenous capitalists. This facilitates the importation of much-needed capital and at the same time acts to prevent a local group from entrenching itself and developing a degree of economic independence that may have social and political ramifications in the future.

The accumulation of capital is seen, therefore, as being primarily a responsibility of government. On the one hand, governments can encourage the growth of a network of institutions that accumulate capital but are manipulatable by a central authority, as, for example, marketing cooperatives, and people's banks. On the other hand, governments can seek to encourage private investors to enter the economy in a variety of ways. Private investment, however, is not indiscriminately sought. Both African Socialists and nonsocialists encourage private investment from external sources, but the socialists insist upon greater limitations than do the African nonsocialists. The case of Ghana is, perhaps, most illuminating. The Ghanaians foresee a role for private investors in rigorously defined sectors of the economy and, to a considerable extent, in partnership with government. Although this view has not developed as clearly with other African Socialist countries, all envisage considerable control over the areas within which private foreign capital will be welcome, although there is less agreement on partnerships between foreign investors and governments in various activities. Confronted with the inescapable need for external capital resources and technical skills to foster economic development, none of the African Socialists have formulated rigid conditions concerning external assistance.

A major dilemma of African Socialism arises from the dependence of African economies on the export of primary products. Inheriting in many cases monocultural economies linked to external metropolitan consumers, African Socialism is committed to industrialization and to a reduction of this present dependency. However, as long as African countries remain dependent on earnings from exports of primary products for a major share of their development budgets, they will continue to have a vested interest in increasing such exports. Hence, many African Socialists willingly support international commodity agreements and other trade arrangements which help either to bring higher and more stable prices for primary products or to provide new outlets for ever increased production of these exports.

There exists, as well, conflict over the scale of interterritorial markets for products of industrialization and the means of lessening dependency on exports to Europe and elsewhere. Some African Socialists argue that only through the development of African common markets can a real basis be laid for industrialization, while others argue that the growth of these markets will only increase the dependence of the least developed African countries on those that are more developed. This argument continues to be expressed even among members of an established African common market, such as the East African Common Services Organization, comprising Kenya, Uganda, and Tanganyika. Thus African Socialists and nonsocialists may well prefer to carry on development within the context of their own territorial economies. To date, few practical steps have been taken to lessen the dependency of African states on exports of primary commodities. There exists a vague belief that at some future time "economic independence" will be achieved.

To many, African Socialism has come to be no more than a convenient doctrine which helps to explain, rationalize, and justify governmental involvement in the processes of economic growth.

*The dilemmas of control and class formation.* The drive for independence and for economic development following independence has created serious problems of control for the leaders of Africa's new countries. These problems are centered upon the imperative of obtaining the enthusiastic cooperation of the populace for sustained economic activities that will aid the accumulation of capital without creating new imbalances in the distribution of national income.

For the population as a whole, independence has *not* been a revolutionary experience. The colonial governors have gone and parts of the civil service have been replaced by Africans, but many elements of colonialism remain and attitudes developed in the colonial period continue to be expressed. The end of colonialism has not brought a substantial betterment in the conditions of life to the bulk of the population: urban problems of unemployment and low standards of living continue as before. And there is even less change in the rural areas. Thus, the promises of the nationalist leaders have yet to be fulfilled.

In these circumstances, African Socialism is extremely useful, for it stresses the identity of the African people while seeking to mobilize the entire population for economic development. In this context, it represents a unifying doctrine akin to the nationalism of the pre-independence period. Now that European power has been dissolved, the natural tendencies which bifurcate African society begin to assert themselves. Different interest groups are beginning to form. The political leaders see the example of the class-divided metropolitan powers before them. The divisive tendencies, the beginning of social classes, the competition between groups, all represent situations that are dangerous to the continuation of African nationalism.

An examination of the leaders' references to African Socialism shows an emphasis upon this sense of identity and a depreciation of the notion that separate economic classes should or can develop. The problems of class and stratum consciousness and of control are integrally tied to the differential sacrifices that various groups are called upon to make in order to advance economic progress. One additional function of African Socialism is, therefore, to help create an atmosphere of hard work and self-sacrifice on the part of all elements in the population for the larger collectivity, the nation. African Socialist thought is universally marked by the idea of sacrifice for the larger collectivity. This is frequently put in traditional terms; for example, in pre-European times Africans were tied to collectivities such as the extended kinship group, and made sacrifices for these groups. There is currently an attempt to carry forward this experience and to transform the collectivity from the parochial kinship unit to the nation. In this respect, African Socialism is a unifying doctrine which supports, in the economic sphere, the political changes that have taken place.

The ideology of African Socialism differs radically from that of the West. The view of human nature underlying African Socialism rejects the individualistic philosophy of the West. The African Socialist holds a view of human nature which, he believes, rests on the fundamental characteristics of traditional society: classless, communal, and egalitarian. What is common to these characteristics is the concept that only inside a given society can the individual fulfill himself, that the society gives him shape, form, and cohesion. Further, the society takes on a collective animus of intentions, aspirations, and fears, and the failure of any individual to adhere to this animus gives to the society the right of compulsion to force the individual to be free. Unlike the Western majoritarian conception of democracy, the African Socialist rejects the "will of all" or the will of the majority and adopts the language of Rousseau: the "general will," the "will of the people." In fact, many of the leaders of the independent nations of Africa see themselves as filling the role of Rousseau's "Legislator."

The role of this ideology in shaping their views on a number of subjects can be illustrated by African Socialist definitions of "capitalism." Although in Africa the antonym of "socialist" is frequently ' capitalist," the African Socialist defines capitalism differently from the non-African socialist. Capitalism is defined not simply as private ownership of the economy but as the kind of human relationships that individual ownership can produce. Private ownership, insofar as it heightens individual ambition and produces a desire for personal gain, destroys those characteristics in African society that are most highly prized. Yet it is vital to realize that the African Socialist argues that this "alienation" is not only an essential feature of capitalist society but equally common in communist society.

Like many utopian socialists, African Socialists are fundamentally suspicious of modern large-scale economic organizations. Specialization will tend to fragment human relationships, estranging the worker from the personal satisfaction of his craft. Although the experience of Africa's colonized peoples was essentially one of managerial capitalism, in the last stages of colonialism Africans could see *public ownership* producing very much the same effects. Thus both public and private ownership result in "alienation" (though private ownership both is more closely identified with the evils of colonialism and suffers from the profit motive—that is, is based on private and not public gain). But the exigencies of rapid economic development require the economies of scale of large organization, and this conflict between utopian aspirations and the most efficient use of scarce resources constitutes a major dilemma for African Socialists.

Finally, it must be noted that African Socialism has a function for the African political leaders as they find themselves involved in the world conflict. It permits them to distinguish themselves from both the East and the West. It accomplishes this by delineating their role in the international arena as an independent one. Thus, African Socialism becomes equated with neutralism and other ideologies that reject political domination by either the East or the West.

*The Organization of the Book*

In organizing this volume, the editors have attempted to present as thorough and detailed an analysis of African Socialism as is possible at the moment. It appears to us that such a study should seek (1) to examine the basic trends, defining and exploring them in detail; (2) to examine specific countries and leaders to determine what African Socialism means within the context of specific African nations; (3) to provide some basic documentation of material that is now scattered through a variety of publications, most of which are unavailable to the public.

We have organized the volume along these lines. Part I, "Definition and Exploration," is primarily concerned with the delineation of the parameters of African Socialism, utilizing as primary tools of analysis the disciplines of the social sciences. The contributions by Friedland and Morse utilize the basic disciplines of sociology and economics to examine African Socialism, while Kopytoff employs the tools of anthropology to assess the contention of many African Socialists that their doctrine has deeply established roots in traditional African culture. Nelkin examines the relationships between socialist thinking and Pan-Africanism by analyzing the intellectual roots of the Pan-African movement. Chapters 5 and 6 of Part I examine African Socialism within the framework of more traditional socialist thinking. Roberts studies African Socialism from the context of the pluralist socialism characterized by Britain's Labour Party and, in particular, its Fabian wing. An analysis of African Socialism which follows more directly in the Marxist framework is that of Potekhin. Professor Potekhin has expressed these ideas in a variety of publications, most of which are unavailable to Americans, and the editors believe it useful to have an understanding of the Soviet view of African Socialism. In Chapter 7 Zolberg studies the colloquium held late in 1962 by the Senegalese government on African Socialism. Because this was a major effort to assemble the representatives of various governments to discuss African Socialism, the trends that emerged at the conference are of considerable import.

Part II of the volume is concerned with specific countries, Ghana, Guinea and Senegal, Mali, and Tanganyika. Each chapter examines not only a different country but a different aspect of African Socialism. Thus, Legum examines the influence of socialist ideas on

Nkrumah and the ramification on the Convention People's Party and the various social groups in Ghana. Andrain is concerned with a comparative examination of the approaches to African Socialism of the leaders of Guinea and Senegal. Grundy's study of Mali focuses on the organization of planning within government. In contrast, Burke's chapter on Tanganyika analyzes the meaning of African Socialism by cutting across the many social levels in the country, from Nyerere to Baba Kabwela—the man on the street.

The final portion of the volume consists of basic documentation. Appendix I contains one of the earliest statements on African Socialism by one of the founders of Pan-Africanism. In the late 1950's George Padmore wrote a lengthy history of socialism, from which the material for this essay has been extracted. Padmore's contribution is exceedingly significant, for probably more than any other single figure he helped to draft the shape of African Socialism. This hitherto unpublished statement has had enormous influence in Ghana and probably, in turn, shaped the thinking of other African Socialists. In Appendixes II–VII we have assembled a variety of important and basic contributions by African leaders to African Socialism. These are documents that Africans read and study, and they provide the outlines of African Socialism as Africans see it.

Part I

# Definition and Exploration

Chapter 1

# Basic Social Trends

William H. Friedland

A sociological analysis of African Socialism should be concerned with social structures, institutions, and views of society. This limits the subject matter of the present chapter, since it excludes from consideration important economic manifestations except as they impinge upon social organization and structure. Thus, this chapter will not consider significant developments such as public ownership in African economies; it is specifically limited to sociological aspects of African Socialism.

A second caveat must be noted. The aspects of African Socialism to be discussed here can only be regarded as *trends*.* Up to the present time, few institutions have developed reflecting a socialist organization of society. On the whole, most African societies continue with the social structures inherited from a colonial past. Yet many changes are taking place and new ideas circulating about the future. Although these changes indicate that a number of African countries are developing along socialist lines, they are still somewhat tentative and their direction is not fully clear. This chapter seeks to explore these tendencies even if fully developed institutions characteristic of socialism have not yet made their appearance.

*African Socialism: Four Basic Trends*

Four basic trends in Africa appear to be relevant to any analysis of socialism. These trends are important because a great deal of discussion and considerable action is now being concentrated on them. The trends are: (1) the idea of the social obligation to work; (2) the conversion of labor unions from consumptionist to productionist associations; (3) an orientation toward a classless society or a society with minimal stratification patterns; (4) a tendency

* In discussing these trends, most examples will be drawn from Ghana and Tanganyika. This is being done for the sake of convenience, since these are relatively familiar areas. The trends described hold, however, for a variety of other countries.

toward developing a society that can be characterized as "focal institutional."

These trends exist at different levels: some are more advanced than others in being implemented in African societies. The first two trends are relatively low-level developments of considerable immediate importance. These represent, in effect, solutions to the first dilemmas African political leaders confront when they undertake political consolidation and economic development following the achievement of independence. It is in these areas that a great deal of action and talk is found.

The third trend, the movement toward a classless or minimally stratified society, is somewhat more abstract and of less immediacy. It represents a goal toward which many African leaders are striving, and a considerable amount of energy is being invested in formulating an ideology to encompass it.

The fourth trend, toward a society I have called focal institutional, is least conscious and most abstract. Indeed, the fourth trend only appears as the three more obvious trends are examined. Although least conscious, this final tendency is probably the most significant.

### The Social Obligation to Work

A major theme now widely manifest throughout independent Africa is the idea of the social obligation to work. The basic notion is that men have an obligation to work so as to increase the material well-being of society. Parasitism and idleness, for example, are regarded as social sins.

While the concern of leaders is to increase production in their respective countries, different African leaders discuss the obligation to work in varying ways. Kwame Nkrumah of Ghana, who typifies one approach, contends that the state has undertaken the solution of basic economic problems of workers and that they consequently have responsibilities to the state. As he put it in one speech, after listing the many benefits that workers derive in Ghana:

If we are doing all these things to give workers comfort and satisfaction, we expect in return their loyalty and hard work to build Ghana. In the Ghana we are reconstructing we shall have no room for lazy workers and subversive trade union elements. We must be prepared to make sacrifices for the greater things ahead.[1]

---

[1] Numbered notes (primarily source citations) will be found at the back of the book, on pages 279–306.

The idea of the obligation to labor is manifested in other ways, for example, in polemics against parasitism. Parasitism is ill-defined; it is not certain if the "parasites" are capitalists (in the Marxist sense, i.e., owners of the means of production) or subsistence agriculturists unwilling to increase their production. The careful, if not very useful, Marxist definition of parasitism (which defined the bourgeoisie—the owners of the means of production—as parasites) is rarely used clearly and consciously. Private enterprise continues to occupy an important place in the economies of most African countries, and few African leaders engage in all-out attacks on it. However, a strong sense of anticapitalism underlies many campaigns against parasitism.

Attacks on parasitism are very often directed against elements in African society capable of increasing production but unwilling to do so. The view of work traditionally held by most Africans was not propitious for capital accumulation. Thus, leaders concerned with initiating the process of economic development or of increasing the standard of living of their people continually inveigh against the failure to work. In Tanganyika, leaders often engage in manual labor on community development projects to show that no shame attaches to getting one's hands dirty.

In denouncing parasites, the argument is frequently heard that the obligation to labor is traditional. Julius Nyerere, for example, has said:

In traditional African society everybody was a worker. . . . When I say that . . . everybody was a worker, I do not use the word "worker" simply as opposed to "employer" but also as opposed to "loiterer" or "idler." . . . Those of us who talk about the African Way of Life and . . . take a pride in maintaining the tradition of hospitality . . . do well to remember the Swahili saying, *Mgeni siku mbili; siku ya tatu mpe jembe*—or, in English, "Treat your guest as a guest for two days; on the third day give him a hoe!" In actual fact, the guest was likely to ask for the hoe even before his host had to give him one—for he knew what was expected of him, and would have been ashamed to remain idle any longer.[2]

While Dr. Nyerere is right in stressing the traditional responsibilities to share in the production of food, there is an emphasis here that is probably incorrect. The urgency of work which is emphasized in the speeches of many African leaders is at the opposite pole from the traditional African view of work. The traditional view was probably closer to that of the Greeks, who looked upon work as an evil necessary for survival but not as a social obligation.[3] Somewhat similarly, societies in the West sharing the Judeo-Christian ethic did not look upon work with high regard[4] until recent times. Most African societies had subsistence economies and did not see work as an ethic. Further, intense energies are being invested by African leaders in increasing production, which suggests their conviction that traditional attitudes toward work do not encourage capital accumulation.

The obligation to labor is not simply a socialist idea, of course; Weber noted it in *The Protestant Ethic*.[5] The notion has been labeled here as socialist for several reasons. First, classical socialism held that the exploitation of man by man was indefensible and that all men consequently had an obligation to labor. In this respect, the socialist obligation to work is different from that of the Protestant ethic, where the obligation to work is personal and success at accumulation confirms membership in God's elect. Second, work has become an important theme in communist societies, where it is held to be a moral *and* a legal obligation.[6] In addition, socialist and semisocialist societies have created taxation systems aimed at avoiding the perpetuation of wealth from generation to generation, thereby imposing an obligation to work. Thus, the social obligation to work can be regarded as one emergent feature of African Socialism.

The obligation to work in Africa is mainly being implemented by propaganda, and little has been done to make this *a legal obligation*. Political leaders, however, continually make speeches on the subject, and much of the activity of community development in the former British territories and "human investment" in the former French territories is concerned with the creation of an institutional apparatus pressuring people to work. In these cases, *work* is defined in community terms for specific projects such as road building and construction of schools, and not in the sense of a more general obligation to labor for society. While work has been defined, in these cases, as a voluntary obligation to the community, there is some evidence that substantial informal sanctions have been brought to bear against those refusing to contribute their labor to community projects.

On the whole, however, while there has been a great deal of community development and "human investment," the population generally has not yet developed the systematic work habits necessary for rapid economic growth.

### The Conversion of Unions into Productionist Organizations

Most unions on the African continent became significant during the struggle for independence. Although many unions were economically oriented, their political functions were always of considerable importance. In the early period of their development, although they followed Western models, the consequences of their *consumptionist* activities tended to make them part of the nationalist, anticolonial, antiforeign-domination movement. By *consumptionist* is meant that, like unions in the West, African unions became primarily concerned with increasing the ability of their members to consume by raising the standard of living. These activities fitted well with the anticolonial political movement because most employers were considered to be foreign exploiters tied to the colonial power.

With the achievement of independence, however, a distinct shift in orientation can be noted, as unions voluntarily or not so voluntarily become *productionist*.\* More and more, unions are being converted into instruments for increasing the productivity and production of workers.

In some cases, the reorientation of the unions toward productionist activities has ostensibly been voluntary and internal to the union. Thus, John Tettegah, General Secretary of the Ghana Trades Union Congress, has contended:

The workers' struggles do not always and everywhere assume the same form. There was a time when in fighting their employers, the workers smashed machines and set fire to factories. . . . In Ghana today, as in Israel ten years ago, we have not the factories to smash; it is our responsibility to help create them and to give work to the masses of the people.[7]

In other cases, the pressures to convert unions to productionism are largely external. This is true in Tanganyika, where the government and the governing party, the Tanganyika African National

---

\* The distinction in union functions between "consumptionist" and "productionist" is based on Isaac Deutscher, "Russia," in Walter Galenson, ed., *Comparative Labor Movements* (New York: Prentice-Hall, 1952), p. 505.

Union (TANU), have been in serious conflict with the Taganyika Federation of Labor (TFL). Underlying this conflict is the concern of the TANU government that the unions should not become a drag on economic development by continuing their consumptionist activities.[8] During the course of this conflict, productionism has been urged on the unions by Mr. Nyerere.

It is one of the purposes of trade unions to ensure for the workers a fair share of the profits of their labor. But a "fair" share must be fair in relation to the whole society. If it is greater than the country can afford without having to penalize some other section of society, then it is not a "fair" share. Trade union leaders and their followers, as long as they are true socialists, will not need to be coerced by the government into keeping their demands within the limits imposed by the needs of society as a whole.*

Underlying the conversion of unions to productionism is the idea of a classless society, which is dealt with below. For the moment, it is important to note that unions in a "classless" society are conceived of as being different from those in class society. Both Nkrumah and Nyerere view unions as part of the anticolonialist movement. Prior to independence, in the class society of the colonial system, it was understandable that the unions undertook consumptionist activities. While classes are still found in Africa, these are now viewed as anachronisms. The activities of the unions should shift, therefore, reflecting the fact that African society is ostensibly evolving along nonclass lines.[9]

The shift to productionism in Africa follows the model of the Soviet Union after the Russian Revolution. At the 1921 Congress of the Communist Party it was argued that unions were not necessary to defend the interests of workers in their work places in a socialist society. It was held that the instrumentalities of workers' control (the soviets) directed the state and the means of production, and therefore independent institutions to protect workers

---

* "Ujamaa," Appendix II, p. 245. Interestingly, the standard of comparison used by Nyerere in this case is *the nation*. That is, he relates the standard of living of workers to that of other groups within the nation. A different standard is utilized in other cases. Thus, when the general secretary of the TFL attacked the government ministers for driving big cars and having "fat salaries," the publicity secretary of TANU replied that Tanganyika's ministers were the lowest paid *in Africa*. (See *Tanganyika Standard*, July 26, 1962, p. 3.) The comparison was not with other groups in Tanganyika but with comparable units in Africa.

were unnecessary. Instead, a new function for unions emerged in a socialist society: unions should help to increase the material wealth of the society.[10]

The Soviet view is now being widely adopted in Africa.* This orientation holds that, since African society is essentially classless and the party represents the interests of the nation, unions should be primarily concerned with increasing production rather than demanding ever-increasing standards of living for their members.

In contrast to the social obligation to work, the transformation of trade unions from "consumptionist" to "productionist" has been given a firm legal basis. It has been most clearly set down in Ghana and Tanganyika, where government and the ruling political parties have established control over the trade unions. In Ghana, this was accomplished through the passage of a law that imposed on the Ghana Trades Union Congress (GTUC) a "new structure" placing authority firmly in the hands of the Congress as opposed to its affiliates. To enforce merger, unions that failed to amalgamate along prescribed lines were deregistered. The new structure of the GTUC weakened the affiliates and centralized power in the hands of the GTUC. At the same time, the Convention People's Party (CPP) dominates the GTUC through informal means. Thus, by legal and informal controls, the activities of the unions in Ghana have been brought under control of the ruling party.†

The shift in the functions of the unions can be seen by the change in their activities. The unions have tended to place a damper on strikes and have emphasized productionist activities. When, in 1960, Nkrumah instituted compulsory savings and was confronted by a strike of railway workers, the GTUC failed to come out either against compulsory savings or in defense of the strike leaders who were imprisoned.

### Classless or Minimally Stratified Society

The third theme prevalent in African Socialist thinking is antagonism to class society. Social class is regarded with repugnance by many African leaders, who see this as a European import. Ideally, society in the precontact traditional period is seen as having been unstratified. As Léopold Senghor has expressed it: "There are

---

* Without being attributed to the Russians, however.
† The changes in Tanganyikan unionism since the above was written will have exactly the same consequences as has been the case in Ghana.

no classes in our society." However, in discussing the difficulties of the independent African states whose unions continue to demand higher standards of living, Senghor notes that "analysis reveals a certain tendency, a 'real movement' toward the *formation of classes.*" By this is meant that the gap between the standard of living of organized workers and that of the rest of the population has become so disproportionate that "the proletarian is not necessarily the one who claims the title."[11] Similarly, Houphouët-Boigny gave as one reason for breaking with the Communists the fact that "the class struggle, which lies at the base of communism, has no meaning in a classless society."[12]

Antagonism to class society also exists in trade union circles. When the Confédération Générale du Travail Africain (CGTA) was formed in 1956, a resolution was adopted accepting the idea of "the dialectic," but the CGTA "rejects the class struggle, because of African social groups' identity of living conditions and lack of differentiation into antagonistic classes."[13] This is not to contend that Africans fail to see classes within African society; indeed, at times they do. This is considered to be an anomaly, however, which is usually the product of conquest; genuinely indigenous African society is viewed as being economically homogeneous and unstratified.[14]

Not all African leaders see precontact society as being homogeneous. Some leaders recognize the existence of stratification in traditional society but have socialist explanations for its functions.

In traditional African society everybody was a worker. There was no other way of earning a living for the community. Even the Elder, who appeared to be enjoying himself without doing any work and for whom everybody else appeared to be working, had, in fact, worked hard all his younger days. The wealth he now appeared to possess was not his, personally; it was only "his" as the Elder of the group which had produced it. He was its guardian. The wealth itself gave him neither power nor prestige. The respect paid to him by the young was his because he was older than they, and had served his community longer.[15]

Thus society was seen, in the past, as being essentially unstratified.*

---

* Fallers notes a similar phenomenon among the Soga of Uganda. When the Administration pressed the Soga to institute a graduated tax system, the (African) District Council did not see the existence of rich men or wealthy farmers, although the Council members were, in Fallers' estimate, wealthier than other segments of the African population. "The crucial point was that, relative to other countries, . . . Busoga was poor. Differences in wealth within Busoga were less important

This provides the basis for a view of emergent African society that holds, essentially, that there should be no classes in African society *or,* if there must be classes, that the number of strata should be small and the differentials between the strata should be minimal.

The true socialist may not exploit his fellows. So that if the members of any group within our society are going to argue that, because they happen to be contributing more to the national income than some other groups, they must therefore take for themselves a greater share of the profits of their own industry than they actually need; and if they insist on this in spite of the fact that it would mean reducing their group's contribution to the general income and thus slowing down the rate at which the whole community can benefit, then that group is exploiting (or trying to exploit) its fellow human beings. It is displaying a capitalist attitude of mind.

There are bound to be certain groups which, by virtue of the "market value" of their particular industry, will contribute more to the nation's income than others. But the others may actually be producing goods and services which are of equal, or greater, intrinsic value although they do not happen to command such a high artificial value. For example, the food produced by the peasant farmer is of greater social value than the diamonds mined at Mwadui. But the mineworkers of Mwadui could claim, quite correctly, that their labor was yielding greater financial profits to the community than that of the farmers. If, however, they went on to demand that they should therefore be given most of that extra profit for themselves, and that no share of it should be spent on helping the farmers, they would be potential capitalists![16]

A similar idea has been expressed by Léopold Senghor, when confronted by wage demands of government employees in Senegal.

The most important objection stems from a comparison between the respective standard of living of city dwellers—government employees, workers, and laborers—and of the peasants, who constitute more than 90 per cent of the population. It could not serve the public interest to increase the disproportion between the living standards of the classes now in the process of formation.[17]

The dangers of class formation are warned against also by Dr. Nyerere:

than their undoubtedly exaggerated impression that . . . most Europeans were much wealthier than any one of themselves . . . ; from a modern European point of view, differences in wealth within Busoga are substantial." (Lloyd Fallers, *Bantu Bureaucracy* [Cambridge: W. Heffer & Sons, n.d.], pp. 217–18.)

As nationalism becomes successful, the chances of the Europeans and the Asians of maintaining a permanently privileged position in our countries will tend to diminish. But the chances of the educated Africans to become a new privileged class will multiply. Yet this will not be so obvious while the Europeans and Asians are so strikingly wealthier than the Africans. The would-be African exploiter can masquerade as a great social reformer by concentrating the attack on European and Asian privilege. Before we know where we are, what is now an essentially dying-out privileged class will have been replaced by a permanently privileged class of educated Africans.[18]

The TANU government sees cooperatives as replacements for the Asian middlemen. Personnel within the cooperatives will not have the opportunity, it is reasoned, to constitute themselves as a middle class.[19] The development of cooperatives is regarded not as anti-Asian but rather as intended to create institutions amenable to capital accumulation without creating a new class system. The Tanganyikan case holds for other African countries. The salient approach of many African leaders is hostility to the creation of social classes and the formulation of an ideology antipathetic to class formation.

The view of society as classless or minimally stratified is creating a great deal of strain within the modern-day African states. The problem boils down, of course, to the relative economic positions of different groups. This accounts for the recriminations of political leaders and unionists against each other.[20]

The problem of income differentials is obviously important for political reasons. First, if workers obtain increasingly higher wages and benefits, there will be serious effects on capital accumulation and on the standards of living of the rest of the population. Political leaders therefore have cause for trying to keep wages in hand. Second, the increasing differentials in the standards of living of the urban and rural populations accelerate movements to the towns already burdened with problems of unemployment. The presence of large numbers of unemployed accessible to demagogues poses a dilemma for those concerned with maintaining public order. It is understandable, therefore, that leaders like Senghor and Nyerere worry about disproportions in living standards. It must nevertheless be noted that the arguments against continuation of the disproportions are couched in the language of economic egalitarianism, of socialism.

While the ideological formulations are hostile to class formation, it is still possible to denote a number of tendencies in this direction among those who condemn the formation of classes. In Ghana, where socialist rhetoric has been widely used by leaders of the Convention People's Party, this has not prevented the amassing of personal fortunes and the building of palaces by some leaders. The golden bed of Mrs. Krobo Edusei is a most obvious example.

Even where there is more modesty, however, it appears somewhat naïve to expect those with economic and political power to be satisfied with equal access to material wealth as those with no power. It is interesting, in this respect, to see that the same confusion over the definition of social class that exists in the Soviet Union is present on the African continent. The argument is frequently stated that African society will be classless because the state will eventually own the means of production. That there will continue to be strata within society and that invidious distinctions will exist between the strata seem to go unrecognized. In the Soviet Union, which is theoretically "most socialist," there are enormous discrepancies in the manner of living of Premier Khrushchev, a university professor, a skilled worker, and a street sweeper. The socialism of the Soviet Union has eliminated private property as a significant factor, but groups with power take larger shares of material benefits than those without power. It appears to this writer, therefore, that the "exploitation of man by man" continues. It is true that accumulation of material possessions from one generation to the next is *somewhat* minimized, since it is difficult to accumulate personal property that is productive. Children can inherit nonproductive personal property (money, houses) but not productive property, the "means of production" (factories, machinery). There is relative accessibility to the educational system, so that Soviet society is comparatively mobile. Thus, Soviet socialism is marked by considerable social stratification, even though there is little significant private ownership of property.

The possibility that Africans can create a society with little or no stratification must be viewed with some skepticism. The undeveloped state of most African economies creates, instead, great demand for stratification. Because skilled manpower is in short supply, African countries must continue to pay premium prices for skills necessary for economic development. As increasing numbers of nationals become trained to replace expatriates, it should not be expected that they will lower their demands for payments for their services. As has been discovered in other countries undergoing economic development, there is a world market for skilled personnel, and if an adequate style of life cannot be sustained at home, talented people have found their skills greatly appreciated abroad.[21]

We are led to the conclusion that arguments about classless or minimally stratified society can represent ideological justification for the effective monopoly of material wealth by powerful groups. I am reminded of the moral indignation of some Central European socialists and unionists encountered at a meeting some years ago. A socialist union leader was condemned because he personally owned a Volkswagen. The same leaders that were so firm in their socialist morality left the meeting in their chauffeur-driven Mercedes autos. The distinction existed in their minds because they did not personally own their cars; they were the property of the unions and the chauffeurs were paid by the unions.

Ideologies can serve as justifications for the exercise of power and the real command of material wealth. While the contentions about classless society may, in Africa, represent the self-justification for the political elite, it should not be interpreted to mean that these are only words with little meaning. Ideologies can become guides to action. Ideas that are conveniences can become directives for the masses. It is because Africa is in such a state of ferment, because its institutions are so new and still unformed, that any contention about the function of the ideology of classless society must be treated carefully.

### "Focal Institutional" Societies*

A "focal institutional" society is a plural society whose institutions are penetrated and dominated by a single institution which becomes, in effect, the focal institution upon which all others depend. The concept can, perhaps, be clarified by contrasting different types of plural societies with simple preliterate societies.

Very simple societies with low levels of material culture have, by comparison with modern societies, an institutional apparatus that is coterminous with the kinship system. There are no institutions that cut across the single institution of kinship (i.e., age-grades,

---

* In the original draft of this chapter, I used the term "monist" rather than "focal institutional." See the shortened version of this chapter published in *Africa Report*, VIII (May 1963). The reason for the change is made clear below.

associations, religious groupings, etc.). Thus, a simple preliterate society whose social structure is, in effect, equivalent to the kinship system can be characterized as *monist.*

Complex modern societies are, in contrast, plural: there are a multiplicity of institutions cutting across one another and men are segmentally attached to many institutions. While all modern societies can be called plural, there are different types of pluralism. Where power is genuinely dispersed among the various institutions so that no one dominates society, one form of pluralism exists. I propose to call this "genuine pluralism." Where a single institution penetrates all others, undermines their integrity and autonomy, and dominates them, this constitutes pluralism of a different type. This will be called "focal institutional pluralism."\* The Soviet Union and Hitler's Germany are examples of focal institutional plural societies. In both cases, there are or were a multiplicity of institutions dominated by a single institutional complex. The concept of focal institution does not imply anything with respect to decision making and the centralization of power in the hands of an elite. Thus, while the societies cited as examples have been totalitarian, this does not mean that all focal institutional societies must, of necessity, be totalitarian. The location of decision-making power must be separated from the question of whether the single institutional complex dominates all others. It is *conceivable* that a society should be focal institutional and at the same time be democratic—although this may be somewhat unlikely—but the distinction between who makes the decisions in a society and whether or not institutions are dominated by a single institution can clearly be made.

The prevalent thinking and action of a considerable number of African leaders indicate a tendency toward the development of a focal institutional society. Nkrumah, for example, sees the institutions of modern Ghana integrally related to one another, with the Convention People's Party as the focal unit.

\* My usage of the concept of pluralism differs slightly from that of other behavioral scientists; my justification is that pluralism is the polar opposite of monism. By way of illustration, consider several well-known characterizations of American society. John K. Galbraith characterizes the United States by "countervailing power" and David Riesman by "veto groups." In my terms, they would see American society as genuinely pluralist. On the other hand, C. Wright Mills regards our institutional apparatus as being dominated by the "power elite" and would, in my terminology, regard the United States as focal institutional.

Those who are against the labor movement, the cooperative movement, or the farmers' organizations are against me and the Convention People's Party. There can be no split loyalties. Nobody has the right to call himself a true labor fighter if he is not also an honest and loyal member of the Convention People's Party, because fundamentally, the Convention People's Party is the political expression of the Trade Union movement.[22]

Similarly, Nyerere sees the unions and the party as legs of the same body (the anticolonialist movement) and fundamentally inseparable.

If I try to walk from point A to point B, by the very definition of "walking" my two legs will cooperate in taking me there: I do not even have to appeal to logic. Still less do I have to worry about whether the independence of my right or my left leg is being undermined by its need to seek the cooperation of the other! Either both legs are mine or they are not.

If both are mine they must cooperate; to contemplate anything else is to contemplate an absurdity. If, however, I may indulge in such an absurdity for a moment, the inference is obvious: if either one of my legs were to be persuaded that too close cooperation with the other would be an infringement of "independence," neither one of them would arrive anywhere at all!

Similarly, either the trade unions and the political organizations are prongs, or "legs" of the same nationalist movement, or they are not. If they *are,* then the question of whether they should or should not cooperate in getting the country from point A to point B does not arise. They *must* cooperate.[23]

Léopold Senghor has expressed the same view.

Our Negro African situation is not identical with the situation in France, where the salaried folk are struggling to snatch, from a bourgeois State, a larger share of the national income. In Africa, we and you are the State. At least the governments are composed of Africans and government employees [*sic!*] in the overwhelming majority. It is against themselves that the labor unions, particularly the government employees, are struggling. This is an unnatural contradiction.[24]

Essentially the contention is that the people equal the party, which equals the unions, the farmers' organizations, the cooperatives, and the nation. The institution that emerges as the focal unit in this complex is the single party.[25]

The interpenetration of institutions and their domination by the party is remarkably illustrated by Cowan's discussion of the Parti Démocratique de Guinée (PDG).[26] Cowan shows how the PDG dominates the government and penetrates into every level of social life of the country. Through a network of village and urban local committees, the party mobilizes the masses on a geographical basis. The work of local committees is integrated by the party structure, and there is great homogeneity in the problems handled by the committees. The party not only organizes on a geographical basis but has a variety of functional organizations: trade unions, the youth, women, and the army. "Thus, virtually every organized group in the country—the army, youth, women, and labor—is directly related to the party through the presence of their heads in the Bureau Politique [the political bureau, the leading body of the PDG]."[27]

The penetration of the existing institutional framework by the focal institution is marked by hostility to independent and autonomous institutions. One index is the hostility of modern political leaders toward tribes and tribalism. While political leaders emphasize traditionalism in certain contexts,[28] they are intensely anti-tribal. Tribalism is, of course, an outmoded form of social cohesion, but it remains an important attachment for large numbers of rural Africans unaccustomed to pluralism. Because attachments to traditional institutions impede the attachment of individuals to the new nation-state (via the party), modern political leaders are almost invariably hostile to tribalism. The consequence of their antitribalism is to make individuals increasingly dependent upon the single, central focal institution and to undermine the integrity of competing institutions.

The formation of a focal institutional society originates in the exigencies of the present as well as having historical roots. First, Africans coming from traditional societies are accustomed, to a considerable extent, to the idea that society should be centered upon a single complex. Although this complex was the kinship system in the past and is changed to the political party in the present, there are parallels, and it may be that there is considerable transferability from the kinship system to the political party. Second, the colonial period was marked by a tendency for central government to emerge as an important and dominating element in the lives of Africans. Although central governments were not omnipresent and had little direct relationship to the lives of the bulk of the population, they represented a major source of monolithic power.

The trend toward a focal institutional society has its exigencies mainly in the present, however. Basically the trend is related to the difficult economic and political position in which the political elites find themselves. Confronted by a relatively unproductive rural population and an urban population of considerable power clamoring for costly social benefits, they have an overwhelming desire to modernize and provide their masses with a standard of life appropriate to the twentieth century. It is easy to turn to the amenable and accessible instrumentality of the mass political party to move society toward capital accumulation. Recalcitrant and competing institutions can be undermined by co-optation, coercion, and the mobilization of the masses, who continue to maintain their loyalties to the parties that won independence.

The tendency toward this new society is not a product of planned choice as much as it is the consequence of many decisions taken by the political leaders as they come to grips with the difficult economic, political, and social problems of independence.[29]

### Antisocialist Tendencies in Modern Africa

While significant developments are unfolding in Africa that have been characterized as socialist, the observer must recognize that existing social structures are pressing and will continue to press in a contrary direction. This does not contradict Morse's argument that significant economic development in the future will be through public investment.* While the public sector will unquestionably be large and important, this should not be interpreted as constituting socialism. If socialism is defined solely in terms of the nonexistence of private ownership of the means of production, then most African nations—Liberia and Ethiopia among them—may be characterized as somewhat socialist. The mind instinctively recoils from such a prospect, as it does from accepting the idea of Stalin's Russia, with the largest slave camps in the world, as socialist. While socialism has, admittedly, come to be defined as the elimination of private ownership of the means of production by some people, this writer would contend that this is only *a necessary but not sufficient condition* for the establishment of socialist

---

* See Chapter 2, "The Economics of African Socialism."

society. It should be recalled that the founders of modern socialism, Marx and Engels, focused upon the elimination of private owner- ship because they saw it as the vehicle that permitted the continu- ation of exploitation. The founding fathers thought that exploita- tion would disappear with the end of private ownership; they were obviously mistaken, since even in the Soviet Union, with the elimi- nation of private ownership, substantial exploitation continues to exist. Thus, for this writer, socialism cannot simply be defined as the end of private ownership: as long as men continue to make invidious distinctions materially and nonmaterially with respect to other men, socialism does not exist.

It becomes increasingly apparent that socialism has other mean- ings than the end of private property. If socialists in Europe and America have not come to grips with these meanings, it may be left to Africans to do so. In a sense this is what people like Nyerere are searching for. His contention that communitary socialism existed in traditional society is largely correct in that there was little occupational differentiation or extensive division of labor in such societies; the imbalance in wealth between the richest and the poor- est was, in many traditional societies, very small—indeed, infinitesi- mal by comparison with modern industrial society.

But as society increases in complexity, occupational groups, status groups, and classes are differentiated. There is no time here to enter into a discussion of the functional theory of social stratification,[30] but it is a historical fact that societies, including those that charac- terize themselves as socialist, have different social strata, and in- vidious distinctions are made between them that correlate signifi- cantly with occupations.

As African societies modernize, the fissiparous tendencies will be- come more marked as social groups are differentiated as a result of the spreading division of labor. Thus, even if much of the economy of a nation develops in the public sector, one important aspect of antisocialism exists and will become increasingly entrenched: the economic inequality of different groups in African society. Not all groups have benefited equally from independence, and the im- balance of rewards has led to considerable dissatisfaction that may be reflected in institutional change.

The group that has benefited most materially from independence has been that comprising the politicians, the leaders of the inde- pendence movements. Moving from tenuous economic statuses

into the highest positions in parliaments, the government, and administration, they have experienced a rise in the standard of living
that must be described as astronomical.

In contrast, those most disaffected, in all likelihood, have been
the African civil servants and the formally educated elites who
have seen the top positions in the society taken over by their less
educated but politically wise countrymen.[31] In country after country, the growing disaffection of the civil servants has been notice-
able and significant. In most cases, the economic condition of this
group has remained somewhat static. Thus, while independence
has not cost them anything, their relative deprivation has been
great. In the past, this group constituted the top echelon of African
society; above it were the Europeans or other foreigners. Now,
the top is occupied by other Africans and, to add insult to injury,
relatively uneducated ones. This has created considerable unrest
among the civil servants and the educated personnel. If formal
movements or expressions of dissatisfaction have not yet become
manifest, this does not mean that there is no disaffection. The sup-
planting of this group as the top layer of African society serves as
a structural source of discontent.

Equally unhappy in many countries are the trade unionists, even
where the top echelons have been "captured" by the party apparatuses. Workers have come to expect certain kinds of behavior from
their leaders, and even though the upper echelons have been co-
opted by the parties there are still pressures on the unions to continue the consumptionist activities that gave them their start in
Africa. Even in Ghana, where the capture of the union leadership
has been most thorough, workers continue to expect that their
unions will defend their standards of living. This helps explain
the sharp resentment of workers at the passage of the compulsory
savings scheme in 1961 and the subsequent strike of railway
workers that saw a considerable number of workers' leaders jailed.
In Tanganyika, Victor Mkello, head of the Tanganyika Federation
of Labor, supported the TANU-sponsored legislation that cut the
power of the unions and personally led the drive against the anti-
TANU unions, but was nonetheless banished when, in response to
pressures, his own plantation workers' union conducted a number
of unofficial strikes. Thus, the expectations of workers continue to
act as a substantial pressure on the union leaders; and, in spite of
continual co-optation of union leaders to ministries and ambassa-

dorships or the application of coercive measures, the unionists continue to represent a semi-independent source of power for the time being. Workers in Africa, like those in the United States and many other countries, want "more," and the fact that a country's economy can ill afford it is always less significant than the ever-present higher standard of living of the politicians, the civil servants, and the foreigners.

Somewhat similarly, other groups can be delineated in African society. On the west coast the development of an African middle class has now reached significant proportions in a number of countries. The presence of a considerable number of African entrepreneurs has provided the basis for a new social group in society and one that will not cease to exist voluntarily. If African Socialism means that all private trade and commerce should be in the hands of Africans, then a peculiar form of inequality will be brought into existence.

Even in Tanganyika where the indigenous middle class is very small, TANU and Nyerere have been greatly concerned about them. Special action had to be taken in 1960 and 1961 to undermine a small group of African entrepreneurs who were beginning to compete with Asian traders and, more significantly, with the TANU-supported Victoria Federation of Cooperative Unions. The African traders felt that *uhuru* should mean that *they* could supplant the Asians in trading; unfortunately for them, TANU wished the supplantation to come through the cooperatives. The fact that the co-ops pay lower prices to growers than the private traders does not bother TANU, since the co-ops represent a force useful for capital accumulation. If higher prices are paid to farmers, capital will be dispersed for consumer goods. Thus, in Tanganyika, two groups are at least potentially present: the traders who are willing to pay higher prices and the farmers who want higher prices.

The large numbers of students now in training in foreign countries will hardly expect that their standard of living, on returning home, will be the same as that of urban unskilled or semiskilled workers or rural agriculturists. These returning students, the present civil servants, the new urban middle classes, the peasant farmers as they become more involved in production for markets, all constitute incipient status groups and classes.

A variety of groups is therefore already present in modern African society, each having different economic, social, and political interests. For the moment, the differences between the groups continue to be submerged by the impact of independence and the continued power of the single-party systems. It is doubtful that these differences can remain submerged indefinitely.

All of this emphasizes the tentative nature of African Socialism. Just as African Socialism is a relatively empty ideological vessel into which a great variety of ideas can be poured, it can be expected that the ideology will be as malleable in the future as it has been in the recent past—the brief past that African Socialism has experienced.

The fact that fissiparous tendencies—the tendencies inevitable in the pluralism of modern industrial society—have been noted does not mean, however, that African Socialism is significant only as an ideological doctrine. Africa is an enormous complexity, and the forces that are at work are only beginning to be defined. The fight for independence is just about over; now the next stage begins. What that stage will hold cannot yet be revealed, because the ferment and experimentation on the continent is such that tendencies appear in a great many directions. Pan-Africanism, political and economic regional arrangements, African Socialism, and single-party systems are only some of the many tendencies presently visible. No one can predict which of these trends will be most significant in the future. The analysis of the trends implicit in African Socialism are important, however, for understanding the mushrooming significance of this movement. Although socialism appears to exist largely at the ideological level, it is important to remember that ideologies have become instrumentalities for moving men—once men come to believe in them. Accordingly, it is well that students of Africa understand the current tendencies implicit in African Socialism.

Chapter 2

# The Economics of African Socialism

Chandler Morse

To replace premodern social and economic structures with modern ones is a task confronting all of the new countries in Africa. Those countries whose leaders are avowedly attempting to guide them along the path to socialism may be presumed—as an initial working hypothesis and in the absence of explicit statements of objectives—to aim at a form of economic organization in which private ownership of the means of production is either precluded, or confined to a more or less limited range of activities, or subjected to a variety of constraints and requirements designed to promote the attainment of certain social ends; and in which, as an expected consequence of the foregoing arrangements, there will be only minimal conflicts of economic interest.* Other countries, while not pursuing these goals, will nonetheless follow a pragmatic policy of employing public initiative and enterprise as a substitute for private when the latter are found wanting. They are thus likely to wind up with more public and less private participation in, or responsibility for the results of, economic activity than is consistent with the traditional concept of capitalism. Despite the differences in political, economic, and social philosophy between these two groups, it is by no means certain that the ultimate differences between them will be as wide as their leaders and many foreign observers now appear to expect. In some cases, perhaps, the differences will be found to have resided mainly in the extent to which leaders chose to employ socialist rhetoric to justify governmental measures which inevitably had much in common because they reflected similar compulsions.

* In Potekhin's terms, the hypothesis is that the countries are striving to create "socialism in Africa," not "African Socialism." This may be more applicable to some countries, such as Ghana and Guinea, than to others, such as Senegal and Tanganyika.

### The Socialist Goal

Because the path to socialism in Africa has not been clearly defined, and because in any case it would not be easy to follow, the African Socialist countries face two difficulties, one conceptual in origin, the other practical. The conceptual difficulty reflects a certain vagueness, or variability, in interpreting socialism. The practical difficulty arises out of the objective realities that now exist, and will be brought about by the processes of economic and social development: realities that are responsible for a measure of conflict between what is recognized as expedient or growth-promoting and what might be conceived as socialistic. The two difficulties together help to explain why the avowedly socialist countries often adopt policies more for reasons of expediency, or to promote economic growth, than because of the conviction that they will lead to socialism.

Ideologically, the African Socialist countries considered here (i.e., Ghana, Guinea, Senegal, and Tanganyika) have chosen a middle road, lying somewhere between what they regard as the extremes of capitalistic organization, exemplified mainly by the United States, and of communist organization, chiefly exemplified by the USSR. But this middle road itself is rather wide, as a consideration of certain conceptual differences and similarities will show. Senegal and Tanganyika have sometimes seemed to stress the attitudinal aspects of socialism, viewed as growing naturally out of traditional African communalism, while Ghana and Guinea have gone considerably further in attempting to create socialist institutions.

Nyerere, for example, begins an important statement of aims with the assertion that "socialism is an attitude of mind," and his subsequent remarks suggest that he considers the inculcation of proper attitudes, where they do not already exist, to be the main task.[1] The implication is that socialist structures will arise out of socialist ideals, not the reverse. At the other extreme we find Sékou Touré, the most avowedly Marxist of the African leaders. He, too, is idealistic: "We have placed Man at the head of everything." But for Touré this is mystique, not method. When he, like many other African leaders, says, "Our political revolution would not be complete without an economic and social revolution," he intends the second revolution to be more than a transformation of society from premodern to modern. It is to be that, but the modern form is to be socialistic, not capitalistic. Exhortation is important, but structural changes are crucial and must be pressed with determination. A similar view of the need for change in the structure of economic relations appears to be shared by Nkrumah but, reflecting his Anglo-American education, with less invocation of the humanistic aspects of socialism and less concern with doctrinal issues.* The Senegalese leaders, though acknowledging the value of Marxist principles of organization, stress idealism more and revolutionary change less than Sékou Touré. In substance, though not in their modes of expressing themselves, which are distinctively French, they stand closer to Nyerere.[2]

These variations, which reflect differences in the personal experiences and temperaments of the leaders, and in the historically determined conditions to which they must adapt, are significant mainly for two reasons. First, they indicate different views concerning the nature of socialism and how to achieve it. Some of the leaders appear to regard socialism as merely a humanistic type of economic development, while others believe that the humanistic feature will be lost if and to the extent that considerations of private gain guide the processes of production and distribution. Second, they suggest that there will be differences in policies; or, even when policies seem to be similar, that they will be pursued with differential intensity and effect.

*Economic Policies Compared*

The fact that none of the countries accepts the USSR as a model, that none is following, or currently planning to follow, a well-defined "totalistic" path to socialism, helps to explain the range of dissimilarities among them. In the countries with Marxist leadership this may, of course, be only a transient concession to reality, to the lack of trained cadres technically capable of planning and operating an economy in which no major means of production are left in private hands. But it appears likely to reflect also the influ-

* Perhaps it would be more accurate to say that Nkrumah's aims tend to be expressed in more concrete and operationally definable terms—increased standards of living and welfare, greater equality of income and opportunity, opposition to neo-colonialism, achievement of unified African institutions. In his latest and most ambitious published work, *Consciencism,* which is subtitled "Philosophy and Ideology for Decolonization and Development with Particular Reference to the African Revolution" (London: Heinemann, 1964), there are eight index references to "egalitarianism" and only one to "humanism" (although the concept appears in two or three other places).

ence of Western values, assimilated through British and French
channels, and a consequential reluctance to incur the initial human
costs which, on the Russian showing, appear to accompany efforts
to effect a complete socialist reconstruction within a generation.[3]
Even Yugoslavia was unacceptable as a model to Mamadou Dia,
formerly the leading economist-politician and Prime Minister of
Senegal. Following a visit to the Scandinavian countries, Dia expressed a preference for their kind of society.[4] Israel, too, is often
taken as a model. For what it is worth, there is the late D. K.
Chisiza's intuitive observation that neither capitalism nor communism is likely to be adopted in pure form in Africa, where "the
tendency is toward a pragmatic approach which discards the irrelevant and incorporates the best from both systems." But, lacking
a clear model, both the criteria of what is "best" and the ensuing
policies will inevitably vary.[5]

A second policy line, corollary to the first, is that all of the countries contemplate some role for private enterprise, both indigenous
and foreign, at least for so long as it behaves in a manner consistent
with their aims. The 1962 Program of Ghana's Convention People's
Party and her first Seven-Year Development Plan[6] both proclaim
socialist aims but envisage no general take-over of economic activity
by the state. Rather, socialism is to be achieved by steady expansion
of the public and cooperative sector. At a minimum, this seems to
mean that peasant farmers and indigenous traders and industrialists will be permitted to continue functioning more or less as before,
and that foreign capital and enterprise will be accepted as a matter
of necessity. Indeed, all of the socialist countries have found it expedient not only to accept private foreign capital (and aid from capitalist governments), but to welcome it. Ghana and Senegal early declared themselves against nationalization as a general policy, imply-
ing (or stating) that this was intended as an assurance for foreign
capitalists. Ghanaian policy, after some vacillation, seems to have
been stabilized by the investment law of April 1963. Guinea found
it necessary to take similar steps. Statements of policy were followed (in April 1962) by legislation of an investment code.[7] Guinea's earlier assurance against nationalization of the Fria operation
appears not to have been regarded as a general guarantee; and her
nationalization of two major public utilities early in 1961, and of all
private banks and insurance companies, may have had a scare effect
which it was thought necessary to counteract. In 1962 Mr. Kawawa

(then Prime Minister), acknowledging that Tanganyika will certainly need outside investment, added that his government was taking active steps to attract it; and about a year later a Foreign Investments (Protection) Act became law. But the welcome mat for foreign enterprise does not read "laissez faire" in any of these countries. Restrictions have been sometimes imposed on freedom to transfer earnings, with reinvestment of some portion of the remainder in the host country; and the right to nationalize has been explicitly or implicitly reserved, with some sort of provision for compensation.[8]

Third, the spheres within which private enterprise is to be permitted to operate have been (or will be) defined, although the definitions vary in scope and precision, and sometimes change. Guinea, in addition to the nationalizations mentioned above, early brought all foreign and internal wholesale trade into the public sector and created retail stores to compete in the private sector. But late in 1963 most state retail stores were closed, limited private importing was legalized, and an economic conference stressed the expansion of the private sector.[9] The Second Ghanaian Development Plan listed three categories of industries: the first, which comprised transport, communications, energy, waterworks, and cocoa export, was reserved for public ownership; the second was a narrowly limited group, where government participation, along with private capital, was mandatory; the third was a residual sector freely open to private enterprise provided certain rules were followed.[10] The first Seven-Year Plan does not envisage such precise sectorization, but settles for the statement that "during the transition to a socialist form of society the economy of the country will remain a mixed economy, in which public and private enterprise will each have a legitimate, recognizable, and very important contribution to make."[11] Senegal, according to Senghor, will have a socialized sector, agriculture; a mixed sector, mainly public utilities; and a free sector, banks, commerce, and industry.[12] At the time of going to press it was reliably reported that the Tanganyikan Five-Year Development Plan—the first to be drafted under the aegis of the new Ministry of Development Planning—would specify the scope of planned public investment in traditionally private types of activities and the areas to be left to private initiative.

Fourth, the freedom accorded private enterprise is limited by defining the standards of behavior that must be followed as a condition for being allowed to operate. The Second Ghanaian Development Plan was explicit. It said:

At the present stage of Ghana's development, our major interest lies not in reserving some particular industries for government operation, but in ensuring that all industries, whether private or government, observe certain rules. These rules are: to recognize trade unions, to train Ghanaians for superior posts, to employ Ghanaians for superior posts wherever feasible, and to develop the use of local raw materials wherever possible.[13]

The provisions of Ghana's Seven-Year Plan, and of the 1963 investment law, are less explicit but are consistent with these rules. Senghor, having said that private capital will not be scorned but rather sought, specified that the free sector would be "oriented toward the objectives of the plan and, to a certain extent, controlled" by the offering of tax advantages to private businesses. "In return, capital in this sector will be expected to accept social legislation and even to cooperate in building the social infrastructure."[14] Sékou Touré spoke of the necessity for private employers to recognize that the labor movement is not clandestine, and to concern themselves with the future of the country.[15] Tanganyika has attempted to persuade private employers to provide better working conditions, improved labor relations, and wider opportunities for training and promotion, but reluctantly contemplates legislation if voluntary reversal of typical pre-independence policies does not proceed more rapidly. None of these prospective limitations on private enterprise is particularly socialistic, unless one interprets every departure from strict laissez faire as a step toward socialism. Indeed, they seem to be little more than warnings to business to accept principles of behavior similar to those that have evolved in the West. Yet they could also be interpreted as tactical steps which, though not socialistic in themselves, are regarded as essential to the conduct of an undeviating socialist strategy under limiting conditions.*

---

* Such a strategy is most evident in Ghana. The Seven-Year Development Plan calls for the eventual achievement of a socialist organization of the economy by "productive" government investment "until by the end of the [20-year] transition period the state will be controlling . . . the dominant share of the economy" (p. 3). There is already an important cadre of state enterprises in banking, manufacturing, construction, agriculture, fishing, forestry, mining, and electric power. Some have already achieved profitability. See also various references below to Nkrumah's speech of March 11, 1964, presenting the Plan to Parliament.

Fifth, it appears to be the intention, in some of the countries at least, to modernize agriculture without altering the communal basis of land tenure where this persists. That is, the peasant is to remain an individual operator of land to which he holds no transferable title. Nyerere has said, "We must reject . . . individual ownership of land," go back to the traditional African custom "where one is entitled to land if he uses it."* Also, an important role is envisaged for agricultural cooperatives, not only in Tanganyika but in the other three countries. Ghana decided in 1962–63 to experiment with state farms. About a hundred now exist, four being supervised by Soviet and two by Israeli technicians.[16]

Finally, we may note a certain ambivalence in the attitudes of African Socialist leaders toward labor. On the one hand, labor unions are regarded as the vanguard of socialism. On the other hand, the tendency of workers to stress their own narrow economic interests is recognized as a problem. Strikes, economically motivated or (as is sometimes alleged) politically motivated under outside influence, have been dealt with vigorously in Guinea and Ghana; analogous disciplinary measures were taken against a Tanganyikan trade union leader in the early days of the Republic.[17] Senghor exhorts labor unions to become more integrated into the national framework;[18] and Nyerere, perhaps mindful that organized labor is peculiarly able to gain economic advantage, calls on wage earners, along with peasants, students, leaders, "all of us," to make sure that the "socialist attitude of mind is not lost through the temptations to personal gain; . . . or through the temptation to look on the good of the whole community as . . . secondary . . . to the interests of our own particular group."[19] In February 1964, following an abortive attempt in November 1963 to "integrate" labor and government, a "national union" was formed under official aegis.[20]

It is too early to determine, by examination of policies and achievements, how much socialist substance there is behind the rhetoric of the African Socialist leaders. That there is some, especially in Guinea and Ghana, there can be little doubt. But many of the policies that have been adopted are not distinctively social-

---

* Nyerere, "Ujamaa." Title to land was formerly in the chief, who held it on behalf of the people, and allocated it according to need. Now title is in the state, and local authorities perform the chiefly function. Private titles are permissible, and require payment of rent to the state.

istic, and it is not possible to predict that, in the aggregate, the paths being followed will lead surely to a form of society that will generally be regarded as socialistic.

This is not to say that the socialistic rhetoric is meaningless or futile. One of the great needs of countries making the transition to modernism is solidarity: a sense of community, and a consequent willingness to subordinate private interests to those of society as a whole. Nationalism, and its cousin, Pan-Africanism, help to create solidarity, but of a specialized and limited, or vague and ambiguous, sort. The sense of community promoted by socialist rhetoric, on the other hand, is related specifically to the needs of developing countries.

Socialism, because it focuses on economic relations, on the relations of men to wealth and of man to man in the productive context, has things to say that are widely thought to be relevant to the processes of economic development. The processes of development are, in a fundamental sense, divisive, involving functional and structural differentiation of the kind epitomized, in Adam Smith's phrase, by the division of labor. And so, for this reason, there is a tendency toward what Marx called alienation, and a corresponding need for the evolution of integrative mechanisms.[21] How great the need, and what the most effective way of meeting it, is hard to say. No one, I believe, has tried to identify and measure the quantitative effect of alienation, or of the various integrative antidotes that men have devised (e.g., trade unions). Indeed, such considerations are ignored in conventional economic theory, where labor appears as a freely manipulable commodity, a mere tool of "appropriately" motivated managers and entrepreneurs, whose need for profit as an incentive to perform their function must be respected if growth is to continue, but whose methods are not at issue. Yet intuition, and respect for mankind, suggest that labor's motivations must be respected too, and attention paid to the worker as a person. Otherwise, his use of that instrument of last resort, withdrawal of effort, may have an important effect on productivity, and presumably has done so in many situations. Socialism, with its emphasis on the needs of man rather than the rights of property, and on cooperation rather than competition, has a humanistic appeal that its proponents hope will limit labor's propensity to indulge in the slowdown.

That this is the hope of African Socialist leaders is clear from many of their pronouncements (see William H. Friedland's chapter in this volume, for example). It is thought that by providing the masses with a sense of participation in an effort to modernize the economy for the common good, socialism will combat the sense of being manipulated for the benefit of others that workers in private enterprise societies often feel. African elites, familiar with the less savory features of industrialization in Europe and the United States, and themselves emerging from a traditional society structured more to maintain and solidify human relations than to manage the environment for productive increase, recognize the inherently divisive tendencies of competition as a regulator of economic activity and have sought ways to mitigate the conflicts of interest over distribution. Precisely because of its primary concern with this problem, and its potential ability to mobilize cooperative effort, socialism has had wide appeal in the sympathetic and favorable African environment. However, too great emphasis on socialist reality as opposed to rhetoric may retard development, at least for a time, by alienating entrepreneurs. If entrepreneurs are to function effectively, the private sector cannot be confronted with the threat of early nationalization. Nor, alternatively, can the heads of small private enterprise be converted wholesale into managers of large, authoritarian, impersonal state enterprises. Thus rhetoric has some advantages over reality during the transition. Indeed, socialist rhetoric has a kind of reality of its own, since it may smooth the road to economic development while pointing the path to eventual socialism.[22]

Even if it does not constitute a prelude to the achievement of a socialist organization of society, therefore, socialist rhetoric may make an important contribution to the achievement of modernism. Socialism in Africa must therefore be interpreted as at least partly a charismatic effort to rally support for policies that will promote economic and social development, whether or not they promote a progressive socialization of production and distribution processes.

### Obstacles to Achievement of Socialism

What paths will actually be followed, and where they will lead, will depend only partly on the conceptualizations and policies so far considered. To a considerable extent, the outcome will depend on the conditions which the countries inherited, especially the degree to which commercial and other forms of indigenous private enterprise had already become well rooted during the colonial era. Possibly to an even greater extent, the outcome will be determined by new forces generated by the processes of growth and development during the first several decades of independence. Despite differences in initial conditions, these new forces will confront all of the African Socialist countries with a number of closely similar conflicts and problems which are likely to have considerable influence upon their success in creating a socialistic organization of economic activity. I shall discuss four of these areas of potential conflict: those centering around foreign private capital and enterprise, indigenous private capital and enterprise, labor unions, and agriculture.

Before speaking of these four problem areas, it is important to recognize that, in each case, conflict stems from a difference between the inherent logic of a truly socialist form of society, which the pronouncements of the leaders suggest is desirable, and the logics according to which economic groups function in private enterprise societies. Socialism, in its ideal conceptualization, is a cooperative form, in which the functions of individuals and groups are conceived to contribute directly to the welfare of all, and only indirectly to private welfare—not the other way around, as under competitive private enterprise. The latter, despite much slippage of gears, rewards the initiators of productive activities and innovations with a more or less competitively determined share of the resulting increment of output, and assumes that society as a whole will benefit because the share will not exhaust the increment. Socialism assumes that if all seek to promote the good of all, rather than their private welfare, the resulting benefits, when parceled out according to more or less egalitarian principles, will suffice to invoke continued productive effort. Under idealized socialism there is thus no conflict of economic interests, no competitive struggle of man against man, sector against sector. There may be problems, but if so they arise from some different cause than built-in, structural economic rivalry. The society, to use a favored term, is economically integrated; it is a cooperative system without antagonistic economic classes, the form of social system that African Socialist leaders frequently assert is traditional to African society and characteristic of at least the rural sectors of their countries today.[23]

Assuming that a relatively integrated form of cooperative system is what the socialist leaders of Africa wish to create, one must concede that the structural specifications for such a society are not well defined. Public ownership of the means of production is the traditional criterion, but when one considers Yugoslavia and the Soviet

Union, to make only one comparison, it appears that public ownership can achieve a variety of forms. Socialism, moreover, does not
necessarily follow upon nationalization, and expropriation is not
the only method of bringing private property under social control.
Where agriculture is concerned, experimentation with socialistic
forms has been active but notable successes have been few, Gezira
and the Israeli *kibbutzim* being among the rare examples. In these
days, therefore, a socialist, even a Marxist, label does not indicate a
particular form of social organization toward which to steer, and
each group of leaders must come to grips with this problem on its
own terms. To the extent that this has not been done there will be
a tendency to talk in terms of broad goals like integration, and to
stress avoidance of the mistakes of others. One finds Dia, for example, asserting that development is something more than mere
growth. Therefore, "it does not suffice to replace archaic structures
by those of a capitalistic mercantile economy, . . . to replace . . .
rudimentary techniques with advanced ones. It is necessary that
the structural modifications . . . be translated into a true integration of the national economy with the various strata of the population."[24] Analogous sentiments are expressed in the writings of
Nyerere, Senghor, and others.

But a vision of Utopia is one thing, and working out a suitable
itinerary for the journey is quite another. In our brief review of the
highlights of economic policy we have seen that private capital,
both foreign and indigenous, is to be accepted, even welcomed and
encouraged. Public and mixed sectors are also being established,
and provision is made, in Ghana, Guinea, and Tanganyika at least,
for public participation with private capital in certain industries.
We have also noted that labor unions are approved. And we have
observed that peasant agriculture and perhaps also communal land
tenure are to be perpetuated, while technology is modernized and
production and distribution commercialized with the aid, as a rule,
of cooperatives. The question is whether the institutions that will
take shape under the guidance of these policies will produce societies that, in any substantial and meaningful sense, conform to a
socialist image.

Even if one recognizes that in Africa socialism most often means
"mixed society," there is room for wide variation in the mix. To
attempt at the present juncture to predict the ultimate blend would
be rash. In particular, it would be unwarranted to assume that

adoption of a socialist label suffices to predetermine the outcome. In the following paragraphs I shall present some thoughts concerning the obstacles likely to be encountered, while recognizing that in so doing I may exaggerate problems and underestimate the strength of the forces favoring development along socialistic lines, forces that are largely political and, therefore, of possibly overriding importance. Perhaps it is unnecessary to say that I am concerned only with internal influences, and so avoid involvement in the effects of the contest between East and West for African allegiance, important though these may turn out to be as a determinant of Africa's future.

Consider first the case of private enterprise and private capital, both domestic and foreign. One can hardly question the correctness of the judgment that these are needed if adequate rates of economic growth are to be achieved. But traditional socialists, whether Marxist or not, would see an incompatibility between this concession to capitalism and the aim of developing along socialistic lines. African Socialists, on the other hand, seem to take a different view. Senghor refers to what he calls a "semblance" of a contradiction, but contends that it is "only superficial" and can be resolved, if, indeed, it really exists.[25] He does not, however, explain and justify these optimistic judgments. Nkrumah is more explicit. Speaking at a dinner for businessmen early in 1963, he expressed the conviction that "our ideas of socialism can coexist with private enterprise," but he also stressed that the problem was how to permit private capital investment while keeping "sufficient control to prevent undue exploitation" and preserving "integrity and sovereignty without crippling economic or political ties to *any* country, bloc, or system."[26]

I shall not attempt to review the pros and cons concerning the compatibility of private ownership with various concepts of socialism, for to do so would carry us into deep and imperfectly charted waters, but I would like to remark a couple of possible paradoxes: first, that the development of foreign private enterprise may represent less of a threat to the achievement of socialist objectives than the development of domestic enterprise; second, that a policy of Africanization of foreign enterprises, though important for economic development, may be more of a hindrance than a help to the evolution of socialism.

The first paradox arises from a basic criticism of foreign enterprises as they have operated in premodern societies, that they often tend to be externally rather than internally oriented, constituting foreign economic and social enclaves within the economy. This is another way of saying that foreign enterprises have failed to become closely integrated into the structure of the host society. To the extent that this continues to be the case, as it may be especially in the extractive industries which are of leading importance in Africa, there will be few if any indigenous businessmen or politicians in the next generation who have risen to affluence on the coattails of foreign enterprise, and who might therefore rise to defend it against eventual nationalization. To this extent, the road to socialism will be easier. This assumes also that there are few independently wealthy local capitalists and landlords who exercise important political power and influence. If there were such a group, or if it were permitted to develop, the transient foreign managers might forge effective social and economic links between the foreign enterprises and these representatives of local power. This has often happened in Latin America, and accounts in part for the difficulty of bringing about social change there. The pattern has emerged in Africa hardly at all, however, and the African Socialist countries are sure to be on guard against it. For example, in his speech of March 11, 1964, Nkrumah said that Ghanaians would not be permitted to purchase shares in foreign-owned enterprises. Foreign capital may thus operate in these countries without creating a local class or group with a vested interest in the perpetuation of foreign ownership.

This is not true of domestic private capital and enterprise. By definition, they cannot make a substantial contribution to economic growth without creating a group or class with a vested interest in perpetuating its privileges. Moreover, as already noted, such a class might form an alliance with foreign enterprise. Whether, and if so how, an indigenous private sector might eventually be socialized is a question requiring considerable thought and political skill. Too much socialization now will discourage development of this aid to growth; too much laissez faire will make eventual socialization difficult. Ghana, again, is aware of the problem: Nkrumah, in the above-mentioned speech, said that the advance to socialism would be hampered by encouraging Ghanaian capitalism, yet recognized that small enterpreneurs exercise useful initiatives. So he promised them encouragement, but with limitations on size, and specified that "Ghanaian businesses . . . modeled on . . . colonial exploitation" would be denied access to bank credit.

The second paradox is corollary to the first. For if the top echelons of the foreign enterprises should be Africanized, this might create an able, sophisticated group or class with a vested antisocialist interest. To delay Africanization on this ground would be unthinkable. The problem is thus to Africanize foreign enterprise without creating a managerial class with a capitalistic orientation. If they can get away with it, which is surely doubtful, the African Socialist countries may be led to insist on government participation in all enterprises that owe their existence to private foreign initiative. In this way, it might possibly happen that the African officials would become used to thinking of themselves as representatives of the public interest, as servants of the state, and would therefore be more amenable to eventual nationalization than if they had known only the experience of working for a wholly private firm.

Labor unions also create a dilemma. Although the unions in the countries we are considering have often had leaders with Marxist orientation, and in the colonial period the unions were conceived by these leaders as instruments of political change, the basis of their appeal for membership was presumably more economic than political. Now that independence has been won, and a socialist orientation has been adopted by the governments of the countries under examination, the politically minded leaders have come to regard the unions as an instrument to help promote socialism. But the rank and file is more likely to think in terms of higher wages and better working conditions, and to be restless under appeals to sacrifice their own group interest for the alleged welfare of all. This is especially true, perhaps, in the ex-British countries, where the bread-and-butter function of trade unions has been respectable, but not the political function.*

Certain points may be made in evaluating the importance of this potential conflict. First, labor unions have usually been thought to have no function in societies without class antagonisms.† Second, in a society trying to grow and develop along socialistic lines, politically oriented unions can play an important role in disciplin-

* French and other West European unions have had a tendency to be radical political organizations more than bargaining units. But Elliot Berg ("French West Africa," in W. Galenson, ed., *Labor and Economic Development* [New York: Wiley, 1959], p. 222), says of French West Africa in the 1950's: "In practice, the union movement has, in a basic sense, been businesslike and reformist. Its orientation is toward the improvement of African wage levels and working conditions within the framework of the prevailing economic and political system. . . . The labor movement remains fundamentally 'trade unionist,' as the French use this term, rather than 'syndicalist.' "

† See Chapter 1 for a discussion of this point, and an unorthodox view.

ing the work force, especially in restraining demands for higher wages and promoting positive attitudes toward work. However, third, the very existence of unions is an invitation for the membership to employ them as tools to pry economic gains out of a resistant society. Therefore, fourth, there is an ever-present tendency for the rank and file to regard the labor movement as an economic bargaining instrument, especially if private enterprise is permitted to exist and to expand. This, in a nutshell, is why Guinea and Ghana have taken strong steps to prevent strikes and to stress the political function of unions and why other leaders have asked labor to moderate its demands. With a lack of shrewd countermeasures the outlook for conflict between the labor movement and the socialist governments would thus seem to be fully as good as for harmony, especially if foreign interests with particular axes to grind should gain influence over the African unions.[27] Ghana, for one, seems to recognize this possibility, and has taken steps to reduce the likelihood of conflict.*

Finally, consider agriculture. As already suggested, there is a feeling among at least some of the African Socialists that, because of its communal organization, African agriculture is inherently socialistic.† All that needs to be done, therefore, is to build on this foundation. Since peasants are by far the most numerous occupational group, it seems to follow that socialism is the destined form of society for Africa. Senghor calls agriculture a "socialized sector," as though this were an obvious fact that required no explanation. And Nyerere, referring to land tenure, said, "We must . . . regain our former attitude of mind—our tradition of African Socialism."[28]

Yet the fact is that the agricultural sector has been highly resistant to collectivization in every country that has attempted it (with the possible exception of Israel). Although the Russian peasant village had a form of communal organization, the *mir,* the Soviet Union did not attempt to build on this somewhat disintegrated base.[29] It turned to collectivization, and has had trouble with agricultural productivity ever since (though partly because of inferior com-

---

* Among these steps are integration of the Trades Union Congress with the monolithic Convention People's Party, disaffiliation of the Congress from world labor groupings, efforts to bring about the disaffiliation of other African labor movements and their affiliation with the All-African Trade Union Federation, and Nkrumah's announcement (March 11, 1964) that "workers' management" would be tried in several state enterprises, presumably to give workers a tangible economic stake in socialism.

† The following chapter persuasively disputes this view.

binations of soil and climate). Poland and Yugoslavia have so far permitted private peasant agriculture to remain the dominant form of rural organization because they have been unable to devise, or unwilling to run the political risks of introducing wholesale, an operational socialist alternative (although in Yugoslavia land is slowly being taken into state farms and cooperatives as peasants leave it for urban work).[30]

African countries that wish to become socialistic might well contemplate these experiences and consider whether it is, in fact, likely that they can modernize and commercialize peasant agriculture, (a) while maintaining a system of land tenure that is communal in any meaningful sense, and (b) without creating a class of economic individualists who neither think like socialists nor believe in socialism. Let me indicate the two main roots of the difficulty I envisage. First, it seems unlikely that sound land management, under which erosion will be controlled and minimized, soil exhaustion avoided, and permanent improvements introduced in the peculiarly demanding conditions found generally in Africa, will become the norm under traditional African systems of land tenure. Modifications of the traditional systems presumably can be devised —perhaps under Tanganyika's system of cooperatives and village settlements they are being devised—which will conduce to sound land management while retaining the concept that land is ultimately held in common for the benefit of all. But such reforms will not be easy to work out or introduce, and they are likely to be continually undermined by the forces of commercialization and individual interest. Cooperatives are thought of as an antidote to these forces, but confidence in this device could prove to be misplaced. The operation of a cooperative, and the manner in which it serves its members, is often so similar to that of a private partnership or stock company as not to constitute much of a step toward, or safeguard of, socialism.[31] Ghana's decision to take the more radical step of setting up state farms in addition to cooperatives, because it signifies a desire to effectuate eventually a wholesale structural transformation of the agricultural sector, will bear watching.

*Conclusion*

The thesis of this paper has been that the road to socialism in Africa is not clearly defined and possibly for this reason is also strewn with obstacles. With one or two exceptions, such as Ghana and possibly Guinea, the policies adopted appear to be more concerned with promoting economic development than with promoting socialism. This perhaps is pragmatic and realistic. The resources of human talent, of man-made capital, and of natural riches do not make it possible for African countries to erect complete socialist structures on the foundations left by colonial administrations. Nor can they forgo foreign aid if they wish to grow. But aid from the West, it is sometimes feared, may require them to temper their socialism even more than is rendered necessary by internal conditions.* The alternative is to rely solely on aid from the Soviet sphere or mainland China, but this they appear to regard as unsuitable for other reasons.

Under the circumstances, while recognizing the possible contribution of socialist rhetoric to economic development, we may also recognize that the policies adopted within the next decade or two are not likely to be singlemindedly socialistic. But policies that are not socialistic may encourage forces that are positively antisocialistic. It therefore seems possible that the socialist-minded countries will develop ultimate social forms that are quite different from the idealized images that currently guide their leaders. The Tanganyikans, for example, have indicated that they do not want to build an African middle class but rather want to work toward a classless society. What they may overlook is that the forces of modernization, especially the division of labor, tend to produce competing groups or classes with different sources of income, different economic interests, and that strong measures are needed if the development of class antagonisms is to be avoided. When Nyerere, for example, says, "Africa is fortunate in that there is still found on this continent a form of organization of society which fundamentally solves the conflict between the individual and the society,"[32] he implies that this initial state of affairs (if, indeed, it still exists) can be perpetuated during and after economic growth and development. This may be true, but it will not be true if self-oriented economic classes such as industrial and commercial capitalists, organized labor, and individual farmers are allowed to emerge.

---

* For example: "It has been said that politics is the language of priorities; a decision therefore to assist a project in one area rather than another is a political decision, and often affects a whole range of economic and social plans. No underdeveloped country really complains about this. . . . But sometimes the type or conditions of aid have a more ideological content. . . . It is because we expect international agencies not to impose these sorts of conditions that we prefer to get our aid through them when possible." (Julius Nyerere, "McDougall Lecture—FAO" [mimeo.], November 18, 1963.)

Nkrumah, for one, has sensed the problem: "The composition of the Party has become socially quite heterogeneous, and there is the danger that our socialist objective may be clouded by opportunistic accommodations and adjustments to petit bourgeois elements in our ranks who are unsympathetic and sometimes even hostile to the social aims to which the Party is dedicated."[33] Subsequently it was reported that Nkrumah saw no prospect in Ghana of a speedy growth of indigenous capitalism like that which has occurred in India.[34] Perhaps he was already devising an opposing strategy.

My point is that in any society that eschews the Russian model but succeeds, nonetheless, in moving steadily along the path of modernization, the forces tending to create economic classes with conflicting interests are exceedingly strong, while the mechanisms required to resolve these conflicts and mobilize a sense of mutual interest are difficult to devise and to create. I suggest that this state of affairs, and the resulting problems, will be increasingly manifest in all of the African countries that call themselves socialist, unless economic and political counterstrategies effectively forestall creation of self-oriented economic groups (as they may in Ghana), or socialism is pursued at the expense of economic growth (as may have happened in Guinea). Elsewhere, there seems to have been either less capacity or less will to press current economic activity into a well-defined socialist mold. Nonetheless, these less aggressively socialist countries may succeed in creating societies of the middle way, along Scandinavian and Israeli lines. If either the more or the less militant countries do succeed in achieving growth and socialism, history may judge the results superior to those achieved in societies that follow what Chisiza called a Pragmatic Pattern of Development. But it is also possible that African Socialism and African pragmatism, both creatures of the second half of the twentieth century and subject to its forces, will come to approximately the same end.

Chapter 3

# Socialism and Traditional African Societies

Igor Kopytoff

One of the recurring themes in discussions of African Socialism is the proposition that African societies are "cooperative," "collectivist," "communalist," or "socialist" in their traditional form; and, further, that upon this foundation a special kind of socialism, deeply rooted in African culture, can and indeed must be erected. The thesis is too well known to require extensive documentation.[1] Senghor summarized it when he stated that from a study of African civilization "we would learn that we had already realized *socialism* before the coming of the European."[2] This paper attempts to interrelate the historical background of the proposition, its role in an emerging African ideology, the extent to which it reflects African reality, and, finally, its implications, from the institutional point of view, for the construction of socialist forms of organization in Africa.

The view that African societies are organized on some kind of communal principle is by no means recent. Historically, it had been advanced for numerous societies on all continents, together with a large number of other stereotypes that inevitably emerge when different societies come into contact and make attempts at mutual characterizations. In a short but telling paper, Katherine George[3] has presented the range of such stereotypes of Africa up to the eighteenth century, and St. Clair Drake[4] has analyzed somewhat more formally the more recent evaluations of African societies. The variations and contradictions in the stereotypes are enormous. The scarcely human beings in the writings of antiquity give way in the early Age of Exploration to stable polities ruled by kings and nobles. Where Arab travelers saw virtue in relation to Islamic influence, the European Enlightenment, alienated from its own social order, created the virtuous, because untouched, "noble savage" from whom Europe could learn in its quest for regeneration. The later images are more familiar, for many of them are still with us. Unbridled lawlessness coexisted with robots in the iron grip of unchanging custom, and witch-ridden paranoiacs under tyrannous chiefs vied with happy villagers living in communal harmony.

The common thread here is ethnocentrism—not, it must be stressed, simply in its restricted and vulgarized meaning of the denigration of other societies, but in its broader, more significant sense of a universal tendency of all people to perceive other culture patterns through the categories and concerns of their own. The resulting myths may be positive or negative. The "savage" was made "noble" to be enlisted in purely European ideological battles. Economically "nonrational" man can be useful to justify exploitation, to indicate mental simplicity, or to prove a superior social consciousness. A certain type of communal organization suggests "backwardness" to a laissez faire Victorian or to a Marxist and the model for an ideal society to a Utopian socialist. Varied though such judgments may be, the biases they reflect derive from a single ethnocentric core which may be called the *social mythology* of the observer's culture, consisting of the assumptions and myths about his own society and, by projection, about society in general. These myths are related to but do not exactly mirror the objective institutional organization of the observer's own society. Social mythology conditions both the inward and outward views and utilizes those bits and pieces of behavior (never its entire range) that are available through circumstance, perceptual bias, and ideological need. Moreover, a social mythology becomes more conscious and more susceptible to reformulation in times of social change or when new models appear through contact with other societies.

In situations of culture contact, ethnocentric myth building by each society about the other is inevitable (see, for example, a survey of a usually neglected subject, that of African stereotypes about the West, in Herskovits).[5] Furthermore, such myths interpenetrate and influence one another, though seldom equally in situations of political domination. Over time, a collection of myths comes into being and different viewpoints draw their sustenance from it. In the case of Africa, the crudest and most negative of these myths have been eroded in recent times. The emergence of modern anthropology, with its reiterated cautions about ethnocentrism, and the changing international situation, as it affects the mass media of information, have been reshaping the Western view of Africa by divesting the negative stereotypes of their scientific and humanistic respectability. At the same time, other stereotypes, positive or potentially so, have, on balance, been preserved or even enhanced.

On the African side, what may be called spiritual decolonization has, at least until now, dealt primarily with the existing collection of myths. Some positive ones have been reinforced or recombined into new ones; some negative ones are still accepted but are relegated to those aspects of traditional culture that should be eradicated (for example, the belief that bridewealth is somehow degrading is tenacious among some African elites); and some old myths are reinterpreted in new terms. Thus, the nineteenth-century view of Egypt as the fountainhead of all civilization was formerly used to deprive sub-Saharan Africa of all credit for indigenous achievement; at present, this scientifically untenable interpretation of Egypt's role in world history is used by some Africans to bolster the historical importance of Africa as a whole.

We are witnessing in this and other discussions the building by the elite of a new Pan-African social mythology whose vocabulary remains essentially Western. This is perhaps unavoidable because the languages used are Western and so are the concepts against which it pits itself. The historic context in which this social mythology is being constructed is relevant. Not so very long ago, "communalism," "primitive socialism," and "the submergence of the individual in the group" were myths supporting the idea of "primitiveness." Kidd's *Kafir Socialism,* for example, published in 1908, made these points in support of an early rationalization for *apartheid.* At the present historic juncture, the adoption of the term "socialism" carries different and, on the whole, positive implications. It is a term that now carries positive connotations in most of the world; it enhances the symbolism of the separation of Africa from the colonial ("capitalist") powers; and, finally, it provides an ostensibly traditional sanction to the construction of a new social order.

So far, we have dealt with the concept of traditional African socialism as a by-product of a specific cultural process. Its significance, ideologically, to the modernizing African nations is clear. It may also be viewed as necessary in the sense that profound social and political reorganization is probably impossible without a body of mythology about both the past and the desired future. The process is a part of that "inventory" of African civilization which Senghor rightly regards as necessary but whose results he seems to define in advance.[6] Since traditional African culture is regarded as providing the means for understanding the way in which practical planning should unfold in modern-day Africa, a closer scrutiny of the communalism of traditional society is in order. What we are concerned with here is not its essential truth in some philosophical sense but its pragmatic utility as a guide to action.

We shall begin with a specific example of the operation of selective perception in the evaluation of African societies. This writer did research among a Congolese group, the Suku, where the functionally most salient social unit, the corporate lineage, cooperated in consumption but very rarely in production, controlled property as a unit, and practiced extensive and mandatory mutual help within its ranks while rigidly excluding from such help members of other corporate lineages. The views of this society among European residents differed as widely as their respective points of contact with it. An agricultural officer, concerned with patterns of production, saw a large measure of "individualism." One missionary, intimately involved with such matters as marriage and religion, in which the unity of the lineage is a dominant principle, saw widespread cooperation and the "coalescence of the individual with his group." Another missionary, whose administrative duties involved working with members of different lineages, witnessed numerous conflicts of interest and saw in them proof of a "crass indifference to fellow human beings." It is also significant that those who saw cooperation regarded it as something to be expected in an African society; those who saw individualism were convinced that the Suku were deviants from the "usual African patterns." Clearly, both subscribed to a common mythology of what an African society should be like.

Even the observation of a single activity may yield different results. In common with most peoples of the Central African savanna, the Suku practice the so-called "communal hunt" of the dry season, when large stretches of the country are burned and several villages participate in the hunt. At this point, one may see cooperation. Then, one discovers that when a hunter catches an animal, he gives a portion of it to the "owner" of the land being burned and another to the particular hunter who shot the animal a second time, but he does not share the game with all the other hunters. Here, individualism comes to the fore, unless we follow the hunter to the village, where he will distribute the meat among a large number of people. But who are these people? They are members of his own lineage and those with whom he has a precise relationship of reciprocal obligations. Which of these aspects is the observer to stress? One can emphasize one or another, through ignorance, preconception, or choice. Arguments as to what "basic" orientation the organization of the hunt reveals are sterile and would only obscure the existing network of social relations. There is no basis here for a cooperative organization in the abstract; co-operation exists in some respects but not others, between some people but not all. "Socializing" the entire activity would necessi-tate a frontal attack on the very basis of traditional organization of the rights in land, of kinship groups, of interlineage relations, and of the system of mutual obligations.

To call the process by which meat is produced among the Suku a "cooperative enterprise" because at some points several persons are seen working together is as much a distortion as calling General Motors a "cooperative" for the same reason. One can observe, to be sure, that the complicated network of distribution does result in sharing each animal, piece by piece, with a considerable group of people. But it must also be observed that the distribution is no more equal than the distribution of money, far-flung as it is, in any in-dustrial society through its own particular network of culturally defined rights and obligations.

Such considerations have made modern anthropology extremely skeptical of the utility of shorthand descriptions of whole societies. They may have their uses as ultimate summary abstractions, which are not meant, however, to lead one back to the specific empirical data on which they are based, in the same sense that in physics the theory of the expanding universe, though derived from observa-tion, does not predict the next phase of the moon. But when social planning is involved, the communal model cannot be substituted for the precise isolation of the existing social units, of the different principles underlying their organization, and of the variety of functions that these units serve. It is highly relevant whether that all-embracing term "community" stands for the family, or the lineage, or the village, or the nation; whether cooperation occurs in production but not in consumption, in fishing but not in agri-culture, in bridge building but not in trade, in the ancestral cult but not in assembling bridewealth. The presence of cooperation in one aspect does not predict, as cross-cultural data indicate, where else it will be found, and cooperation within a corporate lineage is different from cooperation based on strict reciprocity, where each side keeps a tally of what it gives and receives with no less rigidity than a grocer in New York.

Thus, Nyerere is correct when he points to the individual component in African economic relations: "To him [the African], the wage is *his* wage; the property is *his* property." But when he adds, "But his brother's need is his brother's need, and he cannot ignore that need,"[7] the crucial question remains unanswered: Who, in this particular society, is defined to be such a "brother"? The answer for an East African pastoral society is quite different from what it is in a Fulani emirate. Sometimes the recognition that boundaries of cooperation in Africa are often restricted to relatively small groups has led to formulating the problem of establishing socialism as a matter of "extending" these boundaries to larger groups. Phrasing it in this way is equivalent to seeing the problem of socialized medicine in the United States as simply a matter of having the doctors extend the good-fellowship of their families to the wider circle of their patients. The extension of any pattern to another unit does not occur in a vacuum, for it always means overcoming already existing patterns. Some patterns, furthermore, are not easily extendible. It is no accident that lineage segmentation is such a recurrent phenomenon in African societies organized on the lineage principle; beyond a certain size, lineage solidarity in the same form becomes impossible.

Western social mythology about Africa is particularly susceptible to confusion between the institutional arrangements found in African cultures and the ostensible "personality" of the peoples in these cultures. The new social mythology of Africa tends to perpetuate this confusion. Negritude is, perhaps, the outstanding example.) But cooperative institutions do not by definition imply the existence of cooperative personalities in any generalized sense, and any planning that relies on this equation may be questioned. Among the constant themes in the literature on African social change are the readiness to abandon cooperative patterns when their utility for individuals lapses and when sanctions supporting them are removed, and the evasion of kinship obligations under new conditions.[8] By the same token, the attenuation of kinship ties is accompanied by the emergence of new institutions such as credit societies, operating on a reciprocal and contractual rather than a cooperative basis.[9] These changes can scarcely be accounted for by postulating a generalized cooperative African personality in the psychological sense of that term.

The possible sources of misinterpretation we have mentioned are to a large extent laymen's errors. The question to be raised now touches on some fundamental points of methodology and interpretation in the social sciences. It is that of the extent to which the categories of Western social mythology have influenced the social sciences in their analyses of other, including African, societies. These basic categories are well known: economic, social, familial, political, religious, legal, artistic, and so on. Have these aspects been isolated in the first place because Western social experience tends to make them discrete functional categories corresponding rather closely to discrete institutions? Has "religious" become a theoretical category because there are relatively isolated Western institutions called "churches"? Is the "political" a function because other and different institutions regulate the use of physical power? We are, to be sure, increasingly conscious of the fact that Western institutions are not as unifunctional, not as discrete, as we have thought them to be. Our social mythology is out of step with reality, but its strength can be gauged from the frequent designation in the social sciences of the political functions of churches or corporations as "informal."

Applying Western functional categories to other societies has inevitably resulted in a lack of fit between these *a priori* categories and the reality. Thus, a single African institution, such as kingship or the lineage headship, serves a variety of functions that Western social mythology regards as separate. The king is found to rule and also to sacrifice to the national gods; the lineage head manages the budget and is also the priest of the ancestral cult. By ignoring the fact that the king deals with problems in the national cult that are unrelated to the lineage cult, and by putting them together under the single category of "religion," we note that institutional and functional areas overlap. This is then interpreted as proof that the culture and the society are "more integrated": the less the fit, the greater the "integration." A simple artifact of an inadequate methodology is subtly transformed into a qualitative evaluation.

If untrained observers have perpetuated the myth of "communalism," social scientists have often encouraged the stereotype of "more integrated societies." The two myths, it may be noted, reinforce one another semantically, for the idea of "integration" carries a connotation of all-inclusiveness, social cohesion, and harmony.

It may be objected that the analysis we have presented is "institutional" and ignores "those silent forces which make even institutional changes easy or difficult, acceptable or unacceptable, legitimate or illegitimate."[10] These "silent forces" are, to Abraham, an expression of a common African culture underlying a variety of institutional frameworks to be found in Africa. We agree most strongly that a purely institutional analysis of any society, which ignores the cultural factor, is inadequate because *empirically* incomplete and hence predictively weak. Social (as opposed to cultural) anthropology tends to neglect the cultural ideas behind the act and the institution; thus, we often lack data that would allow us to isolate in an empirical way some of the shared traits of Africa as a single culture area. The problem will not be solved, however, by projecting onto a subcontinent the results of the study of a single group, such as the Akan by Abraham or the Baluba by Tempels.[11] Moreover, when such studies are couched in psychologically suggestive terms without any empirical psychological data, their reliability will always be questioned. The difficulties of such a procedure with a single society are great enough already.[12]

There is the further question, whether a methodologically satisfactory construction of a generalized African culture will be useful except by bringing it back into the specific institutional framework of that society—useful, that is, for purposes with which we are here concerned analytically and with which African planners are concerned practically.

Successful social engineering in Africa, as anywhere else, will demand at least as much careful study as is given to the promotion of fisheries and new crops, and the complexities of African cultures and the richness of their variations deserve more than a simple pigeonhole of Western derivation.

The institutional overview we have presented, and the importance of studying the cultural variable in its minutest details as far as specific societies are concerned, lead to certain broad conclusions. The most obvious one is that it is the *restructuring* of existing institutional arrangements, both cooperative and noncooperative, that will meet with the greatest resistance. Regardless of whether a fundamental African communal orientation exists, any attempts to take away existing economic and other functions from, let us say, the lineage, or the individual, or the village, will present difficulties. A communal conception of African culture will predict these difficulties no more successfully than an individualistic conception of American culture will predict the reaction to a transfer of existing municipal functions to larger or smaller units.

On the other hand, when one is dealing with new activities, not present in the traditional setting and hence not directly interfering with existing institutional arrangements (latent interference is another matter), the assignment of such new activities to the government or to other groups becomes relatively easy. Similarly, new functions may be assigned to existing groups more successfully than existing functions to new groups. For the government to engage in dam building, electrification, banking, shipping, or mining (in some cases) does not contradict the existing social mythology of the people at large, which has no provision for such activities. Of course, many of the African development plans are concerned with just such activities. When the state takes on such new functions, there is no outcry from the public; this is not because the public is "communally oriented," but because there is no crystallized cultural definition as to where these functions belong and because there are few powerful nongovernmental vested interests of local origin already engaged in these tasks. One need not point out what would happen, by contrast, should the government attempt to take over the activities of the market women in West Africa. It must also be remembered that what matters is the institutional framework within which the people have been operating for some time but which is, as far as most of Africa is concerned, a blend of precolonial and postcolonial institutions. For the actors in a given social system, the analytical difference between what may be called "traditional" and other elements may not be relevant, for nontraditional elements have become a part of the present social mythology and shape the expectations of people. For example, allowances for the wife and each child in the Congo have by now become a "natural" component of wages.

Another implication of the analysis has to do with the lack of fit between Western and African functional categories. This may facilitate the introduction of forms of social organization which, in terms of Western categories, could be interpreted as "socialist." The fact that the basic social groupings in an African society are not unifunctional in the Western definition of function, that the village, for example, may simultaneously serve some religious, some economic, and some political functions, means that a constellation of functions around a single institution which would not be acceptable in much of the West may be feasible in an African society. Thus, a school may be simultaneously an educational, political, and religious institution without eliciting the kind of negative reaction that such a functional constellation would call forth in the United States. The facilitation of socialism in this case is, of course, illusory since it is simply an artifact of the use of inapplicable Western functional categories.

In conclusion, it must be stressed that the low predictive value of the concept of traditional African socialism in dealing with specific problems has nothing to do with its role as an instrument of policy at the ideological level. The myth of traditional socialism is already being elaborated, and its wider dissemination will shape the readiness of the population at large to accept socialist forms when new institutions, serving new functions, are created or when old institutions are made to serve new functions. Since no society is static, the acceptance of this communal mythology will help, in the long run, to restructure existing arrangements in a socialist direction as their functional utility begins to lapse. For the planners and the political leaders, the sociological usefulness of any myth and its successful manipulation depend, however, on the degree to which they are not themselves entirely captured by it and realize the limitations to its application in specific cases. At the same time, some degree of sincere acceptance of the myth is necessary if it is to be sociologically "real." African political leaders are thus threatened, on the one side, by a potential lack of realism and, on the other, by the danger of political cynicism. But this is an old dilemma that politicians have had to face since time immemorial.

Chapter 4

# Socialist Sources of Pan-African Ideology

Dorothy Nelkin

"Pan-Africanism seeks the attainment of the government of Africans, by Africans, for Africans. . . . Economically and socially, Pan-Africanism subscribes to the fundamental objectives of democratic socialism, with state control of the basic means of production and distribution. It stands for the liberty of the subject within the law and endorses the Fundamental Declaration of Human Rights, with emphasis upon the Four Freedoms. . . . Pan-Africanism sets out to fulfill the socioeconomic mission of communism under a libertarian political system . . . [for] there is slowly arising a . . . strong brotherhood of Negro blood throughout the world."[1]

Three streams of thought apparent in Pan-Africanism—African unity, black nationalism, and socialism—are reflections of the common experience of the movement's early spokesmen. W. E. B. DuBois, George Padmore, and the Africans active in the development of Pan-Africanism, despite their greatly different backgrounds, all shared the experience of alienation, of being marginal members of society. DuBois and Padmore, the guiding spirits of the movement, initially sought a solution in democratic socialism.*

DuBois, upon completing his education at Harvard and Berlin, began his career in 1894 as professor of classics at Wilberforce University in Ohio. Shortly thereafter, he moved to Atlanta University, where he remained as professor of sociology until 1910. His interest in African unity originated in his concern with the race problem in the United States. In 1905 he founded the Niagara Movement, which in 1910 became the National Association for the Advancement of Colored People (NAACP). The movement's platform ad-

---

* Marcus Garvey, by contrast, who contributed indirectly to Pan-Africanism through his chauvinistic appeal to such people as Nkrumah, and who is sometimes spoken of as a Pan-Africanist, rejected all socialist movements as "inherently prejudiced against the black race since they were dominated by whites." See E. A. Cronon, *Black Moses* (Madison: University of Wisconsin Press, 1962), p. 196. DuBois dismissed Garvey's "back to Africa" movement as "bombastic, wasteful, illogical, and almost illegal," and harmful to the development of Pan-Africanism. Nkrumah himself ultimately rejected Garveyism, and it will not be considered further here.

vocated "freedom of speech and criticism, . . . the abolition of all caste distinctions based simply on race and color, . . . the monopoly of no class or race, . . . the belief in the dignity of labor."[2] In 1910, he became editor of *Crisis,* the NAACP magazine.

DuBois's education and early thinking were conservative. Only after founding the Niagara Movement did he begin to think in socialist terms. But by 1907, he had made his choice: "In the socialist trend . . . lies the one great hope of the Negro American. . . . Our natural friends are not the rich but the poor, not the great but the masses."[3] Using *Crisis* as a sounding board, he aired his views on the race problem and increasingly looked to Africa as a "forum for Negro propaganda."[4]

By the end of World War I, DuBois was focusing his attention on Africa and the possibilities of Pan-Africanism as a solution to the racial problem, which he now saw as international. Pan-Africanism had been formulated as an anti-imperialist ideology by Henry Sylvester-Williams in a small Pan-African conference in London in 1900, in which DuBois took an active part. In 1919 DuBois redefined the concept in international terms, and between 1919 and 1927 he organized four congresses in an effort to find the right formula for a Pan-African movement. The congresses met with an apathetic response. The resolutions of all four were similar except for their concern with current situations: broadly speaking, they held that government should exist for the benefit of the natives, and should prescribe conditions of labor, provide education, regulate investment of capital to prevent exploitation, and hold land in trust for natives until they could develop it.*

The First Congress (1919) was very small and was attended by only 12 Africans out of 57 delegates. The Second Congress (1921) had a representation of 41 African delegates out of a total 113 and was strongly supported by the British socialists, including Sidney and Beatrice Webb, with whom DuBois discussed the importance of labor solidarity between white and black workers.[5] The second session of the Congress was held in Brussels; *Neptune,* a Brussels newspaper, accused the delegates of serving Moscow and hinted that they were out to stir up native unrest in the lower Congo.[6] The

---

* "DuBois's Pan-African Congress," *Crisis,* XVIII (1919), 271–74. In referring to the congresses, DuBois's and Padmore's numbering system has been utilized. This begins with the 1919 Congress. Colin Legum, in *Pan-Africanism—a Short Political Guide* (London: Pall Mall Press, 1962), calls the 1900 Congress the first.

Third Congress (1923), officially supported by the British Labour Party, was attended by many British socialists, including Lord Olivier, Harold Laski, and H. G. Wells. Only 13 countries were represented. It voiced the usual demands for an African voice in government and an economic organization to provide for the "welfare of the many rather than the enrichment of the few."[7] The Fourth Congress, held in New York (1927) and attended by representatives from 11 countries, was ridiculed by the Communists as representing petty bourgeois black nationalism.[8] DuBois planned to hold the second session of this Congress in Tunisia, but this was vetoed by the French authorities. No further congresses were held until after World War II.

Beginning in 1919, a depressing year in terms of racial strife in the United States, DuBois's thinking underwent important changes. For several years he alternated between enthusiasm for Communism as a "most amazing and most hopeful phenomenon"[9] and criticism of the Bolsheviks as a "horde of scoundrels . . . ready to conquer Africa."[10] Finally in 1926 he traveled to Russia, where he wrote his well-known editorial for *Crisis*: "If what I have seen with my eyes and heard with my ears in Russia is Bolshevism, I am a Bolshevik."[11] In 1927 he watched with interest the development of a "workingman's psychology."[12] The terminology of the resolutions from the Fourth Congress reflects this interest, and the session was closed by thanking "the Soviet Government of Russia for its liberal attitude toward the colored races and for the help which it has extended to them from time to time."[13]

It is hard to say to what extent DuBois was directly influenced by Marxist and socialist ideas. He knew many socialists and Communists, but seems not to have read Marx until the early 1930's. He did conduct a seminar on Marx at Atlanta in 1933, and his editorials in *Crisis* in the 1930's utilized many Marxist formulations; yet Marx and Marxist terms were popular during the Depression with many people who had only the dimmest grasp of Marxism.* His book *Black Reconstruction,* published in 1935, took an essentially Marxist approach to the events following the Civil War. Yet throughout this period, DuBois had no commitment to doctri-

---

* Francis L. Broderick, *W. E. B. DuBois, Negro Leader in a Time of Crisis* (Stanford, Calif.: Stanford University Press, 1959), p. 148, discusses DuBois's reading and remarks that his writings in the 1930's have "the once-over-lightly form of an undigested summary of *Capital* and the *Communist Manifesto.*"

naire Marxism and had continuing disagreements with the American Communists over the Negro problem in the United States.

Indeed, DuBois saw the racial problem fundamentally as having nothing to do with economics. He felt that the Russians displayed an "abysmal ignorance of the pattern of racial prejudice."[14] What use was the theory of class struggle if white workers hated Negro workers and Negro capitalists indifferently? "While Negro labor in America suffers from . . . the capitalistic system, the most fatal degree of its suffering comes . . . from [its] fellow white workers."[15] The revolt of the white proletariat, therefore, would not resolve the problems for the Negro proletariat; more would be accomplished by an alliance between black labor and black capital. This is the crucial point in DuBois's thinking: the necessity of unity among Negroes of *all* economic levels. DuBois used the word "class" in a non-economic sense, to distinguish between a "class" of white laborers and one of black laborers.[16] His definition of racial segregation as the "modern counterpart" of class structure[17] represented a distinct break with existing socialist ideas.

On the other hand, within the framework of a black nationalist ideology, he continued to believe in socialism, and there is a curious parallelism between his ideas in the 1930's and the American Communist Party's proposal for a Negro Republic.* In contrast to his earlier integrationist motivations in forming the Niagara Movement, DuBois turned to a philosophy of separatism, the development of a distinct Negro culture, quite compatible with the Black Republic proposal, though residential separation followed his thinking only by implication. "Why does not the Negro race build up a class structure of its own, parallel to that of the whites but separate, and including its own social, economic, and religious in-

---

* The Communist Party of the United States began formulating, during the ultra-left "Third Period," the idea of a Negro Republic within the United States. This Republic was ostensibly based on the application of Stalin's principle of self-determination, and called for the right of secession from the United States. The proposal is thought to have originated with Otto Kuusinen, the long-time Finnish Communist. Cf. Padmore, *Pan-Africanism or Communism?*, p. 306. It was propounded in the United States by a commissar, John Pepper, sent in 1928 to help the American Communists "clarify" their line. Cf. Wilson Record, *The Negro and the Communist Party* (Chapel Hill: University of North Carolina Press, 1951), pp. 58–59. James Allen, American Communist Party spokesman on the Negro question, published details of the proposed Negro Republic in *Crisis*, XLII (May 1935), 135ff. For a full discussion of DuBois's position, see the "Postscripts" throughout *Crisis*, XLI (1934).

stitutions?"[18] This segregationist position was in opposition to the platform of the NAACP, and after some controversy DuBois resigned in 1934. He still rejected, however, the concept of inevitable revolution. "I stood . . . between paths diverging to extreme Communism and violence on the one hand, and extreme reaction toward plutocracy on the other."[19] In turn, the Communists saw him, if sometimes as an ally, more often as "chaining the Negro people to the chariot of American imperialism,"[20] and they criticized his "disdain for the mass, his stewardship of the elite, his reformist-nationalist darker-race program."*

This was the situation until World War II. The four Pan-African congresses of 1919–27, reflecting DuBois's approach, had stated the problem in terms of racialism and the consequent need of government and economic reform. As yet, neither independence nor nationalism had been discussed as a solution to the problems of colored peoples, and nothing of any interest had been said about the African worker.

The Fifth Congress (1945) changed this pattern markedly. Though DuBois was present and active, the new approach reflected the influence of George Padmore. Padmore, a Trinidadian journalist, joined the Communist Party as a young man in the 1920's. He went to Russia, where he became chairman of the Profintern, the trade union branch of Comintern. He then became executive secretary of the International Trade Union Committee of Negro Workers and editor of the *Negro Worker,* a Communist newspaper. Padmore broke with the Party in 1934 when the Negro Trade Union Committee was liquidated "in order not to offend the British Foreign Office," which wanted no unrest stirred up in England's African colonies.[21]

Beginning with the Second Comintern Congress in 1920, the question of nationalism and self-determination had been an important theoretical issue for the Russian Bolsheviks. Broadly speaking, the Bolsheviks identified the struggle for self-determination in

* Broderick, *W. E. B. DuBois,* p. 211 (quoting from *The New Masses*). There was basis to the charge of elitism. DuBois had led the "Talented Tenth," a group of young intellectuals who had been responsible for the formation of the Niagara Movement. An elitist psychology had been carried over to the NAACP as well. DuBois justified it in terms of the needs of black leadership, and it is indeed consistent with his idea of the benefit of an alliance of black labor and black capital. He was, however, critical of the tendency of elites to separate themselves from the masses.

colonial countries with the world proletarian struggle. Self-determination was seen as the "instrument for the political education
of the masses in the spirit of internationalism."[22] The Bolsheviks
therefore supported self-determination. Lenin, for example, though
he opposed "Pan-Islamism and similar trends as combining the liberation movement against imperialism with the strengthening of
established bourgeois elements,"[23] strongly recommended forming
temporary alliances with nationalist movements so that Soviet cadres could operate and train the masses in a revolutionary spirit. In
the end, the goal was to fuse the workers of oppressed nations with
those of the oppressing nations and not with their own national
bourgeoisie.[24]

After Padmore's break with Communism, he became convinced
that Marxism derived solely from Western experience and was
largely inapplicable to colonial questions. Much of his concern with
the distinctive racial aspects of the African problem was based upon
reasoning similar to that of DuBois in the prewar period. In 1937,
in a response to the Italian invasion of Ethiopia, Padmore helped
to create the International African Service Bureau (IASB). The
IASB included among its officers T. R. Makonnen of British Gui-
ana,[25] C. L. R. James from Trinidad, a Marxist historian, and Jomo
Kenyatta, representing the Kikuyu Central Association. It attracted
young intellectuals with Marxist views, but consciously turned
away from Soviet influence. It "oriented itself to Pan-Africanism
as an independent political expression of Negro aspirations for
complete national independence from white domination—capitalist or Communist."[26] It published a journal, *International African
Opinion,* edited by C. L. R. James and William Harrison, an American Negro, formerly a student at Harvard but then studying with
Harold Laski. In 1944, the IASB merged into the Pan-African Federation, the British section of the Pan-African Congress Movement.
This Federation formulated a program "in conformity with the
broad principles proclaimed at all the earlier Pan-African congresses," but it added a demand for "self-determination and independence of African peoples and other subject races from the
domination of powers claiming sovereignty and trusteeship over
them."[27] This was the first call for African independence in the
Pan-African movement.

It was this period, when DuBois's movement and Padmore's
IASB joined to organize the Fifth Congress, that was most important in the development of present-day Pan-Africanism. This was

the time when many modern African leaders learned political theories and "built upon the pioneering work of DuBois [to] formulate a program of dynamic nationalism which combined African traditional forms of organization with Western political party methods."[28]

Among the Africans active in the Fifth Congress were Kwame Nkrumah, J. S. Annan (secretary of the Gold Coast Railway, Civil Servants, and Technical Workers Union, and later permanent secretary in the Gold Coast Ministry of Defense), Nnamdi Azikiwe (represented by Magnus Williams), Makonnen, and Kenyatta. Nkrumah, who had been a student in America since 1935 and had been attracted to the American Communists, met Padmore in London in 1945. They participated in the organization of the Fifth Congress along with DuBois, still in America, who had ceased fighting the American Communists during the war. Encouraged by Russian sympathy for the Chinese, DuBois wrote in *Color and Democracy* (1945), "Democracy . . . is the unloosing of the energies and capabilities of the depressed. This is what the USSR is accomplishing in its own land. . . . The record of Soviet Russia in the matter of racial tolerance has been extraordinary."[29]

The differences between the 1945 Congress and those that preceded it are remarkable. First of all, it was well attended. It was scheduled to coincide with the second conference of the World Federation of Trade Unions (WFTU). The newly organized colonial trade unions were sympathetic to nationalist ideas, and, by bringing together the nationalists and the trade union delegates, the Congress was assured of broad representation. Indeed, according to Padmore, the Congress no longer consisted of an intellectual elite but was "an expression of a mass movement. . . . Alliance between the progressive middle-class intellectuals and the ordinary people was cemented."[30] Second, this was the first congress to be largely organized by Africans and to enunciate the importance of self-government. "The struggle for political power by colonial and subject peoples is the first step toward, and the necessary prerequisite to, complete social, economic, and political emancipation."[31] Using the leftist terminology of the 1930's, the Congress urged a "united front" between intellectuals, workers, and farmers. "Colonial workers must be in the front of the battle against imperialism. . . . Today there is only one road to effective action—the organization of the masses. . . . Colonial and subject peoples of the world, Unite!"[32]

Despite the terminology, this Congress, which established the pattern of events that followed in Africa, was by no means Marxist. The class struggle and violence were rejected as inapplicable to racial problems. The Congress approved of the socioeconomic goals of Marxist socialism, but rejected Soviet totalitarianism. "Nationalism, political democracy, and socialism" were to be the three principles of Pan-Africanism.* While praising Asian national freedom movements and recognizing the "oneness of the struggles of the Coloured World,"[33] Padmore stood firm for a nationalist ideology as opposed to the international ideology of Marxism.

Following the Congress, Nkrumah organized the West African delegates into the West African National Secretariat to implement the resolutions of the Congress. These were primarily concerned with achieving self-government, but were also pledged to promote a West African Federation. Following the Bolshevik tradition, a vanguardist subgroup called "The Circle" was organized by Nkrumah for the "destruction of colonialism," and members trained themselves "in order to be able to commence revolutionary work in any part of the African continent."†[34]

While the Congress refocused the orientation of the Pan-African movement on the achievement of national independence, it did not abandon socialism. The Congress endorsed both nationalism and "the doctrine of African Socialism based upon the tactics of positive action without violence . . . and advised Africans and those of African descent wherever they might be to organize themselves into political parties, trade unions, cooperative societies, and farmers' organizations in the support of their struggle for political freedom and economic advancement."[35] Nkrumah interpreted the ideology of the Congress as "African nationalism—a revolt against colonialism, racialism, and imperialism in Africa."[36] It was perhaps because the delegates to this Congress were Africans, concerned with practical questions of colonialism in their home countries, that the Pan-African concept—the commitment to continental unity—took a secondary position to nationalism. It was, for example, only *after* Ghanaian independence in 1957 that continental unity became a key element in Nkrumah's thinking.

* Padmore, *Pan-Africanism or Communism?*, p. 181. Note the resemblance to Lenin's statement that the goals of self-determination are "democracy, *inter*nationalism, and Socialism" (*Selected Works*, V, 289).

† The influence of vanguardist principles is discussed more fully by Colin Legum in Chapter 8 of this volume.

That Pan-Africanism was developing a nationalist orientation incompatible with doctrinaire Marxism did not pass unnoticed in the Soviet Union. In 1950, the Soviet Africanist I. I. Potekhin warned that the African bourgeoisie would support the anti-colonial movement only until it was successful, and would then seize power for itself and enslave the masses. He cited Nnamdi Azikiwe, an active champion of Pan-Africanism, as following the "ideology and policy of petty bourgeois national reformism."* Soviet journals called Nkrumah's party a "screen covering up the domination of English imperialism."[37]

After 1958, the Soviet line became more ambiguous. While approving the Pan-Africanists' pursuit of national liberation, Potekhin noted the "completely erroneous counterposing of scientific socialist theory to African Socialism."† The Soviet press equivocally supported both Balkanization and Pan-Africanism: "Africa needs unity, but not just any kind of unity is in the interest of its peoples."[38] Pan-Africanism was by this time too popular to oppose, but it does seem likely that the Russians continued to see it as inimical to their interests. In Brzezinski's words, whereas "the emergence of a Pan-African formation could impede the Communist takeover in individual states . . . , a setting of disunity [would] create openings for external intrusion."[39]

In the period following the 1945 Congress, DuBois became increasingly committed to the Russian Communist brand of Marxism. He participated actively in Paul Robeson's Communist-inspired Council on African Affairs, an activity for which he was later indicted by the United States government. By the time of the Sixth Congress (1958), there was little left of his early humanitarian socialism, and his speech, given by his wife, was a plea for the programs of the Soviet Union. "Your bond is not merely color of skin but the deeper experience of wage slavery and contempt."[40] His influence had long since waned. Padmore, by contrast, remained basically a non-Communist Marxist in his thinking. He never wavered once he became convinced that national independence was the route to continental African unity. Nor did he ever again trust the Communists; indeed, he imparted his suspicions to

---

* Vernon McKay, "Changing External Pressures on Africa," in Walter Goldschmidt, ed., *The United States and Africa* (New York: Praeger, 1963), pp. 99, 101. See also Chapter 6 in this volume.

† See Chapter 6 in this volume.

many Africans who emerged as leaders of the independent African nations.

Both DuBois and Padmore were concerned simultaneously with continental unity, nationalism (oriented toward political independence but with racialist overtones), and socialism. Given various emphases by different African leaders and groups today, these themes have become the foundation for current unification programs. An understanding of their balance helps illuminate the relationships between socialism and Pan-Africanism today.

In the past few years, three lines of Pan-African activity have been prominent with modern Africa's leaders: (1) action for the complete liberation of the continent from colonial rule; (2) the development of expressions of cultural unity; and (3) experimentation with political, economic, and social forms leading to unification in order to further internal development and establish a position in international affairs. The commitment of individual nations or leaders to these activities has taken a variety of forms, but the burning issue for all is the first. Liberation has become the specific translation of Padmore's dictum concerning the importance of obtaining national independence.

Also following Padmore, almost all today's Pan-Africanists* are socialists, in the sense that they subscribe to an African Socialist ideology based on the following premises: (a) Africa has a single "traditional culture"; (b) all regions of Africa have suffered the common fate of colonial exploitation; (c) there is an economic basis to the need for unity, namely, that Africa's resources should be exploited for the benefit of Africans; and (d) rational continent-wide planning is needed for the unique African situation in order to achieve progress.

Indeed, in all attempts to create supranational institutions on the African continent, African Socialism has served as the unifying ideology. At the same time, the realization of the objectives of Pan-Africanism—liberation, a sense of common identity, and a continental perspective—is considered by Pan-Africanists to be a precondition for the success of African Socialism in realizing the goal of continent-wide economic development.

The first two concerns of Pan-Africanism—liberation and cul-

---

* I am using the term broadly to include all concerned with unification movements and not merely the group surrounding Nkrumah.

tural unity—are common to all the unification programs. On liberation, countries rigorously oriented toward Pan-Africanism—Ghana, Guinea, Algeria, etc.—have tended to take the most militant approach. The Algerians, for example, have contributed to the military training of liberation fighters, whereas the more conservative Nigerians have stressed nonviolent approaches to the liberation of southern Africa. Nonetheless, all independent African nations are committed to the liberation of the entire continent.

African expressions of cultural unity have most frequently taken the form of mystiques. In many respects, Nkrumah's "African Personality" and Senghor's "Negritude" are little more than the social and political theories of DuBois and Padmore with metaphysical overtones.[41] According to Senghor, "Negritude is the whole complex of civilized values . . . which characterize the Negro-African world. All these values are essentially formed by intuitive reason . . . the sense of communion, the gift of myth-making, the gift of rhythm."[42] Nkrumah, reflecting Padmore's approach, defined the African Personality as a symbol of African political unification, an expression of "the community of aim and purpose . . . [which] will allow us to speak with concerted voice in the cause of peace and for the liberation of dependent Africa and in defense of our national independence, sovereignty, and territorial integrity."[43] The emphasis is very different, but the idea is the same.

It is in practical moves toward organization on a continental level that the widest differences among Pan-Africanists appear. At one extreme are the militant and more idealistic Pan-Africanists led by Nkrumah, influenced chiefly by Padmore's teachings; at the other extreme are the pragmatic Pan-Africanists, oriented toward limited transnational economic structures of the European Economic Community variety.

The militants* have continually emphasized that their goal is nothing less than the creation of a United States of Africa. They firmly reject regionalism and national sovereignty. A Marxist internationalist orientation—such leaders as Nkrumah and Sékou Touré are trained in Marxism—is evident, although it is expressed

---

* I am aware of the inadequacy of the terms "militant" and "pragmatic" in characterizing the difference in approach between these two groupings. There have been a variety of terms used at different times. The group I have called the "militants" has been variously labeled "idealists," "romantics," and "radicals." The "pragmatists" have been called "realists," "moderates," and "conservatives." No terms can adequately classify the two orientations.

in *continental* rather than *international* form. The so-called Casablanca group was one of the important manifestations of the militant orientation. The Casablanca group was formed in 1961, when Morocco, Algeria, and Egypt joined with the Union of African States (UAS), created in 1960 by Ghana, Guinea, and Mali, to call for the early creation of continental political organs. (The UAS had already stressed political unification as a prerequisite for economic unity,* and considered itself the nucleus for a United States of Africa.)[44] Because of their supranational outlook, the Casablanca powers were soon at odds with what later emerged as the more conservative Monrovia group.

The militant outlook was predominant in the three All-Africa Peoples Conferences (AAPC) held in 1958 in Accra, in 1960 in Tunis, and in 1961 in Cairo. The primary goal of the AAPC has been to encourage nationalist political movements in the remaining colonial areas, but only as a means to continental unity based on socialism.

Aim for the attainment of the Political Kingdom—that is to say, the complete independence and self-determination of your territories. When you have achieved the Political Kingdom all else will follow. . . . But this power which you will achieve is not in itself the end. . . . Coupled with this will to independence is an equal desire for some form of African union . . . within the milieu of a social system suited to the traditions, history, environment, and communalistic pattern of African society.[45]

Nkrumah, in his address inaugurating the 1958 Conference, enunciated the four stages of Pan-Africanism: national independence, national consolidation, the creation of transnational unity and community, and economic and social reconstruction.[46] Social reconstruction must be "on the basis of African Socialism"[47] and must be free from all external influence. Reflecting Padmore's caution, Nkrumah warned, "Colonialism may come to us in yet a different guise—not necessarily from Europe."[48] The 1958 Conference created a steering committee to consider programs for unity. More specific moves toward unity appeared in the later conferences, which proposed an African High Command and an African Common Market and took a strong stand against regional solutions.

African trade unionism has also been generally militant. In 1956,

---

* This followed two years after the Union of Ghana and Guinea and included a variety of economic agreements.

Touré resisted the Communist-backed WFTU's attempt to organize a Pan-African Trade Union Conference and created the Confédération Générale du Travail Africain as a trade union free of all international affiliations. This led to the organization of the Union Générale des Travailleurs de l'Afrique Noire, the aim of which was "to affirm the personality of African trade unionism."[49] In 1961, the All-African Trade Union Federation, led by the unions of the Casablanca powers, organized a meeting which attempted to disaffiliate African trade unionism from international organizations such as the International Confederation of Free Trade Unions.

In contrast to the militant Pan-Africanists, who have stressed political unification as a prerequisite to any other kind of unity, the more pragmatic Pan-Africanists have been conservative, regionally oriented, and concerned primarily with economic and cultural matters. The pragmatists share with the militants an ideological framework of African Socialism, which is evident in their concern with eliminating exploitation, planning cooperative economic ventures, and preserving traditional African values. Their focus, however, is on limited economic unity within regional blocs.

The pragmatists were first called the Monrovia powers as a result of a conference held at Monrovia in May 1961. This was followed in January 1962 by a second conference, held at Lagos, to which the Casablanca powers were invited but which they did not attend. The Monrovia group felt that the Casablanca powers were premature in calling for the surrender of national sovereignty to an organ of continental unity. According to a Monrovia spokesman, the two blocs had

one basic difference of an ideological nature which should attract the serious attention of all who sincerely advocate African unity: . . . the conspicuous absence of a declaration by the Casablanca powers that they recognize the right of African states to legal equality . . . ; to self-determination; to safety from interference in their internal affairs. . . . The African states can be as separate as the fingers in their domestic affairs, but can be as united as the fist in matters of external and general concern. . . . We shall yet succeed in forging unity of purpose and identity of interests among the diverse peoples of Africa.[50]

The conferences of the pragmatists typically resulted in practical agreements on economic and educational matters. Yet the leaders of the Monrovia group felt that national sovereignty and continental unity were potentially reconcilable. Thus, Dr. Michael

Okpara, successor to Azikiwe as premier of Eastern Nigeria, advocated three stages for the achievement of African unity: (1) division of the continent into five regions cooperating in nonpolitical (e.g., economic) areas; (2) adoption of political functions by the regions; (3) binding together of the regions into a single political federation.[51]

All sorts of regional organizations have been set up, ranging from vaguely defined units such as the Brazzaville community—incorporating the bulk of the former French territories into a series of secretariats concerned with integrating transportation, banking, etc.—to more locally limited groups such as the Conseil de l'Entente. The Conseil, consisting of the Ivory Coast, Niger, Dahomey, and the Upper Volta, was created in 1959 to administer a solidarity fund established to assist member states on the basis of need. Only after its four members became independent in 1960 was there general agreement on matters such as administrative coordination and a concerted foreign policy. Led by Félix Houphouët-Boigny of the Ivory Coast and largely under the domination of that country, the Conseil has been only dimly Pan-African and scarcely socialist at all. Houphouët-Boigny has been unsympathetic toward movements for concrete political federation. Though he allied his party temporarily with the Communists in the late 1940's, he broke with them on ideological grounds and later committed himself to the development of private enterprise and cordial relations with the European Common Market.[52] Yet it is significant that he has never felt that the Ivory Coast could "go it alone," and he has been forced to devote considerable attention to the regional organization of the Conseil.

The conservative spirit of the Conseil is seen also in the Brazzaville group, consisting of the four members of the Conseil and the bulk of the former French territories in Africa. These nations formed the Union Africaine et Malgache (UAM) in 1961. Unlike the militant UAS, the UAM stood firm for the principle of national sovereignty as against supranational organization. "Union must be created within the framework of national diversity and of the personalities of each state. That is why the 12 of Brazzaville intend to lay the foundation of a close cooperation that will not adversely affect the independence of the participants."[53] Since the creation of the Organization of African Unity in 1963, the UAM has, in fact, renounced all political functions and is now primarily an economic cooperative body maintaining some common services.

Senghor, in advocating a "multinational" confederation, expresses similar concerns. "Horizontal inter-African solidarity will gradually be established by beginning at the beginning with economic and cultural relations, while vertical solidarity between ourselves and our European metropoles will be modified but not dissolved."[54]

In East Africa, regional organization has also been a prevailing preoccupation. Even prior to the attainment of independence, the Pan-African Freedom Movement of East and Central Africa was interested in regional cooperation rather than continental unity. Although its perspective was widened to include adjoining areas of Africa and it became increasingly concerned with the liberation of the rest of Africa, this organization remained regional in character. On the more practical level, there is the East African Common Services Organization (EACSO), inherited from the colonial East Africa High Commission. The services provided by EACSO, including transportation, communication, higher education, and research, are the collective responsibility of the heads of government of Kenya, Tanganyika, and Uganda, with the assistance of a Central Legislative Assembly representative of the parliaments of the three countries. The work of EACSO is handled through a central administration in Nairobi. Because of its responsibilities for communication and transportation, EACSO was by 1963 the largest single employer in the region and disposed of approximately 10 per cent of the gross domestic product of East Africa.[55] At the same time, EACSO has not been regarded as a fully satisfactory manifestation of East African unity, and a variety of attempts have been undertaken to create a more organic structure that will be a proper East African federation. A change which must affect the movement toward federation is the political union between Tanganyika and Zanzibar created in May 1964.

A regional agreement between Kenya and Tanganyika may seem a far cry from Nkrumah's militant continental Pan-Africanism, but the motivation and general thinking of Nkrumah and Nyerere are in fact remarkably similar. According to Nyerere, "No true African Socialist can look at a line drawn on a map and say, 'The people on this side of that line are my brothers.' . . . Every individual on this continent is his brother."* For Nyerere, Pan-Africanism is a meaningful ideal, but it is expressed through na-

---

* Nyerere, "Ujamaa." See Appendix II, p. 246.

tional sovereignty. When discussing the structural forms of Pan-Africanism, Nyerere advises: "Nurse it, encourage it, and let it take its own course."[56] Committing himself to nothing more definite, he reflects the pragmatists' avoidance of a preconceived political structure to embody the Pan-African ideal.

That African Socialism has served to bridge the differing approaches to Pan-Africanism is apparent in the participation of Mali and Guinea with the more conservative nations in the Dakar Colloquium.* The Colloquium pointed to the need for a united front in world politics, and general agreement was reached among the representatives of the 18 nations present on the utility of African Socialism as a "means to achieve full development" and on the role of continental unity in facilitating development.

Development requires a complete and conscious association of the entire people, . . . a policy of denationalization of the great industrial centers and of the essential sectors of production for the benefit of common development, . . . the unification of markets, and the abolition of customs barriers, whose harmful and artificial nature nobody can deny. . . . The first step toward the African way of development is the revolutionary rejection of the old [colonial] structures. . . . Our way to development leads also to a community-centered socialism; . . . to a socialism which, after having been the instrument of national liberation, will be that of the liberation of man.[57]

Thirty independent states participated in the Addis Ababa Conference of May 1963 and in the ensuing formation of the Organization of African Unity (OAU). This must be considered a triumph of sorts for the classical Pan-Africanism of DuBois and Padmore and the militant Pan-Africanism of Nkrumah. The OAU not only provided for an annual formal assemblage of leaders but also created some functional committees for a variety of purposes: to plan the liberation of the rest of the continent, to organize economic development and cooperation and to resolve inter-African problems.† However, the continued dissatisfaction of Nkrumah with many of these committees, though not with the spirit of the

* See Chapter 7.
† Examples are the Liberation Coordinating Committee of Nine Nations, the African Development Bank, and the Commission of Mediation, Conciliation, and Arbitration.

OAU charter, indicates the persistence of the schism despite the realignment of some of the nations. Ultimately, what the socialist background of DuBois and Padmore has brought to Pan-Africanism is a humanist mystique rather than a rational political program. Perhaps because the energies of the Pan-Africanists have been expended largely in obtaining national independence or perhaps because the diversity within Africa precludes supranational organization, socialism has not been translated into administrative embodiment. DuBois and Padmore, after all, as non-African Negroes, viewed the African continent with an international racial perspective: their thinking about continental organization was abstract and they mistakenly saw only colonialism and capitalism as enemies of a United Socialist Africa. That regionalism would emerge as a force sufficient to inhibit continental unity was beyond their perspective. Their dream was a compelling one twenty years ago; and although many problems exist, it remains a compelling political force for modern Africa's leaders. For the moment, however, the Pan-African movement is far from realizing the socialist ideals of its intellectual protagonists.

Chapter 5

# A Socialist Looks at African Socialism

Margaret Roberts

Socialism is more than an economic system. It is a conception of a cooperative society in which inequalities are banished by removing the distinction between "haves" and "have-nots." Socialism in Africa, like socialism anywhere else, cannot be judged entirely in terms of the machinery that has been established to govern the economic system. Three questions must be asked. First, what are the ideals and values which dominate modern African political life and motivate its leaders? Second, are these what we would call "socialist" values? Third, what are the realities of African economic and social needs which are seen to govern the machinery devised to implement these ideals?

Traditionally, certain values have been held as universal by socialists outside of Africa. Whatever our traditions and backgrounds, whatever the local conditions which have seeded our socialist beliefs or the machinery devised to embody them, our ideals are agreed. "Socialism denotes a belief in the pre-eminence of certain values, such as *equality, cooperation, collective welfare,* and *internationalism,*"[1] which contrast with hierarchy, competition, individualism, and chauvinism. Stripped of its methodology, the same spirit is apparent in the definition of Professor I. I. Potekhin, Director of Moscow's Africa Institute: "The state's power is vested in the workers. . . . There are *no exploiting* classes, nor does one man exploit his fellows. The *economy is planned,* and its essential aim is to afford the *maximum satisfaction* of man's material and spiritual needs."[2]

African Socialists have expressed the same cooperative ideals. President Nyerere of Tanganyika writes: "Socialism . . . is an attitude of mind . . . which is needed to ensure that *the people care for each other's* welfare."* Tom Mboya of Kenya refers to "those proved codes of conduct in the African societies which

---

* "Ujamaa." See Appendix II, p. 238 of this volume. Emphasis added.

have, over the ages, conferred *dignity* on our people and afforded them *security* regardless of their station in life. I refer to universal *charity* . . . and . . . ideas which regard *man,* not as a social means, but *as an end and entity in the society*."*

But if the distinguishing mark of the socialist is fundamentally a belief in equality and cooperation, the methods chosen to implement the ideals have been many and divisive. The deepest conflicts have been between the democratic socialists of Western Europe and the orthodox Marxists or Communists. Democratic socialists believe that the Communists' methods have so distorted the ideals as to sometimes negate the three great principles which informed Marx's own writings: *equality* has been betrayed to a rigid economic and political hierarchy in the name of the "dictatorship of the proletariat"; *humanity* is regarded as expendable, in principle and practice, in the interests of an illusory future millennium or the power of a single nation; and the application of *science* to economics and politics has given way to dogma in the interests of discipline and material progress. Democratic socialists do not deny their profound debt to Marx's ideals and his analysis of capitalism. But they do not accept that his prognostications or his prescriptions are universally or eternally applicable. Perhaps their fundamental theoretical quarrel is with the Marxist postulation of the Communist millennium, the perfectibility of the classless society, and the withering of the state; for it is this fanatical illusion that has justified Communist cynicism and intolerance and the sacrifice of its humanity.

Writing as a democratic socialist, I believe that the orthodox Marxists have established their own violent antithesis to the capitalist thesis. Communism has not proved to be the final synthesis of social conflict which Marx predicted for it. To the extent that a synthesis can be approached, it must await the scientific application of the universal socialist ideals.

African Socialism, therefore, is of more than academic interest. Conceived as it has been in the pragmatic and scientific twentieth century, free from the romanticism bred of nineteenth-century capitalist misery and conflict, is it possible that African Socialists will be less cluttered than we by the bitterness of past political conflict? Perhaps more important, is it hopeful that African Socialism has been born a triplet to Africa's other two driving forces: na-

---

* See Appendix IV, p. 251. Emphasis added.

tionalism and economic development? African nationalism and Pan-Africanism, which assert a unique African contribution to humanity and which make Africa unwilling any longer to accept the ideologies of others, may help to focus the attention of African Socialists *pragmatically* on their own needs. A similar practical result may be expected from the urgent drive for economic development.

At the emotional heart of socialism is the assertion of the claims of the have-nots in relation to the haves; and nowhere is this more true than in Africa. The African continent feels that it has suffered centuries of deprivation and exploitation in relation to Europe, and it is determined above all to overcome the effects of underprivilege. But the continental scale of this sense of deprivation—the feeling that *all* Africans are "have-nots"—gives to African Socialism special qualities which distinguish it from European socialism. Tom Mboya writes:

We are immersed in a massive transition in which we are seeking new identities at personal, national, and international levels. . . . In and around the world today there are millions of people . . . engaged in a similar venture; the aims they have in view are not very different from our own, but we differ in tradition and background; their position and perspective vis-à-vis the challenge to be faced is not the same as we have. We are thus cast for our own role, and we either live up to it or not.*

What are these "new identities" which are being sought for Africa's have-nots, and what are the implications for socialism of these new African ideals? They may be discussed under three broad heads: the need for rapid economic transformation; Africa's past experiences of capitalism; and the implications of nationalism and Pan-Africanism on the class-war theories of socialism.

### New Identities

*Economic transformation.* Economic development is seen as the indispensable prerequisite for Africa's dignified emergence on a basis of equality on the world scene. President Bourguiba has said: "It is . . . necessary to inculcate a sense of dignity in those of our Tunisian citizens who live in poverty, misery, and hunger. It is clear that they are happy to be delivered from French domination.

---

* See Appendix IV, p. 250.

. . . It is equally necessary that [they] feel the need to improve their living conditions . . . and live honorably as advanced people do."[3] It is a question not only of the absolute level of material wealth but of closing the technological gap between Europe and Africa. Socialism is sometimes acclaimed almost entirely in relation to those objectives. President Senghor's definition at the Dakar Colloquium on Socialism in December 1962—"Socialism for us is nothing but the rational organization of human society considered in its totality, according to the most scientific, the most modern, and the most efficient methods"—might easily be said to be indistinguishable from a fascist approach to development, had he not later added, "More than the use of the most efficient techniques, it is the sense of community which is the return to African-ness." But, at Dakar, it was clearly the developmental aspect of socialism that struck the common chord.*

*Past experiences with capitalism.* But this does not explain why socialism, and not capitalism, is chosen as the best method for development. The reasons are partly historical, partly pragmatic, partly emotional. Africa's experience with capitalism has not been a happy one.[4] Capitalism has been associated with the colonial powers and with their exploitation of the extractive industries and primary commodities to the virtual exclusion of other industry or agriculture. Capital has been largely foreign-owned, and much of the profits of enterprise in Africa has been exported. Africans have been largely excluded from the profits of foreign private enterprise, with the result that, with a few exceptions, no major class has developed with a vested interest in capitalism. The impression has been left that the main effect of capitalism was the buying of African produce at low prices and the selling of European produce at exploitive prices. Finally, the process of colonialism, equated with capitalism, apparently ignored or destroyed African culture and left Africans themselves with its worst aspects only— social alienation, economic rootlessness, and national exploitation.

It also left Africa without a capital-owning and risk-taking entrepreneurial class, which might have provided the political and economic spur to capital accumulation through private enterprise. The result is that the task of capital accumulation devolves upon the state. For only the government has the means and the authority to initiate large-scale investment, accumulate capital in-

* See Chapter 7.

ternally, and elicit large-scale foreign resources. More than this, however, the scarcity of capital resources entails their planned investment according to a carefully prepared set of priorities—much as was done in Europe during wartime. As has been pointed out with respect to Mali, "African Socialists want to avoid *ad hoc,* experimental, and haphazard change."* Socialism is regarded as essentially rational as opposed to haphazard, and as planned and controlled as opposed to arbitrary; for those reasons it gives the best hope of rapid economic transformation.

Planning and state control, moreover, are seen as the only way to avoid both the economic waste and the human dislocation engendered by the development of resources through unfettered capitalism. President Nkrumah draws an extreme contrast between socialism and colonial capitalism:

Ghana inherited a colonial economy. . . . We cannot rest content until we have demolished this miserable structure and raised in its place an edifice of economic stability, thus creating for ourselves a veritable paradise of abundance and satisfaction. . . . We must go forward with our preparations for planned economic growth to supplant the poverty, ignorance, disease, and illiteracy left in their wake by discredited colonialism and decaying imperialism.[5]

Emotionally, too, the socialist solution appears most apt; for it is in tune with the most common African conception of the best in the precolonial past. "African Socialism is a reality which was subjected, for a certain time, to the shock of colonialism: we must now rethink it in its new context. Frightened by the spectacle of Western individualism, we prefer to correct the abuses of our traditional socialism and to retain the community aspects of our civilization."[6] President Nyerere returns frequently to the same theme: the African "saw himself all the time as a member of a community, . . . but he saw no struggle between his own interests and those of his community. . . . Our problem is this: How to get the benefits of European society . . . and yet retain the African's own structure of society in which the individual is a member of a kind of fellowship."[7]

In practice the most common way of implementing this conception of traditional socialism has been the practice of *investissement*

---

* See Chapter 10, p. 177.

*humain,* or community development through voluntary labor. In effect this is an attempt to channel local clan loyalties and methods of working into a planned program of economic development. There have been some interesting results with human investment programs—notably perhaps in Tanganyika, Mali, and Guinea. And far too little attention is given to this aspect of development by economists totting up post-independence development gains. It is perhaps interesting that Nyerere's coining of the word "communitary" to illuminate the traditional aspect of socialist development coincided, apparently fortuitously, with President Sékou Touré's choice of the word *"communaucratique"* to describe the same thing in Guinea.

*Socialism without the class struggle.* Three movements of emotions combine to reject the classic Marxist conception of the class struggle: African nationalism, which represents the political revolt against colonialism; Pan-Africanism, which embodies the desire for continental solidarity and African equality; and African Socialism, which takes up the cause of Africa's dispossessed. Aside from the observable fact that economic classes cannot be meaningfully defined in Marxist terms in Africa, the overwhelming urge both before and since independence has been for unity—the unity of Africa, the solidarity of all the continent's "have-nots." This is not surprising: the African "haves"—the potential "exploiters"— are so insignificant in number as to be scarcely worth bothering about. There are, it is true, African leaders who speak in terms of the existence, or the inevitable growth, of classes; but they are not at present representative. Outside of South Africa, they are confined largely to the Communist-oriented Parti Africain de l'Independence of Senegal, to a small but vocal element in the Convention People's Party of Ghana, and to the few tiny Communist parties in Africa. It is also true that where militant oppositionist trade unions exist, as in Nigeria and the Congo, there are the beginnings of an articulated class consciousness in relation to "the growing gap which separates the class of the privileged of the new regime—government employees, military men, politicians—from the mass of the urban and rural proletariat, the unemployed and the jobless youth."[*]

[*] A. Kithima, Congo-Leopoldville delegate to the Dakar Colloquium. Cited by Zolberg in this volume, p. 121.

But far more representative is the view that the class struggle is irrelevant to African conditions, and that what is important for the African Socialist is to see that it remains that way. Most African leaders are confident that classes can be prevented from arising in Africa, provided that development proceeds along socialist lines. Their hopes are not shared either by Soviet Africanists, represented in this volume by Potekhin, or by American economists, if Professor Morse's views in Chapter 2 may be taken as representative. The process of development, in the Soviet view, must produce more clearly defined economic classes; and to some extent these must come in conflict with each other—at least by making conflicting claims on state priorities. The African answer is that a "socialist attitude of mind," or a sense of unity expressed through joining different sections of society together in a single party, can eliminate such rivalries. This answer is not wholly convincing. The difficulties already experienced in relation to the trade unions in many states are a reflection of sectional, if not class, conflict. This will be discussed later.

In fact, the class struggle is not ignored by African leaders. But they tend to see it as operating on the international, rather than the national, level. President Nyerere writes:

The world is still divided between the "haves" and the "have-nots." This division is not a division between capitalists and socialists, or between capitalists and Communists; this is a division between the poor countries of the world and the rich countries of the world. . . . The rich countries of the world today may be found on either side of the division between the capitalist and socialist countries.[8]

Very much the same sentiments are frequently expressed by President Sékou Touré of Guinea.

This relatively simple view of an international class struggle must not be confused with a recent sophisticated attempt by Soviet economists to reconcile their difficulties about the class war in Africa by associating the "socialist" working classes of the Communist countries with the "peasants" of Africa. G. F. Kim writes:

The states which personify the rule of the workers headed by the working class, allied with the peoples of the young sovereign states which have arisen on the wreckage of the colonial empires—this alliance implements on an international scale the Leninist idea of union of the working class with the many million semiproletarian and nonproletarian masses oppressed by the colonialists. Thus the problem of the alliance of the working class and the peasantry, transcending national limits, has become an international factor.[9]

Past speeches by African Socialists, however, cannot provide Soviet theoreticians with much hope of African acceptance of such a theory, neat though it is. It conflicts with nonalignment and Pan-Africanism, both of which are stronger in Africa today than the need for a solution to the apparent intellectual problems posed by Africa's refusal to fit into the Leninist design. "Socialism can be achieved without a proletariat," said Mali's Minister for Development, Dr. Seydou Badian Kouyate, at the Dakar Colloquium in December 1962. "The political organization of the whole people can bring the country to socialism. . . . It is a question . . . of the whole people organized as a political force to take its destiny into its own hands."[10]

Three key ideals, therefore, may be said to lie at the heart of African aspirations today: economic development, planning and cooperation, and national and Pan-African solidarity. Each of them strikes strong chords in the experience and ideals of non-African socialists, but not all the implications of these priorities may be described as specifically socialist. Each has deep roots in experiences of the past and in the realities of the present. It is worth looking a little more closely at some of the implications of these conditions for the theory and practice of socialism.

### Implications for Socialism

*Nationalization.* Nationalization of existing private enterprise is nowhere given a high priority in state planning, and is seldom regarded as a principle or prerequisite of socialism. On the contrary, state ownership of the "means of production, distribution, and exchange," to use the Marxist phrase, is approached highly pragmatically. Outside of the U.A.R., and Algeria with its exceptional conditions, only Guinea has embarked upon any serious program of nationalization. In Guinea the process has been put sharply into reverse since 1962, on the grounds that it has not produced results. President Touré's pragmatic approach to socialism was illustrated by a Guinean delegate to the Dakar Colloquium who quoted the President as saying: "To speak of socialism is to speak of a complex of structures and economic and social practices. But socialism for us is not an end in itself. We do not define ourselves in relation to it as an end, but rather . . . begin with the needs of specific situations."[11]

Doctrinally, President Nkrumah is perhaps the only prominent African statesman who has been moving toward acceptance of a more conventional Marxist position on state ownership; but even he sees this as something for the future: "Socialism *assumes* the public ownership of the means of production. . . . [However,] not only do the people as yet not own all the major means of production and distribution, but we have to lay the actual foundations upon which socialism can be built, namely, the complete industrialization of our continent."*

Meanwhile President Nkrumah and many others emphasize the present need for a private sector "which will incorporate those industries open freely to foreign private enterprise."[12] "The government stresses that in all sectors of the Algerian economy there will be a place . . . reserved for private industry, which represents a stimulus to public enterprise."[13] "We must encourage private businesses or individuals, Malagasy or foreign, to industrialize our country."[14] "Our choice of African Socialism must not make us enemies of private enterprise."[15]

If large-scale nationalization is raised as an issue, therefore, socialist opinion in Africa comes down heavily at present against it. The emphasis is placed instead upon planning of all sectors of the economy, and upon mobilizing the people, as the only plentiful resource, by whatever methods prove most effective. That the public sector is generally relatively large is due partly to the historical factors already discussed and partly to the fact that sophisticated fiscal and other techniques for controlling and influencing the private sector do not yet exist in Africa as they do in the developed capitalist economies. The solution to this problem is generally found in laying down conditions, usually generous, under which private enterprise may operate, with the aim of controlling, directing, and orienting the economy, rather than nationalizing it.

The same pragmatism is at work in formulating the African Socialist approach to foreign investment. The dilemma, as Africans see it, is that in order to overcome technological backwardness and

---

* "The Basic Needs of African Socialism," *Pan Africa*, April 19, 1963, p. 13; emphasis added. See also Appendix V, p. 260.

dependence, African nations must temporarily increase their indebtedness to foreign sources of capital. But "foreign aid," says President Modibo Keita of Mali, "no matter where it comes from or what form it takes, is never completely disinterested, for it remains tied, more or less obscurely, to the economy and the political [system] from which it comes; or it leads to crushing debts for the nation."[16] The solution is generally sought either in devising schemes of "partnership" between state and foreign private enterprise or in limiting the field and methods of operation given to foreign investment.

The debate on the whole question of the role of foreign aid, government and private, continues. On the one hand, capital attracted from abroad limits the need to accumulate it at home by restricting consumption; on the other hand, capital accumulated at home may be more effective in mobilizing the resources and energies of the people themselves. There is a growing tendency to question the value of large-scale foreign aid, even government-to-government gifts. The answer to this very real dilemma is likely to be the use of foreign aid in enterprises such as education and technical assistance, which will allow Africa's own human resources to expand their productiveness.

*Development and equality.* European socialists are sometimes surprised and even disconcerted by the relative emphasis given by Africans to production as opposed to distribution of wealth. In the words of a Tanganyika student, "Socialism in Europe is to take the wealth and spread it out, but African Socialism is the common effort to create wealth." While most European socialists would claim both objectives for their system, that sentence nevertheless contains an important truth which will help many socialists in the West to understand their African contemporaries. Here we should refer back to the concept of the "have-nots" in relation to the "haves," which permeates all socialist ideals. In Europe it was the vast disparities in property and income within the capitalist economies that stimulated the need for reform. And these conditions in turn dictated the means chosen to implement socialism—the establishment of free and strong trade unions of workers, the reorientation of government spending from the richer to the poorer sections of society, the priorities given to social welfare, public as opposed to private spending, and finally, public ownership of productive property. All these measures were primarily redistributive and conducive to egalitarianism; they were secondarily designed to induce cooperative methods of production and only thirdly aimed at increasing the overall size of the national cake.

In Africa, by contrast, almost everyone is a "have-not"—at least in relation to Europe's "haves." The primary task therefore must be to increase the size of the continental and national cake. The egalitarian and cooperative purposes of socialism, though important, are inevitably of secondary importance. Ben Salah, Tunisian Secretary of State for Finance, summed up Africa's priorities: "The intention of all true socialists is that society should improve production, control it, and distribute it justly."[17]

*Trade unions.* The African conception of the "have-nots" has important implications also for the position of the trade unions. Socialists in the West are often profoundly shocked by the treatment meted out to "the workers" by African "socialist" governments. They particularly resent the tendency to restrict the free bargaining position of the trade unions. But it is important to remember that within most African economies, organized labor often represents the most privileged, not the least privileged, section of society.

This is certainly true of many civil service unions. Organized labor generally represents the only body of people in a position to enforce demands for a larger slice of the national cake, and often already far outstrips other sections of the population in terms of present standards of living, low though these may be. Often, too, the effect of demands made by the unions which seem perfectly legitimate by European standards would, if met, dislocate the entire development plans of a government with a tight budget and carefully conceived priorities. Soon after independence in Tanganyika, for example, wage demands by civil service unions led to open conflict with the government, which reacted by severely clipping the wings of the whole labor movement. It is not generally known that if the unions' demands had been met they would have absorbed virtually all the development capital available to the government from Britain's independence "golden handshake." Little or nothing would have remained to meet the equally legitimate demands of the overwhelming majority of Tanganyikans—the non-unionized workers, the peasants, and the unemployed.

Most African governments have reacted to the threat of active trade union opposition by forcing or enticing the labor movement into the role of a "wing" of the governing party. This is generally justified by insisting that in a socialist society there is no real conflict of interest between the government and the workers.

Where independence gave political power to socialists . . . , trade unions fight for the consolidation of political power under the hegemony of the socialist party. They fight for higher living standards for the workers, but relate this fight to the more fundamental problems of increasing industrial and agricultural output.[18]

Either the party is their [the workers'] party or it is not. If it is not their party, then the problem does not arise; but if it is their party, then the doctrine of "independence" from it is an absurdity.[19]

The workers must actively support their revolutionary party and government for the consolidation of international independence and the creation of the material foundations for the construction and development of a socialist economy. In short the trade union organizations . . . have passed from the stage of destruction to that of construction.[20]

Except to doctrinaire Marxists, such justifications are unconvincing. They simply rationalize a need by the state to prevent organized labor from upsetting development plans. No government, however elected and whatever its ideals, can perfectly represent the interests of all "the workers," much less other groups as well. Democratic socialists insist that the freedom of the workers to organize for collective action in relation to the employers and the state is fundamental under a socialist as well as a capitalist government, although socialists would hope that the former would minimize the conflict between the workers and other sections of society. Thus democratic socialists cannot be expected to approve restrictions in Africa upon trade union freedom. Nevertheless it is important to understand the realities behind such restrictions. It is probably also necessary to recognize that in the present conditions of underdevelopment and with the need to emphasize capital accumulation, trade unions determined to maximize the living standards of their own members are very unlikely to survive anywhere in Africa. But conceivably experience will teach a cooperative relationship between socialist governments and free trade unions.

*"Revolutionary" democracy and the one-party state.* To the democratic socialist, the current African approach to democracy and the party system is perhaps the most disconcerting aspect of African Socialism. It has been explained in terms of the legacy of authoritarian colonial rule, of the need to stamp out tribalism and establish national unity, of the illiteracy and inexperience of the electorate, and of the importance of centralized economic planning. Each explanation has merit; but more fundamental is the revolutionary approach to politics which is the product of Africa's nationalism and the present state of economic backwardness.

Yet when African Socialists talk about revolution they do not mean a "revolution" in the Marxist sense; they mean a technological revolution to "crash" the continent through to the twentieth century. The idea that the advent of socialism into Africa demands a revolution—in the manner that Marxists would consider necessary in Europe—is scarcely entertained. Socialism, they consider, can be achieved by an evolutionary process in Africa. Instead, most African leaders relate revolutionary *methods* to the *aim* of development, and hence to full international equality and economic independence. But these revolutionary methods are easily compared, and hence often confused, with those used by revolutionary Marxists. They involve, above all, the use of the governing party not only for exhortation and mobilization of the people, but for discipline, unity, and the establishment of an identity between the hierarchies of the state and the party.

Generally, the party is conceived as incorporating the people as a whole; in this role it is intended to keep the leaders in touch with popular opinion, to prevent the growth of opposition opinion or action, and to inform and instruct the people in the thinking of the leadership. This is most comprehensively expressed by President Touré: "The Party constitutes the thought of the people of Guinea at its highest level and in its most complete form. The thought of the Party indicates the orientation of our actions; the thought of the Party specifies the principles which ought to direct our behavior, our collective and individual attitude."[21]

President Nkrumah, on the other hand, has recently been moving in the direction of a more strictly Marxist conception of an ideologically elite party, specifically socialist, intended less as a unifying force than as an educative and disciplinary vehicle for government policy: "The composition of the Party has become socially quite heterogeneous, and there is the danger that our socialist objective may be clouded by opportunistic accommodations and adjustments to petit bourgeois elements in our ranks who are unsympathetic and sometimes even hostile to the social aims to which the Party is dedicated."[22]

There are of course other views among African Socialists on the role of the party and the theories of "centralized democracy." Nigeria's leaders proclaim their faith in the multiparty system as the only true democracy, however difficult it may be to operate. In Kenya the militant governing party, KANU, sets out in its manifesto its belief in "democratic African Socialism . . . democratic because we believe that only in a free society can each individual develop his talents most fully." Opposition to the idea of "one-party democracy" is growing among intellectuals and others who feel that their freedom of speech and action is actually or potentially threatened by "centralized democracy." A Ghanaian socialist writes:

Any system of government which does not put the government firmly under the control of the general mass of the people is incompatible with socialism. . . . To argue that the one-party system is compatible with this responsibility [by the government to the people] . . . is to ignore what sociological study has taught. . . . Election within the party, far from preventing the formation of an oligarchy, seems rather to favor it. . . . The only check . . . is criticism from outside the party, and a properly organized group to act as a check *against the party*.[23]

There are, however, few signs that these views will prevail in the immediate future. The revolutionary, exhortatory, one-party approach not only is more widely accepted at the popular level, but may also prove itself, functionally, to be the only system able to meet the needs of the present situation. Neither capitalist Europe nor the Communist East achieved the capital accumulation needed to break through into self-sustaining economic growth without at the same time enforcing mass discipline through a highly restricted political system. It is not easy to see why Africa should prove the exception. The temptation for competing political parties to offer present satisfactions rather than future economic growth is obvious and dangerous; and the temptation for a ruling party to suppress opposition which might succeed in undercutting it in that way is equally clear. On the other hand, a more or less authoritarian system is not necessarily a totalitarian one: one-party states in Africa vary considerably in the extent to which they keep genuinely in touch with the people, or simply govern by overriding all opposition in the interests of an oligarchy.

It is not necessary for European socialists to applaud the one-party state or to describe it as democratic in the sense of providing the electorate with complete freedom of political choice and action. But it may well be necessary to see this system as an inevitable, if hopefully transient, concomitant of Africa's breakthrough into economic independence and self-sustaining growth. It is likely in fact that democracy in the European sense must await what the Marxists scornfully call the "bourgeoisification" of the proletariat, in terms of which they (the Marxists) explain the lack of revolutionary purpose in the Western European working class. For it is that ugly-sounding process which breeds the demand for political freedom as well as economic advance, for a voice in the process of development as well as a share in its benefits. In many parts of Africa today, notably Guinea and Tanganyika, the single party is being genuinely used as a means of expressing the opinions of the people, and not only as a method of enforcing the will of the leaders. This in itself is part of the process of democratic education, and it may prove the best of the limited choices available to Africa today.

A "nonaligned" socialism. Finally, African Socialism cannot be understood without an awareness of its nonaligned character. In one sense this may be seen as part of the wider African search for identity; but, more important, it is the result of pragmatic adjustment to the needs of the local African situation. Marx is valued both for the humanism of his sentiments—because these coincide with the African's sense of his underprivileged status—and for the revolutionary fervor and political organization which he bequeathed his disciples, which fit in with the African's conception of his own revolutionary needs. Marx's economic theories regarding the ownership of property and the requirements of the socialist revolution are either rejected as irrelevant or treated piecemeal and pragmatically. There is virtually no sense of reverence for a historically accurate doctrine, or obedience to the dictates of a dogma—much less to the dictates of the Communist bloc. Thus:

It is both unnecessary and objectionable to narrow the range of choice to two systems: capitalism and communism. As a matter of fact the chances of either . . . being adopted in its unadulterated form are very slim. In Africa, the tendency is toward a pragmatic approach which discards the irrelevant and incorporates the best from both systems.[24]

At the same time, European democratic socialists do not always recognize or applaud what they see in African Socialism either. Many suggest that pragmatism has gone too far when it abandons the principles of democracy and resorts to the use of government machinery for the preservation of the power of a single party. But the dismissal of the resulting regimes as fundamentally unsocialist, even fascist, is superficial, unimaginative, and smug. It does not take into account the circumstances in which African Socialism has been born, the overwhelming *popular* desire for rapid economic growth, and the absence of any practical evidence that this can be achieved without restricting the ability of the people to object to the sacrifices they will be called upon to make.

This is not to suggest that the theory and practice of African Socialism leaves nothing to be desired even in relation to African conditions. The long-term effect of the concentration of power, if it leads to the solidification of an oligarchy and the suppression of popular participation, negates its purpose: political discontent produces instability, and economic frustration leads to apathy, the dissipation of energy, and a decline in growth. The recognition of this point is already agitating the minds of thoughtful African leaders like Nyerere and Touré. They are particularly concerned with maintaining flexibility within the apparent monolith of the party, and above all perpetuating the popular sense of participation in government through the party.

It is too early to say whether they will succeed. At present, where the leadership itself has a genuine sense of democracy, the party serves a useful purpose both in mobilizing the people for development and in reflecting their own needs and opinions. It is providing a compromise between the growing individualism of modernity and the traditional African sense of solidarity and collective action. The line between this admirable cooperative spirit and a deadening coercion is a fine one; and very much depends upon the leadership, in the absence of an evolved machinery of democratic government. The quality of African Socialist leadership is uneven and highly individual. Perhaps the hopes and the dangers of the situation may be summed up by these sentiments:

A synthesis will be possible between individualistic and socialistic values, harmony between them being achieved in the complete human personality. This synthesis of a true socialism and a true humanism, which will rest on African reality and African values while not rejecting the enriching contributions of other cultures, will be genuinely African, but will at the same time have universal importance.

The comprehensive hopes are expressed in the text; the dangers may be deduced from the fact that its author, Mamadou Dia, former Prime Minister of Senegal,* is serving a life sentence for attempting a coup against the President of his country.

* See Appendix III, p. 248.

Chapter 6

# On African Socialism: A Soviet View

I. I. Potekhin

The many and varied opinions expressed on problems raised in my book are grouped around two fundamental questions: (1) Can African countries make a direct transition to socialism, bypassing capitalist development? (2) What is "African Socialism" and what relation does it bear to the theory of scientific socialism?

## On the Theoretical Possibility of the Noncapitalist Development of African Countries

A book with the pretentious and misleading title *Marxism, Communism, and African Socialism*[a] was published in Paris in 1962. The author set himself the task of proving the untenability of my views on the possibility of noncapitalist development for African countries.

In attempting to show that Africa must inevitably pass through the capitalist stage of development, Milon refers to Marx and to his theory of historical materialism.

Marx has always maintained that socialism could not be built in a society which has not been previously transformed and made ready by capitalism, which has left it as a legacy a powerful apparatus of industrial production and a numerous working class comprising the majority of the population. . . . Thus, according to Marx, socialism must inevitably succeed capitalism, just as capitalism succeeded feudalism, and feudalism, ancient society. . . . Capitalism must precede socialism, just as feudalism preceded capitalism. . . . [And further, Marx] affirmed that socialism was unattainable, and that any attempts to

This article originally appeared in *International Affairs* (Moscow), January 1963, pp. 71–79. It constituted a polemical response by Professor Potekhin to two attacks on his book *Afrika smotrit v budushchee* (Africa Looks Ahead), published in Moscow in 1960 and subsequently translated into German and French. The article has been only slightly edited for minor points of style and to remove polemical rhetoric which does not bear on the discussion of African Socialism. THE EDITORS.

[a] René Milon, *Marxisme, communisme, et socialisme africain* (Paris, 1962).

hasten its coming were doomed to failure, until the capitalist system should reach the highest stage of its development.[b]

In order to lend credibility to his views on historical materialism, Milon cites the following quotation from Marx's Preface to *A Contribution to the Critique of Political Economy*: "No social formation ever perishes before all the productive forces for which there is room in it have developed; and new, higher relations of production never appear before the material conditions of their existence have matured in the womb of the old society itself."[c]

It is a known fact that peoples and countries develop unevenly. In the contemporary capitalist world there are highly developed, developed, and less developed countries. African countries belong to the latter group. There is no need to explain why they have lagged behind in their development; this is already clear to all sensible, unprejudiced persons. Yet in contemporary society material conditions have ripened sufficiently for a large group of countries to go over to a new, higher form of organizing social production— to socialism.

Another question arises in this connection: What about those countries in which the capitalist form of organizing social production has not yet reached its peak of development? Does it follow from Marx's teachings that every country and every people must pass through all stages of development: slavery, feudalism, and capitalism?

Let us take a look at history. Many peoples in Europe did not experience the slave-owning mode of production, but made the transition from primitive communism to feudalism, bypassing the slave-owning formation. No one can deny that the peoples of the

---

[b] *Ibid.*, pp. 2, 14.

[c] K. Marx and F. Engels, *Selected Works*, I (Moscow, 1958), 363. In quoting Marx, Milon lets slip an inaccuracy which is of primary importance to the argument: instead of "social formation," he writes "society." There is every reason to believe that this substitution of concepts was intentional on Milon's part: the German original has "Gesellschaftsformation," and the French edition "formation sociale." See *Œuvres complètes de Karl Marx, Contribution à la critique de l'économie politique* (traduit sur la 2-ème édition allemande par J. Molidor, Paris, 1954), p. 30. "Social formation" and "society" are not analogous concepts. The concept "society" can mean a particular society (of a particular country or a particular people) or human society at a definite stage of its development. Marx wrote not about "society" in general, but about "social formation," meaning a definite mode of production— slave-owning (ancient), feudal, or capitalist.

Soviet Far North, for example, the Nentsi, Evenki, Chukchi, live in socialist conditions, yet they experienced neither slave-owning, feudal, nor capitalist formations; they proceeded to socialism, bypassing all these formations. History shows that it is by no means essential for every people to pass through all successive stages of historical development.

Marx and Engels maintained that there is a definite sequence of socioeconomic formations, that it is impossible, for example, for feudal society to succeed capitalism. But nowhere and never did they write that all peoples must inevitably pass through all stages of historical development. On the contrary, they recognized that certain peoples and countries might bypass certain of these stages. There is no detailed theory of noncapitalist development in the works of Marx and Engels, that is, the transition of backward peoples to socialism, bypassing the capitalist stage. The necessary conditions for this did not exist in their lifetime. Lenin and his successors were responsible for evolving such a theory.

### On the Feasibility and Desirability of Noncapitalist Development for African Countries

The colonial policy of plunder has made Africa the most backward region of the world. We shall not weary the reader with statistics on the state of industry and agriculture in Africa—they are too well known. We shall simply give a few figures about living conditions. Average per capita national income for 1952–54 was $740–$780 in Britain and France, but in Kenya it was $60 and in Uganda $50. Average annual consumption of meat per head of population in Britain and France is 41–54 kilograms, but in the former Belgian Congo it is 0.9 kilogram and in Ghana 2.5.

Life expectation ranges from 30 years (Guinea, 1958) to 40 years (Congo, 1950–52), while in Europe it averages 60 years. This also means that in France there are 250 adults for every 100 children, but in Upper Volta there are only 87; that is, each adult in Upper Volta has to feed three times as many dependents as a French adult. The circle tightens: widespread chronic malnutrition, protein hunger, disease, and an extremely low level of labor productivity. What is the way out of this vicious circle? Capitalism? But how much time would be needed for Africa to catch up with Britain and France, if she were to take the capitalist path? The whole world is now aware that the socialist system rates of economic growth are considerably higher than the capitalist. Moreover, can it be said that even in the advanced capitalist countries all members of society are guaranteed a high standard of living, that there is no poverty, mass unemployment, and hunger there? It would be possible to quote much striking evidence on this matter, but we shall content ourselves with one example, Liberia, which the American press is wont to describe as the shop window of capitalism in tropical Africa. The London *Times* has written that "Liberia is a country of free enterprise and if at one end of the scale people appear shabby and rather *farouche*, at the other there is considerable wealth."[d]

This cannot be denied—it is the stern reality of capitalism. *"Capitalism is the road of suffering for the people,"* declares the Soviet Communist Party Program. Intelligent Africans realize this and express themselves in favor of the socialist path of development. There is no need to quote all the numerous statements by such outstanding African statesmen and political figures as Kwame Nkrumah, Sékou Touré, and Modibo Keita along these lines. We shall limit ourselves to recounting the speech of the Tanganyikan Minister of Trade and Industry, George Kahama, in Parliament in June 1962.[e] Tanganyika, he said, had been part of the British Empire for more than 40 years. Soviet Russia, too, had existed for a little more than 40 years. Before the Revolution Russia had been a medieval state with an extremely backward economy and an illiterate population. A comparison of the Tanganyika and Russia of our days, he said, showed that despite the fact that she had gone through two terrible, devastating wars, Russia had become a leading world power, while Tanganyika had remained almost as she was 40 years ago. How could this startling contrast be explained? By the fact that a socialist system of social production had been created in Russia, Kahama declared.

The capitalist path is of course not closed to the African peoples and countries. All the necessary conditions exist for the development of capitalism, the choice urged by the imperialists and their ideological crusaders.

A mission from the International Bank for Reconstruction and Development worked in Tanganyika in 1959–60 and published a

[d] *The Times* (London), January 10, 1958.
[e] *Sunday News* (Dar es Salaam), June 17, 1962.

thick book on *The Economic Development of Tanganyika*. One of its many recommendations is to abolish common ownership of land, to divide the common land among the peasants and turn it into private property. Since they are honest people, the authors immediately point out that any reform of this kind would entail "eventual concentration of ownership of land in the hands of those who have money to lend, and the creation of a destitute landless class."[1]

That's what development along capitalist lines is like: a small section of rich farmers, big landowners, separates off, and the main mass of the peasantry are ruined and have to become farm laborers. Is this prospect to the liking of the African peasantry? They must decide for themselves. Forward-looking Africans have already given their opinion on this matter: they are against the capitalist path of development.

The matter is as follows, then: theoretically it is possible for Africa to go over directly to socialism, bypassing capitalism; the desire to take this path exists. Are the objective conditions present? Any honest person would reply to this question in the affirmative. What are these conditions?

There exists the world socialist system. This is an extremely important condition. If there were no world socialist system there could be no question of socialist development for peoples who had not passed through the capitalist stage.

Besides the mighty socialist system, there still exists in the world another capitalist system, imperialism. The imperialist states firmly oppose the former colonial and semicolonial countries taking the socialist path. Nor do they balk at any methods. They are even prepared to employ intervention and destroy the political independence of these countries. The most recent and most glaring example of this is Cuba.

However, the existence of the world socialist system ties the hands of the imperialist powers and stops them from taking extreme measures. The world socialist system acts as a guarantee of the independence of these countries.

To countries which have freed themselves from colonialism

[1] *The Economic Development of Tanganyika. Report of a Mission Organized by the International Bank for Reconstruction and Development* (Baltimore: Johns Hopkins, 1961), p. 95.

and have started on the independent construction of their life the socialist countries give all-round aid—economic, technical, and cultural. This aid is offered without political strings to all countries, irrespective of which path they have chosen—capitalist or socialist. This aid is also of fundamental importance because it compels the imperialist powers to be more compliant in offering credits and loans on more advantageous, less fettering terms. It is also of fundamental importance because the socialist countries help develop those branches of the economy which are the best guarantee of economic independence, which is the main condition for reinforcing national sovereignty. African government leaders greatly value this aid.

The building of socialism in the Soviet Union and the other socialist countries provides immense and rich experience in economic, cultural, and sociopolitical construction along socialist lines. Each socialist country has its own special features in the building of socialism, each has made a great contribution to this store of experience in socialist construction. What to use from this experience and what to discard is a matter for each people who take the socialist path.

The existence of the world socialist system creates highly important prerequisites for the noncapitalist development of the African peoples. The decisive prerequisite, however, is the condition of African society itself. And this presents an extremely varied picture.

The Republic of South Africa, for example, is a capitalist country, with the peculiar feature, however, that capitalist enterprises in industry and agriculture belong to the European minority. The first task here is to make a people's democratic revolution as a result of which the system of racial discrimination will be abolished and the African population will receive political rights equal to those of the European minority. After the victory of the people's democratic revolution there will open up the possibility of building a socialist society, but South Africa is no longer in a position to bypass the stage of capitalist development, since capitalism already exists here. In South Africa, therefore, it is not a question of noncapitalist development but of the transition from capitalism to socialism.

In the North African countries capitalist relations are also fairly developed already, and the classes of bourgeois society—the national bourgeoisie and the working class—have formed, although old feudal social classes are still preserved; nevertheless the extent of class differentiation is still far less than in the advanced capitalist states. The victory of the anti-imperialist revolution and the winning of independence have given these countries a choice: either to advance further along the path of capitalist development or to call a halt and start on building the socialist system of social production.

In discussing the possibility of noncapitalist development we consequently have in view mainly the countries of tropical Africa. The most typical feature of the social structure of the peoples in this part of Africa is the absence of clearly defined class divisions and the still incomplete formation of antagonistic classes. There is no class of big landowners exploiting a dependent peasantry; some exceptions to this rule are Ethiopia, Buganda, and the northern regions of Nigeria and Cameroon. Neither does the national bourgeoisie exist as a class. There are semifeudal, patriarchal-feudal forms of exploitation, there are capitalist elements which exploit wage labor, but there is no class of feudal lords in opposition to a peasantry, there is still no class of bourgeoisie in opposition to a working class.

Peasants living in dire poverty form the bulk of the population. In conditions of political independence just as in the colonial period, they are subject to savage exploitation by foreign companies, wealthy European farmers, and plantation owners.

The number of wage laborers in tropical Africa is still small in comparison with the developed capitalist countries. In Britain, for instance, in the 1950's, 89 per cent of the total population were wage laborers, in France 67 per cent, and in Belgium 71 per cent, but in the French colonies the figure was less than 8 per cent, and in Tanganyika and the Gold Coast about 16. Only in Northern Rhodesia was the number of wage laborers about 60 per cent of the adult male population.[g] Even so, they were in the main peasants for whom work in industry is a seasonal occupation, and moreover they came not only from inside Northern Rhodesia but from neighboring countries. Migrant labor is a mass phenomenon common to all tropical African countries. Everywhere migrants, semipeasant and semiproletarian, constitute a considerable section of the work-

[g] *International Labour Review*, LXXIV, No. 3 (September 1956), 242–43.

ing class. But everywhere, too, in every country, there is an already considerably skilled proletariat whose members are the main core of the numerous trade unions.

The overwhelming majority of workers are employed at enterprises owned by foreign companies. The exploiter of the working class is not the national, but the foreign bourgeoisie. In the struggle for independence the national bourgeoisie and the working class formed a common front, and since the tasks of the anti-imperialist revolution have not yet been fully accomplished, the basis still exists for joint action in the future.

Countries which have freed themselves from direct political rule by the imperialists are building new industrial and major agricultural undertakings. Owing to its weakness, private national capital has a very trifling share in this process. New enterprises are built either with government money or by foreign companies. This means that in the future, or at least the immediate future, the working class will have as its employer not private African entrepreneurs, but foreign companies or the government. This also means that the working class will grow more rapidly than the national bourgeoisie.

This fact is of primary importance for the transition to the socialist path of development. It is impossible to create a socialist system of social production without socialization, in one form or another, of the means of production. This fully corresponds to the interests of the working class, since it is the only class in contemporary society which is not connected with private ownership of the means of production. The African peasantry, too, is vitally interested in the socialization of the means of production, since there is no other way for it to get rid of poverty. The peasant, however, owns some, although extremely limited means of production; he is attached to his small plot of land and this hinders him from realizing that socialization of the means of production by the setting up of cooperative farms is the only way forward to a happy life.

The African working class has to fulfill a specific historical mission—to take the initiative in establishing a socialist system of social production and to lead the peasantry in this task.

The working class, the peasantry, the intelligentsia, and the large-town petty bourgeoisie (artisans, small traders, etc.), almost the entire population, have no reason to be in favor of the capitalist way of development. Socialism is the only way to happiness for them.

Socialism cannot, however, be built without a struggle. Every country has its own unpatriotic forces—feudal and semifeudal elements, some representatives of the national bourgeoisie connected with foreign companies, etc.—who place their own personal, selfish interests above the general good. They act in unison with the imperialists, the natural and irreconcilable enemies of socialism. The struggle is most acute at the present time in Ghana, where the government is putting through a number of measures which will place the country on noncapitalist lines of development.

*"Socialism is the road to freedom and happiness for the people,"* declares the Soviet Communist Party Program. "It ensures rapid economic and cultural progress. It transforms a backward country into an industrial country within the lifetime of one generation and not in the course of centuries." The vast majority of workers and peasants do not as yet understand this. In this the patriotic intelligentsia comes to their aid. There exists in Africa an intelligentsia which has mastered the scientific principles of socialism and is ready to devote all its strength and knowledge for the good of its people. It has, however, to overcome not inconsiderable difficulties.

Many ideologists of imperialism quite frequently dress themselves up in "socialist" clothing. They speak in favor of socialism, but interpret it in such a way that socialist ideas become a veiled apology for the capitalist way of development. We may take Rita Hinden's book *Principles of Socialism, Africa and Asia*[h] as an example. Under the guise of "democratic socialism," the author defends the principles motivating contemporary capitalist society.

Progressive sections of the African intelligentsia oppose this kind of camouflage and help a large number of the masses to distinguish the true supporters of socialism from all kinds of false socialists. Herein lies the great historic task of the African intelligentsia. May we wish them success in their noble work.

### *"African Socialism"* or the African Road to Socialism

My opponents include not only opponents of socialism but also supporters of socialism, people who sincerely desire to transform

[h] Rita Hinden, *Principles of Socialism, Africa and Asia* (London: Fabian Commonwealth Bureau, 1961).

modern African society into a socialist society. One such opponent, Alion Sen, who has been most severe in criticizing my book, published an article "The Future of Our Continent" in the Senegalese magazine *Unité Africaine* on May 14, 1962. Sen concludes his article thus: "We do not wish to erect an 'iron curtain' on the path of our ideological evolution; on the contrary, we want to be present at a rendezvous where there is give-and-take." I welcome such a rendezvous. It would provide the opportunity for a fruitful exchange of opinion which could lead to mutual understanding.

A completely erroneous counterposing of scientific socialist theory to "African Socialism" has gained wide currency among African Socialists: scientific socialism is not suitable for African reality; we shall build our own, African Socialism, is what they say.

"What is "African Socialism"? No single, complete theory of this concept exists. Each individual advocate of "African Socialism" has his own ideas about it and gives a different meaning to this concept, but they are all united by a common desire: to abolish the exploitation of man by man. Yet it is precisely this which is the main content of scientific socialism. Therefore, on this point, the main one, there is no divergency of views between the advocates of scientific and "African" socialism. How then can this great and noble aim be achieved? This is where the difference of views begins.

It is evident from history that the exploitation of man by man appeared with the origin of private ownership of the means of production, when a category of people was formed in society which possessed no means of production and was therefore forced to work for those who owned them.

Scientific socialism holds that the decisive condition for abolishing the exploitation of man by man is to abolish private ownership of the means of production and to socialize them.

It should be stressed, however, that what is intended is socialization not of all and every kind of private ownership but solely and exclusively ownership of the means of production. Only on this basis is it possible to establish a socialist system of social production excluding all possibility of man being exploited by man.

The advocates of "African Socialism" overlook this cardinal question, and it therefore remains uncertain how they think the exploitation of man by man can be ended. Some of them even openly acknowledge the possibility of private capitalist enterprises

existing under socialism. Here the influence of "democratic socialism" may be seen. Rita Hinden, for example, writes that "public
ownership has not proved a panacea for social ills."[i] She thinks it
possible to do away with exploitation while preserving private
ownership of the means of production.* This is a Utopian, false
idea designed to preserve capitalism.

Some advocates of "African Socialism" imagine socialist society
as a society of equal petty producers. They draw the following picture: everyone will have his own means of production in sufficient
quantity to produce all the necessities of life; everyone will manage
his own farm or business independently of others and will exchange the products of his work; if someone suffers misfortune,
the rest will help him.

This type of society, however, is simply impossible with the present state of technology, which requires large-scale production (factories, mills, railways, etc.). This is, in effect, a call to return to
the past and reject all mankind's achievements. This "ideal" petit
bourgeois society is impossible for yet another reason. Private ownership of the means of production leads inexorably to the division
of people into rich and poor, the enrichment of some and the
ruination of others, which in the final count gives rise to exploiters
and exploited.

A legitimate question arises: Why are people who sincerely wish
to build a socialist society and abolish the exploitation of man by
man unwilling to accept the scientific theory of socialism, tested
in practice, and instead engage in a search for some other kind
of socialist society? The reasons are many.

The main one is the effect of anti-Communist propaganda. The
theory of scientific socialism was first put into practice in the Soviet
Union and later in a number of European and Asian countries. The
Soviet Union is quite correctly regarded as the chief practical ex-
ample of this theory. In order to lessen the impact of the Soviet
Union's example on other peoples still living under capitalism,
the imperialists employ all means of propaganda to denigrate it.
Christian missions, acting according to the instructions of the im-

---

[i] *Ibid.*, p. 5.
* Potekhin's inversion of Hinden's argument is worth noting. Hinden says, in effect,
that public ownership does not eliminate all problems. Potekhin turns this into a
statement, in effect, that Hinden thinks that it is possible to solve all problems and
still have private ownership. THE EDITORS.

perialists, exploit the Africans' religious feelings to set them against socialism. Still the Africans are drawn toward socialism since they realize that this is the only way to happiness and so, frightened by anti-Communist propaganda, they try to discover some special kind of socialism.

Propagation of false socialist theories, like the "democratic" socialism of the British Labour Party, has created much confusion about true socialism. The French right-wing socialists and British Labour Party leaders had unlimited opportunities to spread their ideas in the African colonies; not only did the colonial authorities not prevent them, on the contrary they offered them their cooperation. This reveals a great deal: the colonialists, who dreamed of preserving their rule over the enslaved peoples of Africa, helped to spread "socialist" ideas. Surely this is proof that the "socialism" propagated by the British Labour Party leaders and French right-wing socialists is fully acceptable to the colonialists?

The latest invention of U.S. imperialist propaganda is the "pragmatic pattern of development." The African-American Institute has recently published D. K. Chisiza's book *Africa—What Lies Ahead*.[j] The author proposes rejecting the alternative, capitalism or socialism, which he finds "very narrow," and choosing the "pragmatic pattern of development," which even at a cursory glance is obviously nothing more than a fancy title for the same old capitalism.

African statesmen and political figures are educated, mature people. They fully comprehend the real purpose behind anti-Communist propaganda. All the same some of them appear to be to some extent receptive to this kind of propaganda. There are two reasons for this.

Some African leaders are connected through ties of kinship and in some instances by economic interests with the privileged, exploiting upper echelons of society. They think of the good of their people and overcoming the backwardness of their country, and realize that it is impossible to achieve this by taking the capitalist path of development. They think of socialism. But the establishment of a socialist system of production, founded on socialization of the means of production, contradicts the interests of the priv-

[j] D. K. Chisiza, *Africa—What Lies Ahead* (New York: African-American Institute, 1962).

ileged, exploiting circles which are close to them. Hence the search
for some form of socialism which would make it possible to overcome backwardness and raise the people's living standards and
at the same time would not affect the interests of the top circles.
Other African leaders are mistaken in exaggerating the importance of the specific features of African life.

Very often, advocates of "African Socialism" assert that African
society in the past, before the arrival of the colonialists, was socialist. The colonialists destroyed this socialist society and therefore
the task now is to restore it. Reference is made to the fact that in
tropical Africa there has never been private ownership of the land,
that land even today is the collective property of the peasant community, that mutual aid has always been widely practiced there,
etc. All this is true. But it is also true that for many centuries now
private production has been the rule on common land and for
many centuries property inequality has existed.

Tropical Africa has not known the slave-owning mode of production, but slavery existed before the appearance of the European
slave traders. Tropical Africa has not known the feudal formation,
but for many centuries feudal exploitation has existed; in some
regions feudal exploitation was more developed, and in others less
developed, but it was fairly widespread. Many African peoples
before the appearance of the colonialists lived in a primitive communal society, knowing neither exploitation, nor the class division
of society. If there was equality among these peoples, it was equality
of poverty, while socialist society is a society of abundance.

Advocates of "African Socialism" usually maintain that modern
African society is a classless society. They follow this up by arguing: Marxists preach class struggle, but we have no classes and
therefore Marxism cannot be applied to our reality.

These arguments contain two mistakes. Marx said: it is not I
who have the honor of having discovered classes and the class
struggle. Classes and the class struggle in fact existed long before
Marxism. Marxists simply provided the scientific explanation of
the existence of classes and the class struggle. In contemporary capitalist society the class struggle is inflamed by the bourgeoisie which
does not wish to satisfy the legitimate demands of the exploited
classes and which is impeding social progress.

We have already said that although the process of class formation is not yet complete in tropical Africa, there are feudal, semifeudal, and capitalist exploiting elements. Now, with independence, the national bourgeoisie has acquired certain new opportunities to develop. A new stratum of the local bourgeoisie is emerging which may be called bureaucratic; they are high-salaried civil servants. It is utterly impossible to call modern African society classless.

There is indeed much in Africa that is original and unlike other, non-African countries. This is not simply a result of the backwardness caused by colonial oppression. It is the result of many specific features in the history of the African peoples. The forms of transition from contemporary society to socialism, the ways of transforming contemporary society into a socialist one, can also be extremely varied. There can be no ready-made patterns here; everything depends on actual conditions.

Marxists have never said that all the peoples of the world should make the transition to socialism in faithful imitation of everything that has been done in the Soviet Union. Each of the East European countries made the transition to socialism in an entirely different way from the Soviet Union, although as regards their level of socioeconomic development, the East European countries were very close to prerevolutionary Russia. China is taking its own way to socialism.

Lenin always fought against a dogmatic approach to theory and always demanded its creative application. In his speech to the second All-Russian Congress of Communist Organizations of the Peoples of the East, he said:

You are now confronted with a task which has not previously faced Communists throughout the world: while relying on general Communist theory and practice, you must, by applying them to particular conditions which do not exist in European countries, know how to apply this theory and practice in conditions when the vast mass of the people are the peasantry, when it is necessary to accomplish the task of the fight not against capital, but against survivals of the Middle Ages.[k]

Sen mixes up two different questions: the final aim and the means of achieving this aim. There is only one final aim: to build a new social system based on socialization of the means of production whose main law of development is not extraction of profits

[k] V. I. Lenin, *Sochineniia,* XXX, 140.

by the capitalist method of exploiting the working people, but maximum satisfaction of man's material and spiritual needs. The ways of attaining this great aim may vary.

The Soviet Communist Party Program says: "The development of the countries which have won their freedom may be a complex multistage process. By virtue of varying historical and socioeconomic conditions in the newly free countries, the revolutionary effort of the masses will impart many distinctive features to the forms and rates of their social progress."

Countries which have won their freedom will proceed to socialism along tried and tested paths, and along paths discovered by the popular movement. There are no grounds therefore for counterposing "African Socialism" to scientific socialism, if by "African Socialism" we mean the specific ways and means of the transition to socialism in keeping with African reality.

This, alone correct, understanding of the question is constantly gaining ground in Africa. Take, for example, the evolution of opinion in the Convention People's Party of Ghana. The party rules adopted shortly after the winning of independence spoke of "African Socialism" as the main goal. Over the following years a lively discussion about socialism was conducted through the pages of Ghanaian newspapers. In a speech made on April 22, 1961, the founder and leader of the CPP, Dr. Kwame Nkrumah, spoke no longer of "African Socialism" but of socialism in general, saying that socialism "assumes the public ownership of the means of production."[l] The new CPP program adopted in 1962 acknowledges that its ideology "is based on scientific socialism."[m] In a talk with the author of this article on December 8, 1962, Dr. Kwame Nkrumah said that "there is only one socialism as a particular system of social production."

At the recent congress of the Sudanese Union, the ruling party in the Mali Republic, scientific socialism was similarly recognized as the Party's ideological foundation. The congress resolution on organizational questions speaks of the need to set up a Higher Party School, whose syllabus would include "the specific historical, economic, cultural, and social features of the Mali Republic, Africa,

---

[l] *Building a Socialist State,* an Address by Osagyefo Dr. Kwame Nkrumah, President of the Republic of Ghana, to CPP Study Group, April 22, 1961 (Accra), p. 2.
[m] Program of the Convention People's Party, *Work and Happiness* (Accra, 1962), p. 7.

and the whole world, the history and principles of the Party and the principles of scientific socialism, being ignorant of which no leader can effectively solve the problems of building socialism in our country."

The great historical service rendered by the founders of scientific socialism is that "they substituted science for dreams."[n] Socialist ideas sprang up long before the appearance of Marxism, but these were the Utopian dreams of noble people who were concerned at the hard and deprived position of the vast mass of people under capitalism. Today millions of exploited people dream of socialism. But it is not enough to dream; one must know how to make the transition from existing society to socialism. The sole guide in this noble task is scientific socialism.

[n] Lenin, *Collected Works,* II (Moscow, 1960), 20. [The English-language edition is in fact cited by Potekhin here, though he has cited the Russian in note 11.]

Chapter 7

# The Dakar Colloquium: The Search for a Doctrine

Aristide R. Zolberg

## The Spirit of the Conference

Speaking to the press about the "Colloquium on Policies of Development and African Approaches to Socialism" held in Dakar from December 3 to 8, 1962, President Senghor asserted that its goal was to create a "shock" and to attract the attention of African leaders "to the importance of development and the need to choose the most efficient ways and means for this development."[1]

Was this objective realized? Although it is difficult to point to tangible repercussions of the conference on African decision makers, it may well be that, for most of them, the Dakar meeting was primarily a contribution to the growth of a continent-wide network of political communications, a gathering at the foothills while the participants prepared to scale the summit at Addis Ababa in 1963. This spirit was invoked at the outset by President Senghor, whose government co-sponsored the conference with the *Congrès Méditerranéen de la Culture*. He said in a keynote address that a colloquium which brought together diverse views in such an important sphere of governmental activity was a prelude to African unity and augured well for the success of the forthcoming gathering of African heads of states.[2] Many of the speakers echoed this theme, and one of them even suggested that the search for unity was more important than the search for economic guidelines and socialism: "This colloquium must limit itself to an exchange of views. Nothing concrete will come out of it. Its only objective is to enable Africans to seek all that can unite them and to shun all that would divide them."[3]

Since it had been agreed in advance that the conference would not attempt to pass final resolutions, there was no formal occasion for division on issues. Nevertheless, according to the unstated rules of inter-African diplomacy, the acceptance of an invitation to confer with others is a positive act. In this sense, the roll call of participant governments suggested a willingness to overcome some of the cleavages that had become visible since 1958. Although 11 former French territories dominated the proceedings through sheer numbers—perhaps because of the links of the European and African sponsors to Latin culture—the presence of Nigeria and Sierra Leone, the Congo (Léopoldville), Somalia, and Ethiopia indicated that the gap stemming from different colonial experiences was narrowing. Tunisia and the Malagasy Republic testified to the extension of the concept of "Africa" to the entire continent.

Given the current political context and the topics under consideration, however, the participation both of Guinea, which had already taken steps toward a *rapprochement* with other French-speaking African countries,[4] and of Mali, at odds with Senegal since 1960, was most significant. Dr. Kouyate, Minister of Planning and Rural Economy, indicated at the beginning of his speech that he represented his party, the Union Soudanaise, rather than his government, and that he had come to talk about economics rather than about his country's relations with Senegal.[5] Nevertheless, reconciliation was in the air: the possible repercussions of a snub by the Senegalese Press Agency were held in check by the Senegalese government itself,* and Dr. Kouyate's visit was soon followed up by formal negotiations.

From the point of view of African unity, absences were significant as well. On the "Casablanca" side, Algeria, Egypt, Morocco, and Ghana were missing. Only half of the Conseil de l'Entente was there: the Ivory Coast was variously reported as absent or as present without participating; Upper Volta was definitely absent. Gabon and Chad came, but the Republic of the Congo (Brazzaville) and the Central African Republic did not. Liberia and the English-speaking East African countries were not there; neither was Togo. Some of these absences may have been due simply to a lack of interest in what was, after all, an explicitly nonpolitical and only semiofficial meeting. Although some countries may have shunned a discussion of socialism in the belief that it might offend potential investors, the only clear hint of political motivation concerned Morocco, which stayed away because Mauritania came.[6]

---

* The Senegalese Press Agency gave an inaccurate summary of Dr. Kouyate's speech to the effect that "for Mali the problem is simple: there exists only one socialism, that of Marxism-Leninism, to which his country adheres entirely" (*West Africa,* December 29, 1962). The Senegalese government ironed out the incident (*Jeune Afrique,* No. 113).

About 50 non-Africans had been invited personally. The majority of them were French, but others came from Italy, West Germany, Belgium, Czechoslovakia, Yugoslavia, England, the United
States, and Israel. They ranged from economists professionally
concerned with development, such as Father Lebret, long associated with Senegal, and Professor François Perroux, to political
leaders and writers identified with various hues of Western and
Eastern European socialism. Mr. Harris Wofford, special representative of the Peace Corps for Africa, brought up the Square Deal,
the New Freedom, the New Deal, the Fair Deal, and the New
Frontier—without a mention of socialism—and invited African
governments to join in the Peace Corps experiment.[7]

On the whole, the reactions of observers and non-African participants were mixed. In an enthusiastic editorial, *Afrique Nouvelle* acknowledged that the colloquium produced neither a definition of African Socialism nor a full-blown theory of development,
but concluded optimistically that "African Socialism is . . . in the
process of becoming a reality. After the Dakar Colloquium, nobody will be able to smile when the topic is brought up: African
Socialism has now acquired the rights of full-fledged citizenship.
Such results alone wholly justify the organization of the Dakar
meeting."[8] Jean Lacouture wrote in *Le Monde* that "The Dakar
talks . . . will leave a very favorable memory and deserve attention for more than one reason. We must, first of all, remember the
striking moderation of the talks from the rostrum as well as in
private conversations."[9] But in *Jeune Afrique*, while congratulat-
ing the Senegalese hosts for the freedom and the forthrightness of
the debates and acknowledging the value of sharing experiences,
Tibor Mende deplored the ambiguity of the concepts "development" and "socialism" symbolized by their juxtaposition in the
very title of the conference. He wondered further "whether this
colloquium had really better armed our African friends in the
choice of their strategy of development" and to what extent this
obviously sincere search for a doctrine "was compatible with the
opportunism of those—probably the majority—who mouth big
words to hide the dismal betrayal of which they are guilty through
their everyday behavior." He also charged that the participants
lacked realism concerning the need to work very hard to achieve
even modest results and that they underestimated the need for
regional cooperation.[10] In a similar vein, the correspondent for

*West Africa,* while noting that there had been a great deal of useful interchange of views concerning development in general, began his account of the conference with the question, "Who is a socialist in Africa?" and went on to suggest tactfully that "as far as socialism is concerned, it is difficult to acquit some of the delegates of a subtle complacency in paying lip service to an ideal which is not, in fact, pursued in their countries."[11]

The skepticism of some commentators about African pronouncements on development and socialism is similar to an earlier skepticism manifested by critics of African nationalism. Thomas Hodgkin has challenged "the view that African nationalism lacks any genuine theoretical basis—that such ideas as it makes use of are merely gadgets, borrowed to give an appearance of respectability."[12] In the case of nationalism, the doubts of the critics were undermined by the tangible existence of African protest movements and their success in obtaining political control over territorial units. In the case of the language of African economic thought—which preoccupied the Dakar Colloquium and much of the action of present-day African states—the critics are, perhaps, in a less vulnerable position. Although it is possible to find *some* economic growth and *some* movement in the direction of economic democracy, African development is highly dependent, on the whole, on external assistance and brings in its wake new economic differentiation that may lead to a less equitable sharing of national product. Nevertheless, the colloquium revealed a deep concern with the goals and instruments of economic change. Hence, the language of the participants can be analyzed at least as statements of intention, if not as accounts of reality.

### The Language of the Conference

Following a greeting by M. Lamine Gueye, President of the National Assembly of Senegal, and a keynote address by Léopold Sédar Senghor, President of the Senegalese Republic, the representatives of almost all the African governments participating in the conference gave an account of their own country's approach to development and problems encountered or anticipated, usually concluding with an exhortation. There was almost no African participation in the general debate that followed, although, at the very end, Gabriel d'Arboussier, then Minister of Justice, and Mamadou Dia, then Prime Minister of Senegal, attempted a synthesis of the

various themes. Notwithstanding the danger inherent in discussing the thought of a group, the prevalence of common concepts
and concerns was sufficiently striking to allow the use of such a
method in the analysis that follows.[13]

1. *The urgency of development.* The *desirability* of rapid economic development, in the sense of an increase in real national
wealth, is axiomatic in Africa as elsewhere in the contemporary
world. This was expressed through a wide range of target figures:
to double the average per capita income in 20 years;[14] to increase the
annual rate of national growth to at least 4 per cent;[15] to double the
national income in 14 or 15 years;[16] to increase annual economic
growth to 6 per cent in order to double the national income in 10
years.[17] Not only is such rapid development seen as necessary to
ensure internal stability by satisfying the demands of individuals
and groups, but it alone can bring about equality between African
nations and the rest of the world. In this light, the present situation
is critical because "the gap between the developed and the underdeveloped world is growing rapidly. At the present rate, it will
become immense. The real value of raw materials from the underdeveloped areas is declining, while the price of manufactured goods
is growing."[18] Developed nations thus provide the reference group
by whose achievements African leaders evaluate their own progress.

2. *Rationality, planning, and socialism.* The *possibility* of bringing about rapid development is also axiomatic. It stems from a
genuine faith in man's ability to rationally control his human and
physical environment.[19] Operationally, this takes the form of
planning:

Programs enable man to exercise in practice his faculties of analysis,
choice, decision, and action under optimum psychological and technical conditions.[20]

Once independent, the developing countries have almost unanimously
chosen planning as their approach. They have indeed understood, as
have also many developed countries, that the mere interplay of auto-
matic mechanisms does not lead to optimum growth or, consequently,
to development. The generalized use of planning, regardless of content,
is indeed a response to the characteristics of modern economic life.
. . . Planning is, first of all, the introduction of rationality in economic
life. It brings about rapidly or in the long run the gradual elimination
of its mysteries.[21]

The primordial role of government in providing leadership for development is implicit in the emphasis on planning. Neverthe-less, all African plans make room for private contributions from domestic and foreign sources; the result is labeled "partnership."[22] Both in design and in execution, African plans are diverse and eclectic. Summarizing this in his final speech, Prime Minister Dia indicated that while there is general agreement on planning,

we do not always give to this notion the same meaning or the same scope. That is indeed because planning is subject to variations of de-gree and means. For some, the essential role of planning is to afford a satisfactory coordination and linkage of public investments. Others ex-pect their plan to constitute a general framework for the state's eco-nomic policies, or even for the entire economy, and to insure either the best possible cohesion of the partial plans of major economic agencies, or even the dependence of partial programs on the general plan.[23]

Following this trend of thought, the lack of planning, identified with capitalism, is a denial of rationality, and abdication to the uncontrollable mysteries of the market: "In an economy where laissez faire is the dominant philosophy, desired objectives cannot be determined and the future remains an unknown element."[24] By constrast then, rationality and planning are equated with social-ism. Most of the participants expressed this equation, from the delegate who asserted simply that "socialism is a science"[25] to others who elaborated further:

For us, socialism is merely the rational organization of human society, considered as a whole, according to the most scientific, modern, and effective means.[26]

Socialism has been chosen because its scientific method for the analysis of reality will enable us to understand the realities of our nation and hence to transform them rationally.[27]

Socialism is a method for the understanding of social realities and more particularly economic realities. As such it is scientific. Far from being the exclusive property of a single determined ideology, it is the common source of all those who are in search of objectivity. As such it is also, fundamentally, a method for adjustment to realities.[28]

The fervor of such statements suggests that for those who are faced with the overwhelming burdens of government in Africa, socialism is more than a scientific method. It is a modern gnosis which promises to unveil to its initiates the secrets of economic development.

3. *The uniqueness of African Socialism.* The espousal of socialism is understandable because this concept is associated with rationality and modernity. However, the attempt to differentiate "African Socialism" from its more general variety can be understood as but another manifestation of the search for original concepts and the general distrust exhibited by Africans toward formulas which do not take into account African *conditions*: "Foreign solutions cannot be adopted and imposed over African reality."[29]

What is this reality? First of all, it is the fact that the problem of Africa is primarily one of economic decolonization: "In Africa in particular, the specific character of natural and historical givens, characterized by the direct intervention of European capitalism, naturally commands the definition of an African approach to socialism."[30] The second distinct aspect of African reality is the absence of established social classes. Given European conditions, the achievement of socialism involved the mobilization of the propertyless against those who controlled the means of production; this necessitated the creation of an elite vanguard and the resort to violence. In Africa, this is not the case: "Since there is no class struggle, African Socialism will be gradual and peaceful";[31] furthermore, "socialism can be realized without a Communist party because it is the entire people that is being organized and not a specific class."[32]

The search for African Socialism involves for some a rejection of classical Marxism:

It is evident that African Socialism can no longer be that of Marx and Engels, which was designed in the nineteenth century according to European scientific methods and realities. Now, it must take into consideration African realities. This is particularly necessary because Marx and Engels were not anticolonial. Engels defended classical slavery and Marx supported British colonization of India.[33]

For others, there is no real conflict, since Marxism itself puts action before theory:

I must confess . . . that I was at first tempted to conclude that "African Socialism" was an improper term since socialism, being a science, could not be any more African than Chinese or Russian. But, after thinking it over, it is clear that the term "African Socialism" . . . poses the problem of the indispensable adaptation of scientific socialism to African realities. You are all familiar with the simple but famous definition formulated by Lenin: "Marxism is not a dogma, it is a guide for action." In other words, Marxist theory, studied and assimilated by our students, will have a chance to take root . . . only if the youth will take the trouble, from now on, to become more broadly acquainted with the political, economic, and human realities of Africa.[34]

On the whole, however, the findings concerning the relationship between Marxism and African thought discussed elsewhere by Thomas Hodgkin are upheld by the language of the Dakar conference: there are linguistic borrowings, Marxist categories of explanation are used, Leninist ideas of organization prevail, but there is broad adaptation and "the metaphysical aspects of Marxism are either discarded or adapted to suit the needs of the African situation as nationalist leaders understand them."[35]

4. *Economic modernization without alienation.* If there are eclectic borrowings of Marxist linguistic categories, Africans genuinely share Marx's deep concern with the alienation that he saw as a product of capitalist development. The ideal itself is clear. One delegate, modestly acknowledging that since his government did not even have a plan he could not speak about socialist experiments, nevertheless claimed the label "socialist" for his country's approach to development since the government attempted to avoid the development of opposite classes.[36] Other statements expressed similar views:

Democratic socialism has been chosen because it opposes capitalism based on the exploitation of man by man . . . African Socialism wants to enhance the requirements of the common good rather than those of a minority or a faction of the nation.[37]

We believe our approach to be socialist to the extent that we mean to extend the benefits of development to all our peoples to raise their standards of living and afford all the full opportunities for realizing the best in themselves and for the enthronement of the dignity of man everywhere.[38]

In the past, colonialism was the major source of alienation. Now, however, internal dangers loom as well. Realistically, some spokesmen recognized that development proper can bring about the growth of inequality:

The social structure is in a state of effervescence because of increased proletarianization due to the exodus from rural areas and the decline of the artisan class, and an increased awareness among the masses of their misery and the wide gap existing between themselves and the privileged groups.[39]

The greatest threat stems from the political elite itself. For African leaders, socialism thus becomes a self-imposed moral code:

It is necessary that the ruling class, avoiding the temptations of *embourgeoisement,* lead the transition to socialist society.[40]

Socialism is the merciless fight against social dishonesties and injustices: against excessive wages, fraudulent conversion of public funds. It is a moral tension to be kept up from the base to the apex, but especially at the apex.[41]

But for the lone unionist who addressed the colloquium, the leaders' commitment to socialist morality was not enough. In the language of European Marxism, he indicated that the achievement of socialism demands positive actions:

Marx has affirmed and demonstrated that the suppression of alienation could only result from a dialectical process, that is to say that alienation is the consequence of a contradiction between opposite forces: the thesis and the antithesis, the master and the slave, the proletarian and the capitalist, the colonized and the colonizer, and that liberation does not come out of the triumph of the antithesis but only when contrary forces, thesis and antithesis, are overcome by a synthesis.

This means that for us, African Socialists, the end of the colonial regime does not automatically bring about the end of alienation. Franz Fanon understood this perfectly when he stated that the massive, world-wide contradiction opposing colonizers and colonized peoples has been replaced or rather transformed and extended by a series of other contradictions, among which the most virulent is that which opposes the peasants and the rural populations to white-collar workers and people of the towns, who alone have inherited the privileges of colonial society. . . .

Our socialist convictions are in revolt against the growing gap which separates the class of the privileged of the new regime: government employees, military men, politicians, from the mass of the urban and rural proletarians, the unemployed and the jobless youth.

We demand of our rulers a policy of austerity and of political purge which constitute the prerequisites for economic development.[42]

Thus the warning against alienation is clear: the new synthesis of African Socialism demands the creation of a society in which men are fully integrated by virtue of the lack of classes and economic differentiations.

5. *The dilemma of traditionalism and modernism.* Sharply contradictory tendencies were manifested by participants in the conference about aspects of African traditionalism and the need to modernize. These contradictions stemmed from a concern with alienation which is the product of modernization while being equally concerned with accelerating the modernization process. Alienation is seen as stemming from the colonial situation *and* from economic stratification. It occurs when the individual loses his sense of community or when man is sacrificed to the interests of the whole. African Socialism can provide a middle ground: it can be both "man-oriented" and "community-oriented." This solution is found in a "personalist" conception of mankind, inherited by the Senegalese from the French Catholic Left[43] but now formulated by many others:

African Socialism is a humanistic socialism because it is an attempt to bring out the qualities of man . . . African Socialism is thus the complete flowering of man through the flowering of the community in the midst of which he has chosen to live and work.[44]

[The foundations of African Socialism include] a full flowering of man living in the group . . . Our socialism is thus a humanism which does not wish to sacrifice the individual in favor of the collectivity.[45]

The guarantee of this humanistic orientation, the source of protection against alienation, rests in traditional African values.

President Senghor's definition of *socialism* as a *sense of community* appeals to us greatly. He adds that this is *a return to Africanism*; we would rather say this is the *essence of Africanism* which must be preserved at all costs in our endeavor to modernize. In a society which has never really been stratified into classes a redistribution of wealth is a normal process; the provision of equality for all is merely translating into modern terms what goes on all the time and perhaps extending it more consciously beyond the confines of the extended family.[46]

African traditionalism, guardian against alienation, however, can be a mixed blessing: while it helps integration and provides roots, it is a major obstacle to modernization and socialism:

The way to socialism in Africa involves the break-up of economic, social, and psychological structures in order to change our present society into a balanced and harmonious one. . . . It is an established historical fact that traditional political, economic, and social structures have plunged our respective countries into decadence, regression, fetishism, and finally colonization. . . . Economic and social structures at the present stage of the evolution of our countries constitute the main obstacle to our advancement and if we seriously intend to blaze our path toward socialism we must attack these structures. It is here that our first efforts must be applied.[47]

The first step on the African path to development is the revolutionary rejection of old structures. . . . This condemnation and this rejection bear first of all upon the structures which the colonizer himself has created and established. But they must also bear with the same force and the same determination on the archaic structures, on the feudalism which the colonizer preserved and artificially consolidated, while at the same time he subverted them to make out of them the instruments of his own domination.[48]

When the dilemma is recognized, the solution advanced is one of selective conservation. For example, after having demonstrated the role of traditional values in African Socialism, one participant continued: "We also hear that this perpetuates nepotism, bribery, and corruption—this may be so, but our objective is to expunge all these imperfections from our way of life without destroying the *sense of community* which sometimes gave rise to them."[49] Similarly, after arguing for the need to launch a frontal assault upon traditional structures, another speaker qualified himself:

I do not advocate a crusade against traditions: those which represent our past civilization, our attachment to moral values and individual genius, will be jealously guarded; those which are the by-products of declining centuries will be denounced and combated with our last breath.[50]

The search is, therefore, for the best of the old and the new: the old provides integration and social cohesion, while the new establishes modern productive apparatuses leading to higher standards of living.

6. *Mobilization of the masses.* The Dakar Colloquium showed relatively little concern with economic problems of development

per se. In his final remarks, Gabriel d'Arboussier suggested that a future conference would have to deal, among others, with the question of where capital must be accumulated in order to put it to maximum use: must priorities be assigned to agriculture or to industry?[51] Meanwhile, it is clear that in spite of the glib reports of some superficial observers, Africans do not suffer from a "steel-mill complex." The Mali delegate stated that agriculture is basic and that industry can come only later: it must be integrated into agriculture in order to avoid being a foreign body in the economy.[52] President Senghor agreed: "There is need for a plan. But it is evident that agriculture conditions everything else even in developed countries. Marx did not understand this, Lenin had begun to, and Mao Tse-tung understands it fully."[53]

More attention was paid to the human aspects of development. It was generally agreed that human resources were most important: even in a "socialism in search of itself," a major component is "mobilization of the masses."[54] For another spokesman, "the only way socialism can be realized is by mobilization of the masses with the help of all the youth, without exclusion."[55] Elsewhere, the first task is "the mobilization of all energies and vital forces of the country at the service of national construction, at the service of the plan of development, and at the service of our socialist structures."[56] The emphasis on the mobilization of the population was not new; what *was* new, albeit in a negative way, was the failure to discuss "human investment," perhaps because, after many governments encouraged local self-help, "the initial enthusiasm . . . wore off . . . as it became increasingly clear that more planning would be needed to produce effective results,"[57] or even because the use of labor as capital became indistinguishable from some of the more notorious colonial techniques of development.

Although the nature of "mobilization" or "animation" of the masses for development was not fully clarified, the emphasis was primarily psychological. It does not simply involve the movement of citizens along certain prescribed channels, but requires a genuine change in attitudes, a re-education:

It is . . . essential to associate the citizens with the design and the realization of the plan. It is not a matter of gaining their formal support or of mobilizing them by a simple recourse to commands. On the contrary, it is necessary to make the population conscious of the policy of development, to make them experience the problems, to make them will the means, first at the level of village realities, and then, step by step, at the level of regional and national realities.[58]

Mobilization is crucial if development is to be successful. According to Senghor, for example, agricultural modernization must take into consideration not only soils and plants but, perhaps more important, the nature of man and particularly that of the peasant: "The failures of agricultural policies of socialist countries need not be looked for anywhere else."[59]

The political requirements for the success of mobilization were made explicit: "Discipline, authority—but not totalitarianism—a spirit of devotion and of sacrifice, and organization."[60] The major instrument is the mass political party whose functions include, for example, "to bring about the psychological revolution needed to modernize agriculture. This means that the party must be a living body in which sap circulates from the bottom to the top and from top to bottom."[61] Usually, it is argued that the party must have a political monopoly because democracy requires a single-party system to avoid the scattering of forces.[62] Since most of the countries present were in fact single-party states, the question was not really debated. The only governmental dissenter was the Malagasy delegate, who merely suggested that a single-party system was not necessary to bring about development.[63] That the "outs" question the advantages of the one-party system, however, was clearly revealed by the "remarkably violent" intervention of the spokesman for the Fédération des Etudiants d'Afrique Noire en France, which represents many student organizations at odds with incumbent leaders:

Certain members of the opposition cannot return to their country because of the threat of arrest. Student congresses have been forbidden in several African countries and most of the African regimes can be characterized by an absence of freedom of expression, freedom of association, and freedom of the press.[64]

7. *The need for world solidarity.* The success of African Socialism is dependent not only upon the ability of countries to mobilize their internal resources by effecting a transformation of values and attitudes but also on Africa's ability to mobilize world resources by producing a similar revolution in other countries.

Almost all the Africans speaking in Dakar expressed some concern about the dangers of continued dependence upon external capital, and many specified that economic partnership between African governments and outsiders should not be construed by the latter as a license to meddle with internal affairs.* Nevertheless, it was clear that there was an overwhelming concern to secure external partners. Whenever plans were outlined, they specified that a substantial share of capital investment, sometimes amounting to half of the total,† would hopefully be obtained from the outside.

At the very beginning of the conference, President Senghor called for a world conference to consider the urgency of aid to underdeveloped countries; at the very end, Gabriel d'Arboussier also suggested that a future conference would have to discuss the means of world solidarity: how to increase aid, how to make it more efficient, how to make it politically disinterested. The African argument to the world can be stated as follows:

> It is in the best interests of the highly developed countries in the world to help all underdeveloped countries to develop and modernize. In a world becoming more and more closely knit—distance being annihilated for airplanes which could shortly be traveling at three times the speed of sound—prosperity, like peace, has become indivisible and the world cannot long endure half developed and half underdeveloped, half fabulously rich and half abjectly poor. Not to mention the fact that to increase the purchasing power of the people of the underdeveloped countries is indirectly to increase the markets for the goods of the developed countries. So we do not regard external aid as charity—it is merely essential assistance to enable us to help ourselves and therefore benefit our helpers and the world at large.[65]

In the end, there emerges another, perhaps deeper meaning of African Socialism: the natural demands of the poor in the midst of plenty, joining the clamor for justice voiced by the underprivileged throughout history.

### Conclusions

A genuine consensus emerged in Dakar in spite of repetition, verbosity, and lack of precision. African nations want to rapidly increase their wealth while avoiding the discontinuities that led to

---

* This was emphasized particularly in the speeches of the Congolese and Tunisian delegates.

† Dr. Biobaku specified that 50 per cent of the investments needed for the Nigerian plan might be contributed by a world consortium under the aegis of the Bank for International Reconstruction and Development; M. Chaker indicated that Tunisia would accept up to 50 per cent external investments in its own plan.

alienation in industrial countries and without creating social classes. This is seen as possible if political elites learn scientific techniques to control man's environment while avoiding the temptation to apply foreign doctrines that do not consider the human and physical context of the continent. The initiative must come from government, exerting authority without becoming totalitarian, but there must be room for partnership with domestic or foreign sources of capital. Finally, Africa must persuade the Northern Hemisphere of its obligation to participate in a world system which will ensure an equitable redistribution of wealth among countries.

Whether or not this approach to the problems of development can properly be called "socialist" is irrelevant except to the countries themselves. Some African nations which shun the word, such as the Ivory Coast, would nevertheless endorse all of the planks of the doctrinal platform erected in Dakar. To many of the participants, on the contrary, the word is vital because it denotes modernity and democracy in the economic sphere. As indicated earlier, similar questions arose when Africans called themselves "nationalists" and more recently when some began to speak about "Pan-Africanism." From an African point of view, all these concepts are interrelated: the theme of African unity, which dominated the Dakar proceedings from the very first day, was relevant to development as well. Speaker after speaker reiterated that African cooperation and African unity were themselves prerequisites for development. Thus, while a conference on development contributes to unity, a conference on unity contributes to development. In this manner, nationalism, Pan-Africanism, and socialism are woven together to create an overall African ideology of modernization.

Part II

National Programs

Chapter 8

# Socialism in Ghana:
# A Political Interpretation

Colin Legum

"At this juncture Ghana is not a socialist state. Not only do the people as yet not own all the major means of production and distribution, but we have still to lay the actual foundations upon which socialism can be built, namely, the complete industrialization of our country. All talk of socialism, of economic and social reconstruction is just empty words if we do not seriously address ourselves to the question of basic industrialization and agricultural revolution in our country, just as much as we must concentrate on socialist education."[1]

This statement by President Kwame Nkrumah provides several clues to his thinking and to an understanding of political and economic developments in Ghana. It illustrates Nkrumah's commitment to the Marxist aim of state ownership of productive property. It shows that, like all modern Marxists, he cannot conceive of a socialist society which is not also an industrial society.

This chapter examines the consequences of a variety of conflicting forces—ideological, political, economic, and social—presently existing in Ghanaian society. The thesis is that Dr. Nkrumah is both a convinced idealist and a practical realist. As an idealist, Nkrumah is committed to an economic organization of society that can be characterized as Marxist. Nkrumah is also a dedicated Pan-Africanist, concerned simultaneously with ideas of the liberation of Africa from colonialism and economic domination by the European (or other non-African) powers, with the need for continental political organization so that Africa may emerge as a vital world force in the future, and with the organization of the continental economy on a socialist basis.

In contrast to this global idealism, Nkrumah is also a hard-headed realist. On the one hand, he is fully aware of the importance of Ghanaian nationalism as a force for mobilization of internal forces and as a weapon to forge his wider Pan-Africanist ideals. On the other hand, he is sensitive to the existence of powerful forces that provide significant drags on the development of socialism in Ghana. Thus he recognizes that Ghana has neither the resources nor the personnel needed to establish a Marxist society at the present. "Ghana at this time is not possessed of the socialist means."[2] Besides, "socialism needs socialists to build it."[3] These inertial forces are also represented by the presence of conscious, recalcitrant social and economic groupings, within the Convention People's Party (CPP) and outside it, who regard socialism with disdain since they see in it the elimination of whatever privileges they possess.

Like Trotsky in different circumstances, Nkrumah rejects the notion that socialism can be built successfully in a single country in Africa. For him, the building of socialism in Ghana must be accompanied by the building of socialism throughout the continent. This belief rests on the premise that independence in Africa is indivisible, and that there can be no real independence without economic independence, which in turns depends upon socialist development. Hence his advocacy of a continent-wide, single, mass political party.[4]

It is because of these contradictions that Nkrumah has fallen back on a "vanguardist" conception of political organization—a conception that he learned in his early period as an African nationalist and that he continues to employ in seeking to manipulate the recalcitrant and enervative forces presently existing in Ghanaian society. These contradictions as well as Nkrumah's mercurial personality have caused many apparent inconsistencies. Events such as the excoriating attack on certain elements within the CPP in the famous Dawn Broadcast, which was not followed by any significant party or government reorganization, the toleration of *The Spark*'s position—one which was often antithetical to his own—and the many unexplainable ministerial changes make it difficult to present a fully consistent interpretation of the political process in Ghana.

A brief examination of Ghanaian society elucidates the background in which the present political patterns have developed. Ghana's society is characterized by strong individualism operating within ethnocentric communal patterns. This makes for strong tribal and regional interests and for individual enterprise, two factors that militate against socialist ideas. This reaction has been strongest among the peasants, the fishermen, the traders, and the middle class. Although land is mostly communally owned through the traditional system of tribal stool lands, practice allows for individual possession during the lifetime of the occupant, and usually for his descendants. Thus the vital cocoa crop is raised by individual peasant producers. The pattern of cooperative marketing—introduced by the colonial government—was only reluctantly accepted by the cocoa farmers after its practical advantages became apparent. But they resist any idea of collectivization of cocoa production.

Trading patterns are also strongly developed in Ghanaian society. The "market mammies"—a significant force in bringing the CPP to power—vigorously insist on their right to individual trading; every attempt to limit their opportunities has met with strenuous opposition. Independence opened up opportunities for Ghanaians to develop large-scale business and manufacturing enterprises, which were quickly seized by a small but powerful group of traders, mostly supporters of the CPP.

Modern socialism has no popular roots in Ghanaian society. Its present influence is not primarily a response to needs felt by the masses of workers and peasants; it is the result of a deliberate choice of policy by Nkrumah and an elite in the CPP. They see socialism as the best method of meeting the needs of developing African society and of overcoming the problems of colonialism. The task of this elite group has been to popularize the idea of socialism and to win the country over to its acceptance; but they have not hesitated, on occasion, to adopt socialist measures against popular opposition.

The CPP was not originally a socialist party in the sense of being predominantly guided by socialist principles. Its early influence and popularity were supplied by the anticolonial struggle. Although its first constitution speaks of socialist objectives, this policy was not a prominent feature in its earlier years. If there was little effort to make socialism a major plank in the CPP's program during this period, it was because Nkrumah knew that "in order to organize a genuine popular movement it was necessary to build

on all existing foundations wherever this was possible."⁵ But he
was under no illusions about what would happen to a party organized on a mass base to achieve liberation. "The composition of the
Party has become socially quite heterogeneous and there is the
danger that our socialist objective may be clouded by opportunistic
accommodations and adjustments to petit bourgeois elements in
our ranks who are unsympathetic and sometimes even hostile to
the social aims to which the Party is dedicated."⁶

## Major Aspects of Nkrumah's Socialism

The examination of political and economic events in Ghana illustrates the pragmatic approach that Dr. Nkrumah has taken again
and again in seeking to resolve the contradictions between his
idealism and his practical concerns. To a considerable degree this
is reflected as a continual search for ideology, for forms of organization within the CPP and the government, for the development
of economic policies. It appears as both experimentation and vacillation, and, undoubtedly, elements of both are present. Nevertheless, through the many developments certain distinct threads appear which reflect two major themes in Nkrumah's socialism.
These are represented by (1) his vanguardist conception of party
organization as a way to move masses toward socialism; and (2)
his conviction of the need for the proper economic organization
of society through the ownership of the means of production by
the state.

In his autobiography, Nkrumah describes the influences on "my
revolutionary ideas and activities" of Hegel, Engels, Mazzini, and
"particularly" Marx and Lenin.⁷ His Pan-Africanist ideas were
stimulated by Marcus Garvey rather than by the democratic socialist and later Communist Dr. W. E. B. DuBois. But it was George
Padmore who in his own lifetime probably influenced him more
deeply than any other socialist or Pan-Africanist. By the time these
two met, Padmore was a crusader against the international Communist movement, having become converted to democratic socialism as a result of his disillusionment with Stalin's Russia. While
Padmore broke completely with communism, he brought to the
Pan-Africanist movement an only slightly modified conception of
political organization which was essentially vanguardist.

Nkrumah's first work, *Towards Colonial Freedom,* was written
in 1942; but his views had changed so little that he could publish

it unchanged 20 years later.[8] It is a straightforward Marxist-Lenin-
ist tract against imperialism.

Dr. Nkrumah knows that in order to bring about a radical
transformation of Ghanaian society, he must have the active support of his party, and the full backing of the civil service (administration, police, judiciary, and army). But none is an altogether
willing instrument of his purposes, for all reflect the nature of
Ghanaian society. The CPP can be relied upon to echo the leader's propaganda and to join in singing the praises of the Osagyefo,
but not to give its wholehearted energies to revolutionary change
for socialism. The objectives are obscured by people who have
gravitated toward the source of power but who have little understanding of, or liking for, socialism, or for Nkrumah's methods.
The government machinery is likewise staffed with people ill
equipped — ideologically and often technically — to implement
Nkrumah's ideas.

The result is that the President must rest upon a tiny coterie of
intimates for genuine support. But they represent no more than
one or two cells in the honeycomb of the power structure; and
even they do not always support the President's ideas. This conception of a tiny cell of militant intimates has been a close feature
of Nkrumah's tactics in his rise to power and in his struggle to
retain it. So far, he has only once made the mistake of seriously
overestimating the power of these intimates; that was in 1961–62,
when he encouraged them to undertake the task of disciplining
the "capitalist elements" in the Party; he was later forced to a temporary and partial retraction. Generally, he looks upon this group
for the "re-education" of the CPP, of the administration, and of
"the people." For example, they have been positioned by Nkrumah in the different wings of the CPP to conduct ideological education programs.

The history of Dr. Nkrumah's reliance on a vanguardist organization began with the formation of "The Circle" in 1947.[9] A close
examination of the Circle is of special importance because of the
light it sheds on Nkrumah himself, and because its methods and
thinking still operate at the innermost center of power in Ghana
through the nucleus of leaders of the National Association of Socialist Students' Organization (NASSO) and of the Party Vanguard Activists (PVA).

The Circle's motto was "The Three S's"—Service, Sacrifice, and

Suffering. Its two aims were (1) "to maintain ourselves and the Circle as the Revolutionary Vanguard of the struggle for West African Unity and National Independence; [and] (2) to support the idea and claims of the All West African National Congress in its struggle to create and maintain a Union of African Socialist Republics." Its long-term goals were described as follows: "At such time as may be deemed advisable THE CIRCLE will come out openly as a political party embracing the whole of West Africa, whose policy then shall be to maintain the Union of African Socialist Republics." The only change in this goal is that Nkrumah now talks about creating such a socialist party for the whole continent. "I see before my mind's eye a great monolithic party growing up out of this process (of training freedom fighters), united and strong, spreading its protective wings over the whole of Africa."[10]

The theory behind the Circle, as set out in the following passage, later continued to apply to the role given to NASSO and the PVA's:

No movement can endure unless there is a stable organization of trained, selected, and trusted men to maintain continuity and carry its program forward to successful conclusion. . . . The more widely the masses of the African peoples are drawn into the struggle for freedom and national independence of their country, the more necessary it is to have an organization such as THE CIRCLE to establish stability and thereby make it impossible and difficult for demagogues, quislings, traitors, cowards, and self-seekers to lead astray any section of the masses of the African people.

The seventh law of the Circle required a member to declare: "I accept the leadership of Kwame Nkrumah." At the time this was presented, Nkrumah was 30 and still only a student in London. But the concept of *Osagyefo,* the great and unvanquished warrior, was already firmly implanted.

Nkrumah never lost sight of his long-term objective. For him the "political revolution" was only the prelude to an "economic revolution," both in Ghana and in Africa. To achieve the economic revolution he assiduously promoted the concepts of the Circle through NASSO, which was formed in the late 1940's among students in Britain. After Nkrumah's return to the Gold Coast, NASSO took the place of the Circle as an exclusive group devoted mainly to theoretical discussion and teaching; but its members were also useful to Nkrumah in reporting on what was happening inside the CPP and in the country. It was to one of its first leaders—Kojo Botsio, at that time still his bosom friend—that Nkrumah entrusted the special task of guiding, protecting, and encouraging the young socialists in the Party in the early 1950's. But until his death in 1959, George Padmore and his close colleague, Dr. T. R. Makonnen, were its chief ideological counselors. Of NASSO's role Nkrumah later said: "This is the custodian body of the Party's ideology and is composed of the most advanced ideological comrades, torchbearers, of the Party's ideals and principles. NASSO forms the bark of this mighty tree, and cements the physical and organizational unity of the CPP."[11]

It was to NASSO that in 1961 he dedicated the Kwame Nkrumah Ideological Education Training Center and the Positive Action Training Centre at Winneba.

From the early 1950's regular weekly meetings were held at Nkrumah's residence, which he attended as often as he could.[12] However, once it became apparent that the way to Nkrumah's "inner circle" lay through membership in NASSO, the organization began to attract recruits who were increasingly regarded as rather dubious by its original members. The older group objected especially to Mr. Tawia Adamafio, formerly a bitter opponent of the CPP. Adamafio had joined the Party in the early 1950's, obtained a scholarship to England, and soon took control of the influential NASSO branch in Britain. From this vantage point he later moved into two key jobs—secretary-general of the CPP and Minister of Information. In the late 1950's he became a leading figure in NASSO, and was looked up to by the group of socialists who came into prominence after Padmore's death. This new group strongly disapproved of Padmore, whom they regarded as "a Trotskyite and a West Indian." NASSO changed its character under Adamafio's control; a number of its earlier members withdrew because they felt that "opportunism had sneaked into the Party's 'custodian body.'" Adamafio's humiliating downfall after the Kulungugu bomb attempt on Nkrumah's life in 1962 seemed to this group to confirm all their suspicions about his "careerism." But although Adamafio fell, the group that had looked to him for leadership and that now controlled the party press and other important party posts all survived—despite a spirited attack on them in the Ghana National Assembly by their sworn opponent, Mr. Krobo Edusei.

In 1959 NASSO was officially described as the "ideological wing of the Party." But its influence since 1960 has been wielded mainly through the Party Vanguard Activists—the PVA's—whose existence was announced by Nkrumah in his address to the tenth CPP congress in 1959.[13]

Members called Vanguard Activists, drawn from the most politically educated section of the Party, would be trained at special courses to explain the aims and objects of the CPP to those who did not clearly understand them. The Activists would live and work among the common people. They are the salt of the earth. We, the so-called educated members of the Party, must learn from them.

The PVA's were formally recognized in the CPP's Revised Constitution (1959). In 1960 they were established "as a virile functionary unit of the Party whose duty it is to propagate selfless devotion to the cause of the Party."[14] Their role and functions—which bear the unmistakable imprint of The Circle—are defined in Part Four of the CPP's 1962 Revised Constitution. Here the original fears expressed by Nkrumah in launching The Circle, of the dangers that would face a mass party, are recognized as having overtaken the CPP. "The politically conscious leadership is faced with the danger of being swamped by tribal, regional, and other communal ideological influences which are penetrating the ranks of the more backward Party membership." To combat the "ideological menace and factional rivalries" it was decided that "the Party will adopt certain inner organizational measures to safeguard its socialist aims. . . . The Party needs a vanguard of consciously dedicated activists and propagandists" ideologically trained.[15]

It is clear, therefore, that notwithstanding Nkrumah's conscious desire to build a "socialist" party and a "socialist" society, his efforts had been frustrated by social forces within the country and within his party and government. His own efforts had been so largely taken up by the wider responsibilities of office that he was unable to devote himself to the task of "making socialists." His party lieutenants entrusted with this work had failed. Looking back in 1961 over the period covered by the "political revolution," Nkrumah reflected: "For . . . twelve long years, therefore, no conscious consistent effort had been made to provide party members with the requisite education in the Party's ideology of socialism."[16]

*The Role of NASSO and the PVA's*

At every stage since the 1959 CPP congress, Dr. Nkrumah has sought to bring NASSO and the PVA's into greater prominence. He held them up as models to the youth and used them as scorpions to attack the "ideologically weak" older party leaders. He has been careful to ensure their continued "socialist education," but as they tended increasingly to seek Marxist knowledge in Eastern Europe and China, Nkrumah was concerned that they might imbibe "foreign communism" with their Marxism. Thus, when looking for a principal for the new Ideological Institute at Winneba, he asked friends to recommend a person well grounded in Marxism but preferably somebody who had left the Communist Party. In the end, Nkrumah appointed a trusted Ghanaian. His friendship for the Communist countries has always been tempered by his overriding belief in the importance of nonalignment and Pan-Africanism.

When one comes to examine the precise nature of NASSO and the PVA's, it is difficult to delineate any clearly structured organization or, indeed, a precise relationship between them and the CPP. NASSO itself remains a comparatively small elite cadre in Ghana, with branches in countries abroad where Ghanaian students are to be found in any number. It functions both as a discussion group and as a teaching group. They are chiefly responsible for recruiting and training the members of the PVA through the Winneba Ideological Institute and the youth organization. Yet there is little sign that the PVA's operate as an organized unit within the party structure. Having passed through their ideological training, the PVA's are drafted into key positions in the party organization, the civil service, or another branch of activity.

Thus Nkrumah has deployed members of NASSO and the PVA with a strategic eye to the future. With few exceptions, none was given a ministerial post or a seat in parliament. They have been used exclusively to staff the Bureau of African Affairs, the party press, and the radio. The editors of all the party papers (*The Ghanaian Times*, the *Evening News*, *The Spark*, *The Party*, *Labour*, and *The African Worker*) belong to NASSO. The clear intention is that they should be in charge of all the opinion-forming organs in the country. Nkrumah has described them as "the eyes and ears of the Party" and as "the watchdog over Party interests."

The members of NASSO have therefore come to exercise a far greater influence than many of the more senior members of the Party. They write and speak and act with the authority expected of "cadres of the elite." Sharing wholly their leader's fervor for the revolution in Africa as well as in Ghana, they are Dr. Nkrumah's personal apostles; he is their Messiah—a relationship that seems to have survived the "treachery" of their former "top man," Tawia Adamafio.

Ultimately, the vanguardist groups constitute the mechanism whereby Nkrumah hopes to be able to move the Ghanaian—and the African—masses toward an economic revolution. The economic revolution increasingly became a primary objective after 1960, the year Ghana became a republic.

### Nkrumaism—The Expression of Socialist Objectives

Nkrumah announced his intentions of creating an economic revolution on the tenth anniversary of the CPP.

> We stand on the threshold of the second revolution. . . . We must see that our forces are well and truly steeled for the economic battle in which we shall now be engaged. Our Party must be disciplined and well led and fortified by the African Socialist ideology which will reinforce the invincibility of our Party.[17]

Henceforth there was to be a stiffening of party discipline. "All are free to express their views. But once a majority decision is taken, we expect such a decision to be loyally executed, even by those who might have opposed that decision. None is privileged, and no one shall escape disciplinary action." In his address to the Congress Dr. Nkrumah for the first time declared that "the Party is the State, and the State is the Party."[18] To give coherence to this ideology the party organization was restructured to link into a single movement all its "wings": the CPP, the Trades Union Congress, the United Ghana Farmers Council, the National Cooperative Council, the National Council of Ghana Women, NASSO, the PVA's, and the youth organization.

The new orientation emerged as a full-fledged ideology—as "Nkrumaism"—in 1961. Although the ideas were Nkrumah's, its main tribune was his devoted Minister of Defense, Mr. Kofi Baako. Opening the first of his four lectures on Nkrumaism at the Winneba Ideological Institute, Mr. Baako said:

I would define Nkrumaism as a nonatheistic socialist philosophy which seeks to apply the current socialist ideas to the solution of our problems . . . by adapting these ideas to the realities of our everyday life. It is basically socialism adapted to suit the conditions and circumstances of Africa. . . . The African traditional social system is basically communalistic, i.e., socialistic—a society in which the welfare of the individual is bound up with the welfare of all the people in the community. For this reason Nkrumaism is a social idea and a way of life that is completely at home in Africa. I think it is important that I stress that Nkrumanism does not aim at the abolition of personal ownership of your own personal property . . . provided that you do not use what you have to foster an exploitation of man by man.[19]

Dr. Nkrumah's own original definition of Nkrumaism is blandly pragmatic:

In Ghana, we have embarked on the socialist path to progress; but it is socialism with a difference. Some have called it "Nkrumaism." It is not socialism for the sake of socialism, but a practical solution of the country's problems. We want to see full employment, good housing, and equal opportunity for education and cultural advancement for all the people up to the highest level possible.[20]

The early definitions of Nkrumaism did not survive, however. For several years it was widely interpreted by different groups within the Party. Finally, in April 1964, the Kwame Nkrumah Ideological Institute, "in consultation with Osagyefo the President," announced the following definition:

Nkrumaism is the ideology for the New Africa, independent and absolutely free from imperialism, organized on a continental scale, founded upon the conception of One and United Africa, drawing its strength from modern science and technology and from the traditional African belief that the free development of each is conditioned by the free development of all.[21]

Thus defined, Nkrumaism places its major emphasis on Pan-Africanism rather than socialism.

*Nkrumaism as an Economic Program*
The first attempt to give Nkrumaism programmatic content was made in 1962 with the formulation of the *Work and Happiness* program, which later became the basis for the new Seven Year

Plan.[22] *Work and Happiness,* a program "based on scientific principles," rested on two fundamental statements, (1) that socialism, because of the heritage of imperialism and colonialism, is the only system by which Ghana can progress; and (2) that socialism can be achieved only by a rapid change in the socioeconomic structure of the country. To effect this, it is absolutely essential to have a strong, stable, firm, and highly centralized government. This means that power must be concentrated in the country's leadership.

For the first time, the Party committed itself openly and unequivocally to the idea that Ghana should become a socialist society created through "central planning." The mechanism to achieve this goal was to be the one-party state.

*Work and Happiness* was only a prelude, however, to the more significant developments along socialist lines that were forthcoming. Essentially this document laid the groundwork for the emergence of the First Seven Year Plan.

The methods followed in preparing the First Seven Year Plan reflect Nkrumah's pragmatism and his unorthodoxy in Marxist eyes. This plan originated in a study made in 1961 by a team of Ghanaians under the chairmanship of a Hungarian Marxist economist, Dr. Joseph Bognor.[23] This report was turned over in 1962 to a team consisting *exclusively* of Ghanaians, mainly young economists and civil servants. Their draft of the plan was subsequently submitted to an international conference which included economists from both Western and Communist countries.

The Seven Year Plan* advocates a mixed economy for a 20-year transition period. During this transition "public and private enterprise will each have a legitimate, recognizable, and even important contribution to make toward economic growth." The public and private sectors are to be given clearly assigned tasks. It rejects the suggestion that "vigorous state and private sectors within the same economy are incompatible"; this, it says, is "historically incorrect."[24] Nor is nationalization considered appropriate:

As the state finances each year out of budget surpluses a large proportion of the productive investments made in the country, the economy will become progressively more socialized until by the end of the

---

* For a fuller summary of the socialist aims of this plan see Appendix VII, pp. 267–70.

transition period the state will be controlling on behalf of the community the dominant share of the economy. This would have been accomplished without our ever having to resort to such expedients as nationalization.

The place of private initiative is also recognized:

The state's economic activities must never take such a form as to hinder the citizens' own efforts to help themselves. . . . The more private investment in Ghana is contributed by our own people, the less will Ghana be dependent upon foreigners of all sorts, and consequently the greater the degree of her real independence will be.[25]

### 1961—The Turning Point

The period of formulation of Nkrumaism, of programs and plans, all began at a time of mounting social and political crisis which overtook Ghana soon after it became a republic in 1960. Those developments reflected, in part, the social pressures within Ghana and the CPP, and, in part, they were conditioned by these pressures. Up to the time Ghana became a republic, difficulties of the Nkrumah regime stemmed largely from opposition outside of the CPP. The Opposition's last major effort at constitutional resistance to the regime took place with Dr. J. B. Danquah's unsuccessful challenge to Dr. Nkrumah for the presidency. Though not officially proscribed immediately, the Opposition declined as an effective force after the inauguration of the Republic on July 1, 1960. The pattern of politics changed completely in 1961, which is the watershed between the old Ghana and the new. It marked the beginning of troubles *within* the ruling party, and it heralded a new era of violent opposition.

*Middle-class opposition.* Opposition to socialism (and especially to Marxism) was a basic policy of the opposition parties before they were eliminated. They objected to socialism on grounds both of principle and of expediency; their fear was that centralized control over the economy would strengthen the power of the CPP and accordingly weaken their own position. In expressing these fears, the opposition groups spoke for a large section of middle-class Ghanaians, including many who supported the CPP.

Most of the strongly entrenched Ghanaian middle class—lawyers, judges, senior civil servants, lecturers, businessmen—opposed Nkrumah at the time of his break with the United Gold Coast

Convention in 1949; nevertheless a substantial number joined the CPP, especially after independence. They comprised an influential force within the total power structure of the CPP and within the country, being especially prominent in the cabinet, the National Assembly, the civil service, the police and the army, the university, the judiciary, and the Central Committee of the Party.

Ghana's traders, many of them among the earliest supporters of the CPP, resented Nkrumah's initial policy of restricting Ghanaian private businesses to small-scale enterprises. (Significantly, this policy was changed in 1963.) One group of producers actively opposed to the government's policies for cooperative buying and selling was the fishermen of Accra and Cape Coast. While they welcomed the offer of power-driven boats, they bitterly attacked the measures compelling them to sell their catch to a single state-purchasing organization. This particular move was also strongly resisted by the "market mammies," who lost their traditional position as middlemen as a result. The CPP was deeply divided over this proposal, but it was passed in the National Assembly.

That there were so few critics of socialism inside the CPP itself before 1961 is not surprising in view of the lack of emphasis on socialism. Few CPP members took the Party's "socialism" seriously; they were "all socialists" so long as it merely served the Party as a slogan. It was only after Nkrumah embarked on his policy of "ideological education" that the gulf deepened between him and the middle class and that the groupings within the CPP began open conflict.

*The campaign for socialism.* Nkrumah embarked on his new policy of "ideological education" by presenting a series of major statements between February and June 1961.*

Laying the foundation stone of the new Ideological Institute at Winneba, on February 18, Dr. Nkrumah spoke with some heat:

We have reached a point in the life of our nation when it is absolutely necessary to recapture the lofty spirit of our past and bring home vividly to all members of the CPP that the end result of the national task is not individual gain and personal prosperity but service to the country and the masses for the cultivation of popular prosperity.

---

* In view of the suggestion that his extended visit to the Communist countries during 1961 played a part in this new crusade, it is worth noting that all of these speeches were made *before* he had set off for the Communist world in July.

Speaking of the Party's attitude he said: It "has been built up from our own experiences, conditions, environments, and concepts, entirely Ghanaian and African in outlook, and based on the Marxist socialist philosophy and world view." He ordered NASSO "to sprinkle the whole country with party study groups," pursuing the "Cipipification" (CPPfication) of national life.[26]

On April 6, addressing a conference of Teachers' Associations, Nkrumah stated: "It is the aim of my government to create gradually a socialist system of society in which every individual will have the greatest opportunity of developing his talents and ability to the utmost."[27]

Two days later came the startling "Dawn Broadcast,"[28] which shook the nation because, for the first time, Nkrumah publicly addressed himself to the internal problems that were wracking the CPP. He wanted, he said, to look deeper for the causes of the quarrel between different factions of the Party. One immediate cause of the problem was the use that party members were making of their positions "for personal gain or for the amassing of wealth." A second cause was the apparent failure to understand "this socialist structure" that proposed to divide the economy into five sectors —state, state-private, cooperative, private enterprise, and workers' enterprise sectors.

The main part of his broadcast was devoted to an excoriating attack on corruption and nepotism. "Some comrades go round using the names of persons in prominent positions to collect money for themselves. . . . I am aware that the evil of patronage finds a good deal of place in our society." The civil servants, too, came in for sharp criticism. "It amazes me that up to the present many civil servants do not realize that we are living in a revolutionary era." He concluded with a directive limiting the property acquisition of ministers, party officials, and ministerial secretaries.

This was by no means the first time Nkrumah had inveighed against the Party for lack of "socialist principles"; but it was the first time he had trounced it thus in public. The Dawn Broadcast made a tremendous impact on the public; people were keyed up, expecting drastic action against party leaders, or at least a thorough purging of the government. But little actually happened. For one thing, the crisis in the Party had come sooner than Nkrumah had expected, and he was not yet ready to undertake major changes. Moreover, the party crisis left Nkrumah unsure of his own strength in the Party and the country.

Although the Dawn Broadcast was not translated immediately into the purge that many expected, Nkrumah continued the pressure for change. On April 22, he summoned a representative cross section of the party leadership to his official residence at Flagstaff House to attend a Study Group on "Building a Socialist State." He told them the question facing the country was how to achieve the goal of socialism in the shortest time—remembering that "at this juncture Ghana is not a socialist state." Among the ideas he developed was the need to devote more of the national revenue to the erection of basic industries, and to revolutionize "our approach to planning." Hitherto it had been piecemeal and unpurposeful. "Too many governmental and semigovernmental bodies and departments have been concerned in the drawing up and executing of plans. What we need are not reports but plans of action."

Nkrumah announced, at this conference, a revolutionary change in the relationship between the Party and the civil service: in the future, the Party would be the pivot of economic planning. This crucial change in administration was justified on the following grounds:

To attain this laudable end of socialist control we have from time to time to make a review of the administrative apparatus at our disposal, remembering that it was originally bequeathed to us by a colonial regime dedicated to a very different purpose. . . . In our adaptations, because we are embarking upon an uncharted path, we may have to proceed from trial and error. Changes which are made today may themselves call for further change tomorrow.

But, he added, it was not enough to replace the civil servants with party leaders: "If our new economic and industrial policy is to succeed, then there must be a change of outlook in those who are responsible for running our affairs. They must acquire a socialist perspective and a socialist drive keyed to the national needs and demands, and not remain the servants of a limping bureaucracy."

Nkrumah went on to announce similar drastic changes in the structure of the ministerial system, the National Cooperative Council, and the National Council for Higher Education. But he warned: "Without the support of the masses of the people, our plan can fail. The people need to be stirred to a new awareness of their role in carrying forward our national reconstruction. The party cadres [i.e., PVA] must be in the forefront of the educational drive."

Because so many high party leaders and officials in the administration, "able men as they are . . . , are yet without socialist understanding and orientation," he ordered them, by categories, to attend classes at fixed dates at the Ideological Institute. "We cannot build socialism without socialists, and we must take positive steps to ensure that the Party and the country produce the men and women who can handle a socialist program."[29]

*The vanguardist reaction.* The conflict between the different wings of the Party broke surface before the Dawn Broadcast while Dr. Nkrumah was attending the Commonwealth Prime Ministers' meeting in London in March 1961. The vanguardists, however, were naturally much encouraged by Dr. Nkrumah's onslaught against the "reactionaries" in the Party and considered the Dawn Broadcast as license to freely print attacks on the "party capitalists." Although Nkrumah ascribed the quarrel to "certain misunderstandings which led to some regrettable demonstrations" between the Trades Union Congress, the National Assembly, the Cooperative Movement, and the United Farmers Council, at its root was a problem started by the PVA's through the party press and the trade unions about the role of private enterprise in Ghana, and about the business activities of some of the party leaders. Should these leaders be allowed to combine their political functions with their business interests? There was criticism of the corruption and ostentation of prominent members of the government; this was voiced by the PVA's, but more ominously, for the Party at least, by the public as well. Taunting cries of "one man, one house" and "one man, one car" were heard in the streets as a riposte to the old party cry of "one man, one vote." The immediate focus of attention was two palatial residences being built in Accra by two ministers. However, the PVA's singled out for special attention Mr. Gbedemah, Nkrumah's Minister of Finance and his only serious political rival. Gbedemah not only was unenthusiastic about socialism but was reportedly engaging in secret negotiations with party and army leaders to overthrow Nkrumah. The vanguardists were optimistic that the time was ripe to press home the attack on Gbedemah, whom they rightly regarded as their most dangerous opponent and the leading rightist in the cabinet; but at this time

Nkrumah's sounder instincts warned him to consolidate his own position before offering an open challenge to Gbedemah, whose power he never underestimated. Other targets for criticism as "party capitalists" were Kojo Botsio, once the favorite of Nkrumah, who was especially reviled because he had "made a thorough study of Marxist philosophy, and at one time was the Party's Director of Ideological Studies";[30] Ayeh-Kumi, Nkrumah's ethnic kinsman and the outstanding financial brain in the Party; and Krobo Edusei, the tough and colorful Ashanti leader.

The conservatives answered the criticism by expressing open hostility to Marxist socialism. Mr. Patrick Quaidoo, formerly a leading CPP figure and a minister in the government, said in the Ghana National Assembly in May 1961: "Let those who call themselves socialists sit down and study the cultural background of our people and see how best we can adapt these things, instead of wholesale importation of such ideas into our social life."[31] And Mr. Krobo Edusei, then Minister of Light and Heavy Industries, scoffed: "When I get the money, am I expected to throw it into the sea?"[32]

The first significant organizational change was made on May 1, when Nkrumah took over the post of secretary-general of the CPP from Adamafio. This action in no way reflected personal doubts about Adamafio's loyalty but rather was a move to consolidate power before making major changes. Shortly after, Nkrumah replaced Gbedemah with an only slightly less conservative party member, Mr. F. K. D. Goka, as Minister of Finance. Goka was respected, conventional, and obedient, and his position, now that Nkrumah had taken over the country's budget, was reduced to little more than a political cipher, albeit a respectable one.

In July, Mr. Goka introduced the "austerity budget," which had been hastily prepared on the advice of a Cambridge socialist economist, Mr. Nikolas Kaldor. The budget—especially its provision for "compulsory savings"—precipitated a strike among the railway and dock workers of Sekondi and Takoradi; they repudiated the leadership of the Trades Union Congress and attacked the Party as a whole.

Dr. Nkrumah, who had set off in July for a prolonged visit to Eastern Europe and China (having earlier in the year visited the United States and Britain), returned in September to find the

Party at loggerheads, and the country in a state of turmoil. He at once reorganized the army—replacing its British head with a Ghanaian, Major-General S. J. A. Otu—and then his government. Six party leaders, including Mr. Gbedemah and Mr. Botsio, were asked to resign; others were advised to surrender property in excess of £20,000. A few months later Mr. Krobo Edusei was also forced to resign. In October, 50 leading politicians were arrested under the Preventive Detention Act. Although the majority belonged to the Opposition, they also included a number of formerly prominent CPP members. October also foreshadowed a new wave of violence—a bomb set against Nkrumah's statue outside the National Assembly in Accra. The campaign against the "party capitalists" came to its frenetic climax in the "gold bed scandal," which the party press ran for several weeks until, on April 19, 1962, the *Evening News*—with a party flag at the paper's masthead—could happily proclaim: HURRAH FOR THE REVOLUTION: KROBO FALLS FROM GRACE TO GRASS.

*Results of the 1961 crisis.* The whole complexion of Ghana's politics changed as a result of the crisis of 1961. It altered the balance of power in the CPP. The removal of Gbedemah left Osagyefo the undisputed leader. It established the "socialists" as an important if not yet decisive power factor in the party structure; it also made them more feared. It hastened the advent of the one-party state. It brought to a head the long simmering crisis between the old civil service and the new NASSO-oriented elite. It upset the middle-class supporters of the Party: many had looked to Gbedemah for leadership, while others saw ominous signs for their own future in the revolutionary changes in the relationship between the Party and the civil service.

The crisis also had contradictory effects on the vanguardists. On the one hand, it entrenched an inverted power complex among some of the leading members of NASSO. On the other hand, the rediscovery of the importance of "the masses" during the strike of the Sekondi-Takoradi workers was an unpleasant experience for them. Finally, the crisis marked the end of the constitutional phase in Ghana's politics and the beginning of another—that of the assassin's bomb.

In spite of the shift in the balance of power within the Party, the nonsocialists and antisocialists were not eliminated. The fact that, within the year, Krobo Edusei, Kojo Botsio, Ayeh-Kumi, and other dismissed leaders were back in high office shows that Nkrumah had overestimated his capacity to rule effectively by relying on his "socialist cadres." They were not a sufficiently powerful force to be able to hold together the diverse elements in the country. To restore the balance of power and to restore some efficiency to his government (especially in its economic affairs) he was compelled, toward the end of 1962, to make a tactical retreat. Nevertheless, the importance of this campaign was that it represented the first attempt to purge the Party in its highest places and to try to turn the CPP into an effective instrument for Nkrumah's brand of socialism. Once having undermined the more significant leaders who constituted a possible challenge to his socialist direction, Nkrumah could bring back a number of the nonsocialists who were at least personally loyal to himself. He retained his suspicions of them, however, voicing his doubts strongly in *Africa Must Unite* and through *The Spark,* which described the middle-class supporters of the Party as "the backward-looking intellectual elite." Sir Arku Korsah's dismissal as Chief Justice late in 1963 once again brought the simmering crisis between the middle class and the party socialists to a head. "Unlike the open confrontation of the assassins of Kulungugu,* the present forces of reaction are applying insidious tactics of putting cogs in the wheel of the revolution. They have found their way into all popular organs of state nearest to the heart of the people's power."[33] The party press started a campaign similar to that of 1961 against the "party capitalists": now their demands called for the replacement of "the old colonial materials" by "the most revolutionary strata of our society."[34]

But the middle class made no organized attempt to resist the pressures of the new ideologists. Some of their numbers in the police appear to have given support to a further assassination attempt on Nkrumah. The university students—who tend to adopt antigovernment though not necessarily antisocialist tendencies— became more vociferous, but their criticisms carried little weight. Most important, the army leadership remained loyal to the President.

Meanwhile the socialist thrust was not abandoned; its main drive was given over during 1962 to the vanguardist group in

---

* It was at Kulungugu that the first bomb attempt was made on Nkrumah's life.

charge of the Party's press—in particular *The Spark*. From 1962 on, this group became increasingly Marxist in its public pronouncements.

## The Role of The Spark—*The Marxist Approach*

Since it first appeared on December 15, 1962, *The Spark* set itself up as the theoretical voice of the party press. It is published by the Bureau of African Affairs, which operates as a government-sponsored agency for African Freedom Fighters. Its editor is Mr. Kofi Batsa, one of the half-dozen CPP members expelled by Nkrumah in 1954 because of their affiliations with the Communist World Federation of Trade Unions.[35] Mr. Batsa is a prominent member of the inner caucus of NASSO. Although he is the editor, the ideas reflected in *The Spark* are the views of a wider group who write under the collective pseudonym of Julius Sago.

*The Spark* holds ideas on socialism that are unequivocally Marxist Communist, although it continues to speak of Nkrumah's "Marxist socialism." It rejects outright as "spurious" and "neocolonialist" any notions of "African Socialism." Writing of the Dakar Colloquium, it describes "African Socialism" as being invented by the neo-colonialists with a "historic mission . . . to combat and if possible defeat scientific socialism, firstly by introducing elements alien to socialist thought, and secondly by denying some of the foundations of socialist ideology."[36] It also rejects the common African view that the nature of traditional African society is "communistic" or "communalistic." It declares:

The traditional collectivist way of African life is a mere illusion. African society must evolve; it cannot go back to two or three centuries ago. What is the old collectivist way of life in Africa? It wasn't a classless society. Nor were relations in it harmonious. It was a feudal system based on the hegemony of a few big families lording it over less privileged ones and even serfs. Human rights were nonexistent and industrialization was absent.[37]

The application of this Marxist Communist approach to modern Africa is treated with considerable sophistication in a series of eight editorial articles on "Socialist Parties in Africa," which ran in March and April, 1963.[38] This series is seminal in the sense that its ideas have become the basis of the editorial policy of the party press. Its central theme is that "socialist parties in Africa today must make their class struggle clear." The importance of the class struggle is emphasized in the discussion of the role of socialist intellectuals:

They must quickly spotlight and destroy any attempt to revise or even deny some fundamentals of socialism under the guise of creating an "African Socialism." In particular, they must wage unrelenting war against the view that there are no classes in Africa. For classes do exist in Africa both in the sense of economic groups occupying different positions in the production system (that is as employers, self-employed, workers, etc.) and in the sense of different income groups. An added reason is that the denial of the existence of these classes in African society is ultimately a denial of the need for socialism in Africa.[39]

This leads to the question of how the "socialist struggle" should develop in Ghana. For the clearest answer one must go to *The Spark*'s stable companion, *The Ghanaian Times*:

There are two clearly discernible but organically interrelated revolutions making up Africa's struggle. The first revolution is the fight for freedom from colonial rule. It is waged by the national liberation movement. The attainment of political independence by Africans marks the end of Africa's first revolution. But it is, at the same time, the beginning and vital element in Africa's second revolution. . . .
This is the socialist revolution. Its aim is economic and social reconstruction. It is conducted by means of a people's socialist movement. It attains victory with the achievement of total independence—political as well as economic, social, and cultural—from foreign rule and influence. . . . The fight for complete independence in the economic sphere and for social emancipation of the masses is defined as the socialist revolution. Its instrument is the people's liberation movement as distinct from the national liberation movement. . . .
The natural allies of the people's liberation movement in the struggle for the victory of socialism are: (1) the national liberation movements in all colonial countries; (2) the people's liberation movements in all countries; (3) the revolutionary proletarian movements in the advanced capitalist countries; (4) the world movement for peace and disarmament; (5) the capitalist interests wishing economic relations on terms mutually advantageous to themselves and the new nations; and (6) the socialist states of the world.[40]

In attempting an assessment of *The Spark*'s role in Ghana, we are faced with a number of questions. Is it a straightforward Communist paper? How typical are its views of thinking inside

NASSO and with the PVA's? How influential are these groups within the CPP and inside Ghana? How far does Nkrumah share its views?

There is no possible doubt that *The Spark*'s "scientific socialism" stands foursquare behind the ideology of international communism. This much was admitted to me by a leading member of the paper's editorial board. The obvious conclusion to be drawn from this might be that *The Spark* is a cell of the Communist Party in Ghana. But this conclusion is denied by my informant. His explanation can be *paraphrased* in this way:

Inasmuch as we accept the doctrine of scientific socialism we are naturally drawn more closely to the socialist countries than to the capitalist world. We feel that we have an interest in the ideological leadership of the international Communist movement; that is why we believe we should be present at their conferences to express our views. At present our complaint is that the decisions are taken by Khrushchev without sufficient consultation with the international Communist movement; at times this can amount to dictation. We must not simply be the rubber stamp for Russian policies. That is why, when necessary, we feel ourselves free to criticize the policies of the leaders of the socialist countries.

He drew my attention particularly to the criticism of Russian policy in the Middle East.[41]

My informant saw nothing wrong in the CPP's being represented at Communist conferences and stated, in fact, that the CPP was represented at the 1962 conference of 81 Communist nations in the Soviet Union. He continued:

However, we do not believe that the CPP should become a Communist Party, or that it should be affiliated with the international Communist movement. To do so would involve entanglement in the cold war, and it would destroy our policy of nonalignment. For us, nonalignment and Pan-Africanism remain touchstones of our own ideology. It is this that separates us from other Marxist Communists. Thus, although we are aligned to all those who uphold scientific socialism, we are strictly nonaligned with any of the powers in the socialist world. That goes for China as well as for Russia.

Although he claimed that they would, whenever necessary, criticize the Chinese as they had the Russians, I have not found any criticism of Peking in the columns of *The Spark*, other than im-

plicit criticism in its editorial support for the Moscow Nuclear
Treaty, to which Ghana subscribes; even then, their endorsement
was lukewarm. "World reactions to this test ban treaty started
off by being enthusiastic, but have gradually become cool with
the growing realization of the severe limitations of the Moscow
Treaty."[42]

*The Spark* has little popular support either in the country or in
the Party. The paper's circulation is only a few thousand, which
includes a sizable free distribution outside Ghana. The members
form a distinctive, minority cadre not only in the Party and in
the Trades Union Congress, but also in NASSO and among the
PVA's. On the other hand, they have strong (and sometimes
bitter) opponents inside the Party, the cabinet, and the civil service. The older, senior CPP leaders regard them as both a threat to
their own positions and a malign influence on the President. Their
influence comes not from any popularity of their own, but from the
power they derive through their close associations with Nkrumah.
Although he has never publicly endorsed their views, they stand
under his direct protection; and he sanctions the finances on which
they operate. Their precise relationship is subtle, complex, and not
easily defined. What makes it especially difficult to understand is
that *The Spark* was allowed to develop theoretical positions in
conflict with Nkrumah's. At least that was the case in the past;
whether it will be so, now that Nkrumah has evolved his own
definitive doctrine, the philosophy of "Consciencism," still remains
to be seen.

### Nkrumah's Evolving Philosophy

Dr. Nkrumah has never made any secret of his belief in Marxism
and in "scientific socialism." But he is not, and never has been, an
orthodox Marxist. He insists, for example, that religion is not inconsistent with Marxism. He has described himself as "a nonde-
nominational Christian and a Marxist socialist," and says he has
not found any contradiction between the two.[43] He admires the
achievements of the Soviet Union and China but has strong doubts
about applying Lenin's ideas uncritically. He has always rejected
the classic Marxist view that class revolution is essential to the
building of socialism in Africa, and he rejects the notion of a class
struggle in African society. "The African social system," he says,

"is communistic. In the African social system the formation of a pauper class is unknown, nor is there antagonism of class against class."[44] By this definition Nkrumah conflicts with *The Spark* with its heavy emphasis on class struggle.

These growing divergences between *The Spark* and Nkrumah, especially during 1963 and the opening months of 1964, have baffled outsiders. But it now seems clear that Nkrumah was deeply engaged, during these months, in the search for a doctrine of socialism that would be of general application to Africa. His need was to reconcile his own socialist ideas with Pan-Africanism through a philosophy that would establish his position as a messianic leader on the continent. He wished to do for Africa what Marx and Lenin had done for Europe and Mao Tse-tung for China. While willing to learn from them, he was unwilling to accept their philosophies. He therefore established his own Philosophy Club, with Professor Willie Abraham, a Ghanaian Fellow of All Souls, Oxford, as the main theoretician. These philosophers, though sympathetic to Marxism, believed that neither the "scientific socialists" nor the Western philosophers had supplied a doctrine that reflected the needs of Africa: these could come only from an understanding of African society.

Such an approach was not wholly acceptable to *The Spark* Marxists. While they were willing to cloak their "scientific socialism" in *kente* cloth,* they were opposed to thoroughgoing revisionism. They approached Africa entirely through Marxist eyes; the philosophers preferred to approach Marx through African eyes. But while the philosophers were working out their ideas in private, *The Spark* was canvassing its ideas in public. If Nkrumah did not react against them, it was because he was not yet ready to take a public stand.

The moment for doing so came with the publication of *Consciencism* in April 1964. Described by its subtitle as a philosophy and ideology for decolonization and development with particular reference to the African revolution, *Consciencism* is Nkrumah's manifesto for the African revolution. His premise is that in Africa the social-political ancestor of socialism is communalism.[45]

In socialism the principles underlying communalism are given expression in modern circumstances. Thus, whereas communalism in an

---

* Ghanaian traditional dress.

untechnical society can be laissez faire, in a technical society where sophisticated means of production are at hand, if the underlying principles of communalism are not given centralized and correlated expression, class cleavages will arise, which are connected with economic disparities, and thereby with political inequalities. Socialism, therefore, can be and is the defense of the principles of communalism in a modern setting.

Not only does he deny the existence of classes in communalistic society; he denies its inevitability in a modern setting. Also, he denies the necessity for revolution to achieve socialism.

Revolution is an indispensable avenue to socialism, where the antecedent social-political structure is animated by principles which are a negation of those of socialism, as in a capitalist structure (and therefore also in a colonialist structure, for a colonialist structure is essentially ancillary to capitalism). . . . But from the ancestral line of communalism, the passage to socialism lies in reform, because the underlying principles are the same.

Thus, in relation to African traditional society, socialism is historically revolutionary but genetically evolutionary.

Nkrumah's manifesto prescribes five main tasks for socialists in Africa: (1) to seek a connection with the egalitarian and humanist past of the people before their social evolution was "ravaged by colonialism"; (2) to seek from colonialism those elements like new methods of industrial production and economic organization which can be adapted to serve the interests of the people; (3) to seek ways and means of crushing the growth of class inequalities and antagonism created by the "capitalist habit of colonialism"; (4) to reclaim the psychology of the people by erasing "colonial mentality"; and (5) to defend the independence and security of the people. *Consciencism* also seeks to describe the principles, strategy, and methods by which "liberated territories" can achieve their transition to socialism. It proclaims that "while societies with different social systems can coexist their ideologies cannot." Should one deduce from this statement that capitalist ideology or even Western democratic socialist ideology cannot coexist with Nkrumah's Consciencism but that the "scientific socialism" of the Communist world can? There is, as yet, no clear guidance to provide an answer to this question; but the presumption is that this will be so unless the international Communist movements should classify

Consciencism as revisionism, in which case it, too, will fall into the category of incompatible ideologies.

Nkrumah's prescribed method of achieving socialism in Africa is by creating a single mass party for the entire continent. The idea of such a mass party was encountered for the first time in the Circle—but at that period it was to be confined to West Africa. It obtained its continental dimension in 1963 in *Africa Must Unite*. Now, in *Consciencism,* he launches the idea formally; and supplies it with an ideology of its own.

Though Nkrumah's new philosophy rejects many of *The Spark*'s basic ideas, the editors promptly and uncritically accepted the new line. The collective editorial opinion, expressed by Julius Sago, is that Consciencism "will provide the rallying ground for all sincere African patriots who feel that socialist ideology should more closely reflect the African background."[46] They make no attempt to justify their previous views rejecting the need for a particularist socialist philosophy to meet the special needs of Africa. Is this merely a tactical withdrawal, or is their acceptance of Nkrumah's philosophy genuine? It is too early to say. But their new role is explicit. Henceforth *The Spark* will take over its role of acting as the theoretical organ to mobilize a continental mass party. "Be it known that the only sure road to African political unity is a continental mass party, animated by the people, guided by a continental strategy, soldiered by the people, and fighting uncompromisingly for a people's program."[47] They identify three existing forces on which such a mass party can be built: the few African governments "genuinely committed to socialism"; "the popular organizations inside the regimes of neo-colonialism," e.g., the radical political parties, the trade unions, the progressive intellectuals and students, and the popular organizations which demand an end to foreign control of national life; and the national liberation movements in Southern Africa, more especially the revolutionary wings of such movements.

The portents for the future are clear. With the publication of *Consciencism,* Nkrumah has launched himself in his new role as the "Lenin of Africa." While basing himself on "scientific socialism," he avoids aligning himself with the Communist world by revising Marxism to give it particular application to Africa. Nor will he be content with the role of theoretician; he will now seek to play the leader over a continental mass movement whose enemies will be not only the former colonial powers but also those African governments that are categorized as "neo-colonial regimes." In this way Nkrumah will seek to link the struggle to build socialism in Ghana with the socialist forces throughout Africa.

### Summary

Nkrumah's objective for Ghana has always been to convert it into a Marxist socialist state in which the means of production are largely publicly owned. His second consistent objective has been to use Ghana as a base to spread his ideas throughout Africa. For him socialism and Pan-Africanism have *always* belonged together. But, being a realist as well as an idealist, he has been aware that Ghanaian society is not ready for the radical application of socialist ideas and that the African states are unwilling to accept, and even antagonistic toward, political unification. Thus his tactics both inside Ghana and in the wider African context have shifted frequently from using the accelerator to applying the brake. He understands fully the politics of power and the need to keep both his flanks protected. This is especially important in Ghana, where society is unprepared for his kind of socialism. To ignore this reality would be to invite defeat on the home front. His struggle, therefore, has been not only to build a new society in Ghana and in Africa, but to survive politically and physically.

Nkrumah's *Work and Happiness* program and the Seven-Year Plan reflect the distinction that he makes between the aim of a fully socialized society and the methods needed to establish it. The question arises whether this emphasis upon an evolutionary process toward socialism is a genuine reflection of Nkrumah's own intentions, or whether it is a deliberate disguise to avoid frightening away the Western capital necessary for rapid industrialization. The balance of evidence supports the conclusion that Nkrumah would genuinely prefer an evolutionary process of economic change simply because in Ghanaian conditions it is more likely to succeed than a fully authoritarian economic policy. Any attempt to dragoon the peasants would meet with implacable opposition. Moreover, a period of transition would allow Nkrumah to get the best of both worlds by enabling him to maintain a nonaligned economic policy. He knows that if he opts immediately for a fully state-operated and state-controlled economy, he will be forced to rely almost exclusively on aid from the Communist countries; this is something he is determined to avoid if at all possible. He is fully aware of the fact that he does not yet possess either the technological skills or the ideological cadres needed to operate a centralized political and economic system.

Nkrumah's tactics therefore call for great subtlety, and they produce curious paradoxes. What makes it harder to interpret his maneuvers is his vacillating personality. Increasingly he gives the impression of being several different people, each of whom seems to need a different form of expression. The hypersuspicious Nkrumah finds expression through his intimate Circle; the isolated Nkrumah resents and criticizes the secretiveness of cells with their proclivity for plotting; the confident Nkrumah can assert a relaxed and charming leadership, not only over the CPP but also over his traditional opponents, with many of whom he remains on friendly personal terms. Nkrumah's tactics swing violently with his moods and his fortunes; but his objectives do not change. The NASSO-ists, the PVA's, the party press, and especially *The Spark* all belong to the armor of Nkrumah's revolutionary mood. To consider them in isolation invites the risk of exaggerating their power.

Essentially, Nkrumah sees himself as a man of destiny. In his rational mood he sees himself as *primus inter pares* with the revolutionary African leaders who accept the need for a unified Africa. At other times he sees himself as the *Osagyefo,* not of Ghana alone but of the whole of Africa: the all-powerful, all-conquering warrior who will do for his continent what Lenin did for the Soviet Union, Mao Tse-tung for China, and Lincoln for the United States of America. These are his three heroes of "positive action." He sees himself cast in the hero mold: the hero of a free and independent, liberated and unified Africa—an Africa built on socialism; the socialism of Consciencism.

Chapter 9

# Guinea and Senegal: Contrasting Types of African Socialism

Charles F. Andrain

Socialists historically have articulated moral and spiritual, as well as economic, goals. The demands for "justice" and "community"— the elimination of exploitation and alienation—as well as "bread" —the realization of economic abundance—rallied men to the socialist cause in Western Europe. A similar development has occurred in Africa. Here African leaders face problems arising out of a lack of integration in modern African societies. The colonialists helped destroy traditional solidarities, but they failed to establish new systems of national solidarity. The colonial civil servants introduced changes in the urban centers, but at the village level they undertook fewer modifications of the traditional systems. In an attempt to overcome the social strains between the rural-traditional and urban-modern sectors of society, African Socialists stress new symbols of common solidarity.[1]

In two states of French-speaking West Africa, leaders expound an ideology of African Marxism. Léopold Senghor, the President of Senegal, Mamadou Dia, the former Senegalese Prime Minister, and Sékou Touré, President of Guinea, all want to adapt Marxism to African conditions. To appeal to groups subjected to social strains between the rural and urban settings, these three leaders blend the socialist values of the traditional precolonial African society with more modern Marxist ideas. Senghor and Dia strive to transplant the traditional African feeling of solidarity to the national framework. According to Senghor, Negro-African society* rested on a communal basis, "which gave its members, with a single soul, a high ideal of solidarity, in which all communicated. Our new mutual benefit organizations and cooperatives which will

* The term "Negro-African" is more specific than "African." Senghor frequently uses this term, which fits with his philosophy of Negritude and is concerned with the values of Negro peoples in Africa and the New World. He recognizes the existence of non-Negro Africans, such as Berbers and Arabs.

integrate all the peasants will have the same kind of structure and will be animated by the same ideal."[2] Mamadou Dia also praises the feeling of solidarity found in the traditional African society. The new African states must maintain this active solidarity between the individual and the group. The existence of solidarity must remain the basis of economic development:

African development is characterized by an underlying conception of man. Not individualistic man, but *l'homme personnaliste*, who finds his full blossoming in the coherence of a living society, of an organic community. We can, in Africa, rely on the most authentic of our traditional values for achieving such a goal. That is why our way to development leads also to a community-centered socialism; to a socialism not of coercion, but of solidarity, of free adhesion and free cooperation; to a socialism which, after having been the instrument of national liberation, will be that of the liberation of man.[3]

Sékou Touré tends to find solidarity more within the framework of the national state and party than within the traditional culture. For him, solidarity is the essential characteristic of Guinean society. Solidarity lies at the fundamental base of socialist action; it signifies the harmony between all the diverse interests in the nation.[4] Thus, the ideologies of African Socialism espoused by Senghor, Dia, and Touré combine the values of traditional society with Marxist concepts. In the words of Sékou Touré, "Instead of applying society to science, we must apply science to society. Thus, Marxism, which has served to mobilize the African peoples and particularly the working class and to lead that working class toward success, has been shorn of those characteristics which do not correspond to African reality."[5]

### Similarities in Beliefs

This theme of adapting the economic plan to concrete realities pervades the ideology of African Socialism. Senghor believes that Africans must retain the method of European socialism, but not the institutions recommended by European socialists. The socialist method analyzes the realities of a country or area, discovers the contemporary value of the existing institutions and style of life, and then adapts these institutions to the demands of the modern world.[6] Touré has a similar view, although he talks less about the values of the traditional African society. In his opinion, Africa constitutes a third force, a nondeveloped area between the capitalist and communist camps. For this reason, Africans must reject both capitalism and communism and instead adapt their economies to concrete African realities: "Thus, when people ask us if we are for capitalism or for socialism, for the East or for the West, we invariably answer that what we consider first and above all is the Africa we intend to liberate from foreign domination, sickness, misery, and ignorance."[7]

All three African leaders in French-speaking West Africa reject the capitalist approach to economic development. As one who values order, President Touré opposes capitalism because it caused anarchy and disorder in the productive forces. Moreover, in accord with his stress on the general interest, he feels that capitalist organization brought egotism and individualism to Africa.[8] Guinea needs capital but not capitalism. Foreign capital must be integrated into the economic plan: "We have never excluded cooperation with capital; we have only rejected capitalism as a social form of organization because it does not correspond to our stage of development."[9] Since Africa has neither a bourgeoisie nor a large accumulation of capital, the capitalist system has limited usefulness to the new African states.

Mamadou Dia likewise holds that Africa does not have the conditions necessary for capitalist development. The capitalist states of Western Europe and the United States have two conditions not present in Africa—abundant capital and a bourgeois class willing to take risks. Neither precolonial African economies nor capitalism favored the formation of a middle class or indigenous capital. In actuality, European capitalism created in most areas of Africa a "subproletariat," rather than an African bourgeoisie.[10] For humanistic as well as purely economic reasons, the capitalist example has limited utility for contemporary African states. Dia feels that capitalism neglected human needs and African values. Capitalism is based on greed and exploitation; it has failed to satisfy man's fundamental needs: "Since economy is essentially based on human and social relations, since it is in essence socialistic, in the broadest sense of the term, the rule of the accumulation of money—the foundation of capitalism—cannot be the law that will determine the formation of structures in such civilizations."[11] In particular, the capitalists neglected the needs of the African peasantry. Sacrificing agricultural development for mining industries, capitalism neither undertook industrialization nor improved the conditions of the peasant masses. As well as subordinating basic human needs to the desire to maximize profits, European capitalism neglected the artistic, religious, literary, and philosophical values of Negro-Africa. The capitalist philosophy of assimilation assumed that only the European incarnated human values.[12]

As African Socialists, Touré, Senghor, and Dia can be expected to reject capitalism as an economic system for Africa. Yet these leaders also oppose communism, particularly the variety found in the Soviet Union. All three agree that capitalism and communism have striking similarities. President Touré considers communism equivalent to collective or state capitalism. Whereas in a capitalist regime the workers' surplus value goes to the capitalists, in a socialist country the state recovers all or a part of the workers' profits. Since Russian and West European states are highly industrialized, both systems use similar technical means. Neither communism nor capitalism is applicable to Africa, because the Soviet Union, as well as Europe and America, is far more highly developed than African territories.[13] Senghor and Dia have similar views. Dia criticizes Soviet Russia for sacrificing the peasantry to factories run to secure capitalist profits. Senghor suggests that Russian communism has increasingly become more like American capitalism, in that both sacrifice freedom of thought and art for materialistic values.[14]

The most obvious departure from Russian communism lies in Africans' rejection of the class struggle. Sékou Touré regards the class struggle as irrelevant to Africa. The notion of a class struggle has more applicability in the independent countries of Europe, Asia, and the Americas, for there the working class receives a minimal share of the productive goods. In Africa, however, the struggle is not between classes but between the colonized people and the colonial powers. Although conflicts may exist between different social strata or categories, these disputes arise more from a conflict of interests or a lack of political maturity; they are subordinate to the conflict between the African and colonial interests. Those who preach class struggle hence divide the people in the struggle against colonialism.[15]

President Senghor holds a similar opinion. Even if there are castes or strata based on religion, traditional Negro-African society has no classes founded on wealth. Whereas European workers experienced class subjugation, the mass of African peoples came under racial domination. Therefore, African Socialists must seek to abolish the inequalities arising from the Colonial Pact.[16] Contemporary African society faces a challenge not from the capitalists but from the intellectuals. Social groups in a struggle for influence have supplanted warring classes. Class warfare will result, however, if the intellectuals—liberal professionals, functionaries, employers, even workers—are allowed to oppress the artisans, shepherds, and peasants.[17]

This concern for the peasantry and agricultural development represents another departure from Russian communism. Because Communist China has paid greater attention to agricultural production, all three African leaders seem more impressed with economic policies in China than in the Soviet Union. According to Léopold Senghor, Mao Tse-tung did not repeat the mistake of the Bolsheviks, who sacrificed the peasants and agricultural development for heavy industry. Since African territories are mainly agricultural and the peasants comprise the most numerous sector of society, agricultural production must receive equal attention along with industrialization.[18] Although Africans need industrialization to make human progress, they must adapt the methods to the realities of the soil, climate, and race. Industrialists must never forget that they are dealing with Negro-African peasants. In the Negro society, the work of the land is the most noble activity, and the Negro soul remains oriented to peasant ways.[19]

Mamadou Dia likewise holds that African states must not follow the Soviet Union and make industrialization an end in itself:

By principally stressing heavy industry, massive industrialization tends to depress the standard of living and to lower real wages by forcing an increase in importation of equipment and machines at the expense of agricultural commodities and consumer goods, however vital they may be. Thus the realities of the foreign trade of the Soviet bloc reveal that structural inequalities and dependence are far from corrected.[20]

African nations must instead realize a synthesis between the agricultural and industrial sectors. Modernization of the economy without industrialization is inconceivable, since industrialization brings necessary technical advantages to man. But a solid agricultural infrastructure must sustain industrial development.[21]

Sékou Touré follows Dia and Senghor in giving priority to

agricultural development. Essentially an agricultural region, Africa should place maximum effort on production in this area and consider industry a complementary factor of economic development. Guinean leaders must have concern for the peasantry, which comprises over 90 per cent of the population. In Africa the most exploited sectors of society are not the working classes but the peasants and women.[22] The Guinean three-year plan for 1960–63 followed Touré's ideas regarding the complementary nature of agrarian and industrial development. Five-ninths of the budget for production was allocated to agriculture, and four-ninths went for industry.[23]

The two Senegalese politicians attack the Communist states for their authoritarian trends. Mamadou Dia holds that Africa must not adopt the autocratic methods of Russia and China. Traditional African societies were not authoritarian; rather, they placed high value on the individual person and excluded totalitarianism.[24] Léopold Senghor also attacks the Soviet Union for its dictatorial tendencies. There the "dictatorship of the proletariat" became under Stalin an "all-powerful and soul-less monster" which discouraged human freedom. A theoretically temporary dictatorship developed into a permanent dictatorship of the state and party.[25]

### Contributions of Marxist Ideas

What aspects of Marxism do African leaders consider most relevant for Africa? The concept of a dominant party organization occupies the central place in the socialist ideology of Sékou Touré. In his stress on organization, discipline, and control, he demonstrates a closer link to Lenin than to Marx. Like Lenin, Touré asserts the priority of political organization, rather than a spontaneous economic consciousness. Lenin, the political actor, never failed to sacrifice abstract theories to concrete demands of the immediate situation. Sékou Touré adopts a similar attitude: "In Marxism, the principles of organization, of democracy, of control, etc., everything which is concrete and concerns the organic life of given movements, perfectly finds the means of becoming adapted to the actual conditions of Africa. . . . I say that philosophy does not concern us. We have concrete needs."[26]

Touré's concentration on the general political interest, rather than on a more particular class or economic interest, marks a significant deviation from Marxist theory. Like Lenin, Touré empha-

sizes the dominance of the political. For the Guinean leader, socialism means political economy; the economic domain constitutes one
aspect of the political realm: "Political economy is not the adaptation of political action to economic action; on the contrary, it is
the use of economic activities for political ends.[27] Thus, the given
economic conditions are not the purely "independent variables,"
but must be manipulated by political organization.

From the social and economic theories of Karl Marx, Touré
adopts the notion of contradictions in modified form. For both
Marx and Touré the contradictions convey a moral indictment of
the economic status quo. Marx assumed that at a certain state of
capitalist development, the relations of production—organization
of industry, institution of private property, class relations—come
to hinder the forces of production—natural resources, physical
equipment, technological skills, and division of labor. The primary
contradiction revolves around the disjunction between theory and
practice. Whereas in theory the relations of production are based
on private property, in actuality the forces of production are socialized. Touré mentions the notion of a contradiction between the
productive forces and the relations of production. For productive
development to occur, the productive forces—that is, the working
masses—must determine the relations of production. Sékou Touré,
however, does not emphasize this form of contradiction, which
exists principally at a higher stage of economic development than
Africa has so far attained. Instead, he sees the primary contradiction between the African people and the European colonialists.
The colonialists are the capitalists who are hindering the productive forces, or the African masses.[28]

For Touré the contradictions within African society resemble
"cultural discontinuities," rather than things impeding the working out of the logic of the forces of production. Contradictions still
remain in Guinea between the various ethnic groups, religions,
young men and young women, intellectuals and illiterates, urban
workers and peasants, and youth and parents. There are even contradictions within the local party branches and the Bureau Politique National, the highest decision-making organ of the party.[29]
Without a change in the structure left by the colonialists, Guineans
cannot resolve these basic contradictions and thereby contribute to
greater human welfare.

The focus on the welfare of the people, the well-being of collective humanity, expresses Touré's debt to Marxist humanism. Touré believes that the colonialists' economic plans failed because they neglected the human factor. In their concern to reap profits and increase efficiency, the colonialists considered only the technical aspects of economic operations. "Our Plan will succeed because it has the People for its center of interest, because it will be conceived by the People and realized for the People."[30]

Senghor and Dia pay even more attention than Touré to the humanistic note of pre-1848 Marxist theory. For these two Senegalese leaders, the philosophy of humanism marks the most significant contribution of Marxist thought to African Socialism. They focus on the early humanistic Marx, who wrote of the need for ethical, as well as economic, redemption. According to Marx, the capitalist world of mid-nineteenth-century Europe had become oriented to things and abstractions. Man was subordinated to machines. The proletariat symbolized the fate of suffering humanity; the triumph of socialism would redeem humanity from this tyranny of material things and philosophical abstractions. Man would once more conquer nature. Both Senegalese leaders value Marx more as a sociologist and philosopher than as an economist. Rather than setting forth scientific laws of economic development, Marx made his greatest contribution in stressing the effect of industrial economy on modern man. In the opening address to the colloquium on African Socialism held in Dakar, Senegal, during December of 1962, Senghor told the delegates:

We will take care not to forget that a plan of economic and social development is made by men and for men; it is not governed by haphazard development. Its implementation requires first and foremost the conscious will of men and consequently their moral and technical training. This truth is Marx's principal discovery although too many "Marxists" forget about it these days and put greater trust in machines and techniques than men.[31]

In Senghor's interpretation of African Socialism, the Marxist concept of human alienation has a central place. According to Senghor, capitalism brought economic, political, and cultural alienation to Africa. In the economic sphere, capitalism alienated man from his work and the products of his labor; it also dehumanized the workers. In the political arena, there resulted domination of one country by a foreign power. In the social and cultural spheres, one ethnic group became subjected to another; the system of economic and political alienation was thus colored by racism.[32]

Mamadou Dia similarly emphasizes the humanistic contributions of Marx. Originally designed to serve men, economics has become the study of products, techniques, calculations of interest, and quantitative factors. A socialist economy must make man an end, not a means. Although, like Senghor and Touré, criticizing the Marxist ideas of violence, atheism, and philosophical materialism, Dia praises Marx's condemnation of the exploitation of man by man and agrees with his recommendation of how governmental action can equalize relations between the world's dominant and dominated economies. Like Marx, Dia wants to restore man to the center of economics. Man must become the active conqueror of nature, rather than remain the passive subordinate to exterior mechanical forces.[33]

Although Dia supports Marx's humanistic principles, he objects to certain of his economic theories, especially the labor theory of value. An economy that worships work risks becoming an inhuman civilization. An economic science based on human costs has greater relevance than the labor theory of value. The economy of human costs transcends the notion of work, which, in the contemporary mechanized world, appears as alienation.[34] Dia, along with Senghor, believes that the economic theories of Marx have limited usefulness, for they are historically relative to mid-nineteenth-century European capitalism. Despite certain inaccurate predictions, Marxism is more useful as an analysis of the capitalist system than as an instrument for building a humanistic economy.[35]

### Traditional African Economy

In line with the notions of historical relativity and the need to pay attention to concrete realities, these three exponents of African Socialism blend Marxist ideas with the socialist values of precolonial African societies. In contrast to Sékou Touré, Mamadou Dia and Léopold Senghor stress more the "communitarian" values of the traditional culture; they seek to transfer these traditional values to the level of the modern state. For Senghor African society revealed a communal solidarity where man was at the center of the universe. By reason of this community-based solidarity, this spiritual nature of African life, socialism will come easily to Africa: "Negro African society is collectivist, or, more exactly, communal, because it is rather a communion of souls than an aggregate of individuals . . . . We had already realized socialism before the coming of the European. . . . Our duty is to renew it by helping it to regain spiritual dimensions."[36] This feeling of solidarity, the identification of each member of society with the other, was exemplified in traditional culture by the harmony between the individual and the group. According to Senghor, the Negro-African "communitarian" society based its solidarity on the general activity of the group. In a communitarian society, the person feels that he can develop his originality only in and through society.[37]

Like Senghor, Mamadou Dia focuses on the cooperation, solidarity, and altruism found in traditional Africa, where life was communal, animated by a spirit of cooperation. A collective mentality motivated human behavior. There was a complete altruism, a harmony between the individual and general interest. The village formed a group where the interest of each agreed with the interest of all. The land belonged to the collectivity. All productive efforts appealed to the solidarity of every member in the group.[38]

President Senghor also notes the collective nature of work in the Negro-African society. The familial group or corporation owned the means of production and the instruments of work as common property. Under this collective situation, the African worker felt that he labored for something of value to himself. This work satisfied the human needs of responsibility and dignity. Since the work permitted the realization of his personal needs, it was not forced labor but a source of joy.[39] Through work the Negro realized a fraternal communion with his fellows. The nature of the work determined whether property was collective or individual. Collective work resulted in collective property, and individual work produced individual property. Thus, while the products of the individual fields became individual goods, the property of the family fields and herds was considered collective property. Collective work provided for the necessities. Through individual work, the person acquired luxuries and superfluous acquisitions necessary for the realization of his needs.[40]

According to Mamadou Dia, simplicity, rather than luxury, characterized the precolonial African economy. Traditional communalism rested on simple tastes, rather than on extraordinary technical developments. An equilibrium existed between supply and demand. The supply was the enthusiasm which stimulated the members of the collectivity. The demand was based on simple customs. A communitarian principle of life realized an equal sharing of goods and prohibited surpluses and luxurious tastes.[41]

Although Sékou Touré shows less attention to the traditional culture, he too praises the communitarian nature of African culture. Compared with Dia and Senghor, he places greater emphasis on the group-oriented character of traditional life:

Africa is essentially "communaucratic." Collective life and social solidarity give her habits a humanistic foundation which many peoples may envy. It is also because of those human qualities that an African cannot imagine organizing his life outside that of his social group— family, village, or clan. The voice of African people is not individualistic.[42]

In precolonial African cultures, the instruments of production belonged to society. Every man was an element in social production. As a socially responsible worker, he felt an awareness of common interests.[43] This stress on the African features of socialism reflects Touré's concern with articulating a socialist ideology appropriate to African realities. In reply to a question asked at a press conference in Conakry, capital of Guinea, he stated his preference for the term "communaucratie," instead of African Socialism. The term socialism might give outside observers misleading impressions about the Guinean desire to import a foreign ideology. Touré said:

We use the expression "communaucratie" precisely in order to avoid all equivocation and all false analogies. . . . Our solidarity, better known under its aspects of social fraternity, the pre-eminence of group interests over the personal interest, the sense of common responsibilities, the practice of a formal democracy which rules and governs village life —all of which constitute the base of our society—this forms what we call our communaucratic realities.[44]

### Ideology and Economic Development

What is the relation of this socialist ideology to the economic development and political systems of Guinea and Senegal? Compared with the Ivory Coast, Ghana, or Nigeria, neither Guinea nor Senegal has experienced rapid economic growth. When

Guinea became independent in 1958, the De Gaulle government immediately withdrew French personnel and administrators from Guinea and stopped all economic assistance. By 1960 the Guinean economy faced a serious decline in foreign trade, and shortages of consumer goods became prevalent.[45] Although the French intransigence weakened Guinea economically, the ideology espoused by Sékou Touré also contributed to the lack of economic growth. Touré has affirmed the need for political control of the economy; he values party dominance and political ability over purely entrepreneurial skills. Yet those who demonstrate the greatest commitment to the Party do not necessarily possess needed abilities in entrepreneurial activities. Beginning in 1961, the Guinean government took steps to denationalize industry and to re-establish closer economic ties with France and the United States. That year Touré had closed down the two state monopoly trading organizations (the Comptoir de Commerce Extérieur and the Comptoir de Commerce Intérieur), whose operation had not proved successful, partly because Guineans lacked the requisite economic experience. In 1962 the National Assembly voted to relax restrictions on foreign investment. The law provides guarantees against nationalization and sets up more favorable tax and customs arrangements to foreign investors.[46]

Although Senegal has maintained close economic ties with France, Senegalese economic development has also been rather sluggish. In April 1963 President Senghor revealed that industrial and agricultural production had stagnated for over a year. Production of the peanut, Senegal's main crop, had declined. Industrial production was also down. Since 1961 the economic situation has grown worse, and the budget deficit has increased.[47] Although certain aspects of the economic situation, such as a decline in exports outside the franc zone, contributed to this economic deterioration, the ideology of Senghor may partially account for the slow economic growth. Whereas Touré asserts the dominance of the party organization over economic activities, Senghor stresses aesthetic values to the neglect of entrepreneurial skills. The Senegalese president has written that the African renaissance will be less the work of politicians than of Negro writers and artists.[48] The Senegalese have so far shown little interest in purely economic activity; no sizable African entrepreneurial class has developed.

Today Europeans dominate large-scale commercial enterprises, while the Lebanese and other *petits blancs* act as commercial middlemen. Senegalese prefer to enter government service or engage in artistic lines of work, instead of becoming businessmen.[49] President Senghor came to recognize this economic problem in 1963, when he called for the establishment of more technical and specialized schools: "Senegal must train more engineers than philosophers and more economists than poets."[50]

Ideology has a somewhat different function to fulfill in promoting economic development for the Guinean and Senegalese leaders. For Touré, the function of ideology is to mobilize the masses for the political reconstruction of Guinean society. He stresses hard work and has not refrained from using forced labor. He stated in 1958: "I say publicly, we shall be the first African government to institute forced labor. We are not ashamed to say that forced labor will be instituted, since this work will not be done for the benefit of Sékou Touré, the Government, or whoever it may be. This will be done for the benefit of those who are going to work themselves."[51]

Compared with Touré, Dia and Senghor place less stress on the masses and more on the person. Dia believes that a policy of *l'investissement humain* as practiced in Guinea operated solely at the level of crowds. He prefers another kind of human investment, one that pays more attention to the individual person, as does the program of *animation rurale* in Senegal: "The operation occurs at the level of the personal consciousness of each citizen. Each man who does his job with the maximum of conscience, of love for his country . . . creates a real, human investment which is indispensable to the nation."[52] Dia hopes that the program of *animation rurale* will allow greater freedom for the peasantry to satisfy their personal wants. Basically a form of community development, the program stresses cooperatives and the provision of technical skills and civil experience to the villagers. Under this economic program, the function of ideology will be to supply the needed enthusiasm. Economic development needs more than the pursuit of concrete objectives. Africa also needs a doctrine to give the citizens in Senegal enthusiasm, faith, dynamism, and a consciousness of their liberation.[53]

*Ideology and the Political System*

With regard to the political systems of Guinea and Senegal, Sékou Touré's brand of African Socialism tends to encourage a more monistic polity. By stressing the dominance of one party, Touré follows Lenin more than Marx. According to Touré, there is one general interest, one unanimous popular will, and one pre-eminent thought. The Parti Démocratique de Guinée is the definer of this general interest, the custodian of the popular will, and the incarnation of the collective thought of the whole Guinean people: "The Party constitutes the thought of the people of Guinea at its highest level and in its most complete form. The thought of the Party indicates the orientation of our actions; the thought of the Party specifies the principles which ought to direct our behavior, our collective and individual attitude."[54] For Touré the basis of social solidarity lies in membership within the PDG. Through active participation in the party and commitment to its goals, the Guinean citizens will feel a mutual identification with each other.

The socialist ideology of Senghor and Dia rests on a more pluralistic foundation. Compared with Touré, Senghor criticizes Leninist philosophy for its materialism and determinism. Holding that reality is multiple-based, not monistic, Senghor sees many contradictory facets of reality.[55] The Negro-African culture gave the solution of pluralistic unity to political problems. Now the new African states must act on the basis of this indigenous pluralism and seek to blend complementary differences into a new synthesis. Senghor has written, "We have chosen the African path to socialism, which will be a synthesis of Negro-African cultural values, of Western methodological and spiritual values, and socialist technical and social values."[56] Compared with the political situation in Guinea, Senegalese life reveals somewhat greater organizational pluralism. The ruling Union Progressiste Sénégalaise is less dominant in Senegal than the PDG in Guinea. The Senegalese trade unions have retained some degree of autonomy. The various traditional groups, especially the Moslem *marabouts,* exercise economic power outside political controls. For Dia and Senghor, the basis of socialist solidarity lies not in submission to a dominant party but in the sharing and expression of distinctive African values. Dia hopes that when Africans assimilate the techniques of the West, they will not sacrifice African culture and indigenous values to imported techniques: "The modern economy which we want to build ought to permit the safeguarding of the essential values that comprise the originality of Africa."[57]

## Conclusion

In conclusion, although the leaders of Guinea and Senegal have many similar social and economic ideas, their varieties of African Socialism differ primarily in the degree of political control they want to see established over social groups. Whereas Dia and Senghor postulate a more humanistic brand of African Socialism based mainly on pre-1848 Marxist ideas, Touré's ideology reveals a stronger Leninist influence. Guinea has more state control over the economy and is less dependent on French assistance. The Senegalese government has so far allowed non-Africans—Lebanese, Mauritanians, and Europeans—to dominate the economy and has relied more on French subsidies for economic development. The pluralism of the ideology of Senghor and Dia and the greater monistic note of Touré are thus revealed in the political and economic systems of these two states of French-speaking West Africa.

# Chapter 10

# Mali: The Prospects of "Planned Socialism"

Kenneth W. Grundy

African Socialism means many things to many people. It ranges from the increasingly centralized and state-controlled economies of Mali, Ghana, and Guinea to the practically unstructured and somewhat chaotic state and private enterprise admixtures of Senegal and Nigeria. Nearly every African head of state, with the possible exception of Liberia's President V. S. Tubman, Gabon's M'ba, and the Emperor of Ethiopia, has at one time or another paid lip service to some form of African Socialism. Thus, to designate an emerging African state as "socialist" or to say that a leader advocates "African Socialism" tells little about the actual economic and social system or theory existing in a given country. Although there are significant differences among the various theories of African Socialism, the real test of the character of a particular brand of socialism is the confrontation of theory and practice, the juxtaposition of ideology and accomplishment. Consequently, one is forced to look deeper into the realities of economic and social life to understand more fully the content of the particular variety of African Socialism practiced in each country. This chapter examines the operation of African Socialism in the Republic of Mali.

## Malian Attitudes toward Capitalism and Socialism

The officials of the Republic of Mali and its ruling party, the Union Soudanaise, are one of the most Marxist-Leninist-oriented governing regimes in West Africa.[1] This is most evident in the theory of imperialism to which they subscribe and in the ideological orientation of their single-party polity. But it is also reflected in the doctrinal foundations of "planned socialism" (if not in actual practice), and in the rationale behind mobilization of the people for national development. In essence, the leaders of the Union Soudanaise appear intent on eventually bringing most sectors of the economy under state control and ownership. Nevertheless, Malian adhesion to socialist principles is largely pragmatic rather than doctrinaire.

Why have the Malian officials accepted socialism, or at least socialist theory, so wholeheartedly and rejected capitalism so completely? The fact is, capitalism has never been a relevant alternative for this vast, landlocked territory. What little capitalism Malians have known has been predominantly French-owned commercial enterprises. The preindependence *économie de traite* (trade economy) was the antithesis of competitive capitalism found in Europe. Under the colonial system foreign trading companies purchased local agricultural products at the lowest possible prices and sold them to be processed in Europe and America. In return they imported and sold in the country a few manufactured items at inflated prices. The economic development of the African country was regarded as an adjunct of the metropolitan economy to be exploited for the profit of the European trading companies, who usually enjoyed preferred or monopolistic conditions. It was only natural, therefore, that Malian leaders should look at the system through the other end of the telescope. Since they associated capitalism with the hated colonial economic structure, it was never really considered as a live possibility, much less a desirable objective, for independent Mali. In line with the general desire for economic independence and "decolonization," the capitalist system which accompanied the colonial regime was to be supplanted by an African economic system, run by Africans, for the benefit of the indigenous masses.

To attempt to institute an indigenous capitalist economic order would be virtually impossible. There is little capital in the country. Mali's 4,100,000 inhabitants earned about $52 per capita in 1959. The terse reply of Seydou Badian Kouyate, former Minister of Planning and Rural Economy, when he was asked if he was a socialist, is a cogent declaration of why most Africans so summarily reject capitalism: "You cannot be a capitalist when you have no capital."[2] Clearly, few Malians have a vested interest in the creation or maintenance of a system that they regard as inequitable and exploitative. More recently Dr. Kouyate offered another reason for Mali's aversion to capitalism:

. . . the underdeveloped countries cannot follow the same road as the European countries in the matter of the process of their economic development, and that is for evident reasons: slowness of capital formation, subordination of the general interest, and the collective well-being to profits realized by individuals . . . therefore, the only path permitting Mali to develop rapidly and harmoniously would be that of the socialist economy characterized by planning and the decisive role of the state in the economic life.[3]

This explanation is based, first, on the inequities and the uneven and often chaotic fashion in which a capitalist economy progresses, and second, on the speed with which development must be advanced. According to the Africans, the economic development of Europe took too long. Social upheaval and injustice were widespread. The African Socialists want to avoid *ad hoc*, experimental, haphazard change. They are seeking a strategy for development that is rapid, positive, and guaranteed not to create antagonistic forces that seek, for the profit of the few, to retard social change designed to benefit the masses. Capitalism, it is believed, does not satisfy these criteria. One Malian official went so far as to blame the capitalist system for practically all of mankind's ills. In crisp, Leninist terms he declared:

The fratricidal struggles, the civil wars, the general degradation of human relations, oppression, and social injustice are not the fate of men of one race or one continent; they are produced by a system that is born little by little, in the course of an economic evolution determined by private profit.[4]

In still another context the Malians place great faith in the efficacy and adaptability of socialism to the African milieu. In theory, African Socialism is simultaneously a modern approach to economic problems and a continuation of the traditional way of life. It is the adaptation of the "existing cooperative tendency to [a] modernized structure." To illustrate, President Modibo Keita once explained the rationale underlying Malian socialistic principles this way:

We are a country which has been colonized. . . . We have never therefore had an economy controlled by Africans; we have never had an economy controlled by Malians. In Mali the people of the villages work collectively. They have societies, called farming societies, which cultivate the fields of the village in rotation, and sometimes they have one collective field which they work and harvest to cover the common expenses. We consider it would be bad policy to break down this traditional pattern of collective life; on the contrary, we think it should be improved so that it can take its place in the pattern of present-day evolution.[5]

For President Keita, socialism is a "progressive" step in the Marxist evolution of history and, concurrently, an economic organization compatible with traditional African social and economic patterns. When traditional social patterns stand in the way of socialism, as interpreted by the modernizing elite, tradition is abandoned in favor of modernization. The Malian arguments for socialism, like the Ghanaian, Guinean, and Senegalese positions, are of many varieties. Socialism is thought to be democratic, progressive, equitable, and efficient. Planned socialism is regarded as the only road to Malian development. Naturally, planned socialism is to be accompanied by its corollary, the dismantling of those features of the colonial economic system that are not thought to be applicable to African society.

There is a further, perhaps more fundamental, reason for Mali's commitment to socialism. The justifications and explanations for socialism advanced by her officials can be viewed as rationalizations for the adoption of a system that clearly benefits Mali's revolutionary elite.[6] At heart, the Malian brand of socialism is rooted in the social and political character and composition of the new ruling regime. In preindependence Mali there were no indigenous landowning or capitalist classes. Perhaps the closest thing to a Malian capitalist class was the petty trading classes which grew up in the commercial centers. In this regard the Union Soudanaise was particularly fortunate. In contrast to Ghana, Nigeria, and the Ivory Coast, for example, where the colonial power had inadvertently created a small but articulate African bourgeoisie, Mali has no capitalist class of any consequence. Nor is there a well-organized traditional feudal class with which to contend. As a consequence, the revolutionary Union Soudanaise does not spring from a property-owning or bourgeois middle-class background. Rather, it represents the small, Western-educated bureaucratic segment of the population whose power is not anchored to any material economic foundations. During its rise to power, this modernizing elite utilized the issues of anticolonialism and nationalism to sustain revolutionary fervor and rally the interested peasantry to its cause. Once grasping the reins of government, however, the party realized that its control of the state was tenuous. Because of the absence of a broad power base resting on permanent socioeconomic foundations, the ruling elite promptly took steps to solidify its position. Its immediate objective, on attaining independence, was to protect itself against traditional and foreign power centers by emphasizing the merits of national unity and development, and undertaking programs of modernization. In order to achieve its primary objective, i.e., its continued control of the government, and to assure the very existence of Mali as an independent state, the modernizing elite sought to enhance the power of the state. Since it alone controls the state machinery, this approach serves to reinforce its own prestige and power. The chief avenues of increased state power in an underdeveloped country are state ownership of the means of production and distribution and a centrally planned economy. Expansion of state power automatically expands the power of the ruling elite. Like revolutionary ruling groups throughout the world, the Union Soudanaise seeks to make permanent its source of power by restructuring the socioeconomic order to its own advantage. The party also endeavors, by political and ideological education of the masses, to prove to the peasantry, to whom it has turned for support, that it is the most progressive group in the society and therefore rules legitimately. In its appeal to the citizenry, the virtues of the Malian nation, socialism, and the planned economy are extolled to assure broader support for party policies.

### Le Plan Quinquennal, 1961-65

Several strikingly different African states boast of planned socialism. What form does socialism take within the Malian framework? To what extent has state ownership of the means of production been implemented? In centralized control of the economy and state monopoly of the productive forces of society, the Malians are committed to an almost complete socialistic organization. As it was put by Idrissa Diarra, Political Secretary of the Union Soudanaise: "the best means of raising our standard of living consists of controlling, directing, and orienting *all* sectors of the economy."[7] The Union Syndicale des Travailleurs du Soudan, Mali's only labor union, is equally devoted to a centralized economic order.[8] Reflecting such views, the Economic Resolution, approved by the Extraordinary Congress of the Union Soudanaise in September 1960, called for the initiation of several moderately socialistic programs, particularly in foreign commerce and agriculture.[9] Although these party objectives gave only vague indications of what was to lie ahead, they did at least serve as broad guidelines on which party planners could build a program.

Just one year later, the Resolution furnished the foundation for Mali's first "Five-Year Economic and Social Development Plan."

PROJECTED PRODUCTION OF THE DIFFERENT BRANCHES
OF THE MALIAN ECONOMY

(*In millions of CFA francs, 1959 value*)

| Branch of the Economy | 1959 | 1965 | Index |
|---|---|---|---|
| Agricultural products | 20,011 | 33,085 | 165 |
| Food products | 11,673 | 20,291 | 173 |
| Energy | 2,520 | 3,390 | 135 |
| Raw materials | 1,088 | 4,088 | 376 |
| Machinery | 325 | 820 | 252 |
| Textiles, leather | 1,425 | 3,700 | 260 |
| Miscellaneous merchandise | 200 | 350 | 175 |
| Buildings, public works | 4,345 | 16,112 | 371 |
| Service (excluding transport and commerce) | 800 | 1,100 | 138 |
| Total | 42,387 | 82,936 | 196 |

Source: République du Mali, Ministère du Plan et de l'Economie Rurale. *Rapport sur le Plan Quinquennal de Développement Economique et Social de la République du Mali: 1961–1965*, p. 10.

It provided for an 8 per cent annual rate of growth in gross domestic production, to be divided as shown in the table. The increases are sizable, even for a country as economically retarded as Mali. Yet party leaders claim that only by such a considerable productive effort can Mali "emerge from this deplorable state, inherited from almost 70 years of colonization."[10]

At first glance, the Plan Quinquennal, with its projected growth rates and its contemplated social transformation, looms as a preposterous fiction contrived by visionaries rather than by realistic politicians. If viewed strictly in terms of the probability of fulfilling its objectives, its fictional component seems paramount. In Mali, where at least 90 per cent of the people are involved in subsistence agriculture, it is unlikely that sufficient capital for the planned expansion can be raised within the country. On the other hand, it must be recalled that Mali is so economically backward that even a 270 per cent increase in building and public works, for example, does not amount, in absolute terms, to a great deal of economic activity or social change. Still, the overall 8 per cent annual rate of growth envisioned by Mali's planners can hardly be achieved in this five-year period—the economic base simply does not exist. A recent United Nations survey reports that the highest annual growth rate in gross national product during the period 1950–60 was Japan's 7.2 per cent. It also found that in countries where the annual per capita income was $200 or less, the growth rate rarely rose above 2 per cent per year.

Before dismissing the Five-Year Plan as altogether fanciful, however, some fundamental differences must be pointed out between economic planning in the colonial context and economic planning in the context of a newly emergent African country. Colonial planning, at least superficially, was a comparatively sober and professional attempt to divide the available governmental allocations among various sectors of the economy. If progress was forthcoming, the colonial authorities were pleased, but there was little incentive or imperative for rendering basic changes in the social or economic order.

In contrast, planning in the newly independent states is more intimately related to popular attitudes and aspirations. Plans, no matter how grandiose they may appear to the detached observer, are closely associated with the ideology and slogans of development and underdevelopment, and are largely statements of goals. By centralizing dreams and expectations around what is thought to be "scientific" economic planning, development plans become foci of great national efforts.

Centralized planning is placed in a new framework by the modernizing elite—that of immediate national, political, social, cultural, and economic development. To Mali's leaders, planning is the "scientific," "realistic" approach to solving social problems and bolstering the party's regime. Viewed from this angle, planning has a dual utility. First, and most obviously, it is a necessary instrument by which a country can shepherd its limited human and material resources in a more efficient way to achieve predetermined goals. Second, and perhaps more important to the politically conscious elite, planning is a tool for national integration and unification. By rallying many segments of the population behind an ostensibly idealistic plan, major social transformation can be effected with a minimum of resistance. A piecemeal approach to such changes would more likely lead to discontent and unrest. Moreover, a greater measure of centralization of economic and political power can be brought about under the pretense of implementing a plan in which everyone has placed his hopes. Thus, without rendering significant economic progress in statistical terms, social changes can be effected which facilitate centralization of power and, it is hoped by the modernizing elite, ultimate economic development. This is what the Malian officials have in mind when they speak of establishing a "very solid domestic economic policy" in which "profound structural reforms" will be undertaken.*

*Commerce.* One of the most fundamental "reforms" since independence has been the creation of Somiex, the Société Malienne d'Importation et d'Exportation. At least three factors prompted the institution of a state monopoly in domestic and foreign trade. First, an organ like Somiex permits the government to orient commerce to conform with the needs of the Plan and to create new channels of commercial exchange. Second, the state monopoly accords stricter control over imports and exports and affords the authorities the possibility of giving priority to capital equipment rather than nonessential consumer goods. Third, it permits price controls and, more importantly, the appropriation by the state of profits from foreign commerce that would otherwise have been realized by expatriate-owned export-import firms. Prior to Somiex much of the export, import, and domestic retail and wholesale trade remained in such private hands as the Compagnie du Niger Français, an associate of the gigantic United Africa Company operating in the French Sudan. The establishment of Somiex diminishes the influence of foreign entrepreneurs in Mali, and the move dovetails nicely with the general decolonization program espoused by party militants.

In its first year of operation Somiex made a significant impact on Malian commercial life. Business turnover registered by private export-import firms fell from 13.7 billion CFA (Colonies Françaises d'Afrique) francs (about $55 million) in 1960 to 11.6 billion CFA francs ($47 million) in 1961.[11] Some of the loss can be attributed to the dislocation of transportation facilities in the first half of 1961 as a result of the severance of the Bamako-Dakar railroad line. Still more can be traced to the widespread uncertainty of the business community concerning its future in an increasingly socialistic Mali. President Modibo Keita set the tenor for this uneasy atmosphere in January 1961, when he lashed out at foreign busi-

---

* République du Mali, Ministère du Plan et de l'Economie Rurale, *Rapport sur le Plan Quinquennal de Développement Economique et Social de la République du Mali: 1961–1965* (n.p., n.d.), p. 7. One should not underestimate the contributions of various French left-wing economists, Bettelheim and de Bernis among others. Although they provided most of the technical skill necessary for the formulation of the Plan, the goals and broad outlines reflect essentially the aspirations of Malian politicians and theorists.

nessmen who allegedly were attempting to perpetuate colonial domination. In a truculent speech he called on the entire nation to remain "mobilized" in the fight against foreign subversion. Addressing his warnings directly to the French business community, he told the merchants that "the times of profits and superprofits are gone" and if they did not wish to adjust to the new conditions they could leave.[12] In attacking a competing power center which was not wholly subservient to the ruling regime, the party thus sought to circumscribe an element of the population that had heretofore enjoyed relative freedom and an influence substantially greater than its numbers would indicate.

The decline in the activity of the private commercial sector was further precipitated by the granting of monopoly rights to Somiex for the import of basic items and for the export of peanuts. As a result, Somiex did about $8 million in business in its first year. This state monopoly also led to a reduction in the number of private trading firms during 1961 and an overall decrease in both European and African employees. Commerce plays an inordinately large role in the total Malian nonagricultural picture. Since commercial activity was, and still is, largely dominated by foreign interests, Mali's economic dependence is heightened. Few Malians were willing to defend foreign commercial interests, and thus the party's first move to consolidate its power was in the area of export-import trade. Despite the creation of Somiex, the government still does not control the bulk of exports. Cattle and fish are traded across the borders (perhaps as much as 60 per cent of the total real exports), and the resulting imports do not come under governmental control. Moreover, an increasingly active private commercial sector competes with Somiex.

*Transportation.* The state has entered into the transportation business with equal vigor. After the rail link with Dakar had been severed, the government purchased 350 trucks as the basis for the state-owned Transportation Administration. Along with a few privately owned trucking firms, it carries all Malian overland export-import traffic. A Senegalese-Malian Accord was signed on June 22, 1963, which called for the restoration of rail traffic between the two capital cities. Such a development affords the state even greater control of all transportation.

Air Mali, a state-owned-and-operated airline, was established in 1961. Currently operating at a deficit estimated at about $3 million annually, it reflects the economic inadvisability of prestige enterprises founded on pride rather than economic necessity or reality. Another state-owned transportation venture is the Malian Navigation Company. Created in 1961 as the successor to a jointly owned state-private company, it holds monopoly rights on commercial transport on the Niger River. Except for the more primitive modes of transport, Mali's internal transportation system is almost entirely socialized, and promises to be more so as it becomes increasingly mechanized.

*Agriculture.* In the field of agriculture, major politico-economic structural reforms are envisaged and have been initiated in some areas in order "to develop agricultural and livestock production in a socialist framework," utilizing the traditional "cooperative tendency" of the African peasantry. The organization of cooperatives in Mali stems from the idea that agricultural development in economically retarded countries requires a collective discipline.

As Dr. Kouyate observed: "The organisms set in place by the colonial system . . . have yielded only small results. Therefore it was necessary for us to restructure rural society."[13] The Sociétés de Prévoyance to which Kouyate refers failed to produce the results envisioned by their French administrators, yet they did provide valuable experience in the field of rural organization and agricultural production and credit. Consequently, the Malian planners and officials were not creating a revolutionary rural society from scratch.

The village is the basic unit of rural reorganization in the Plan. There is to be a Rural Production and Mutual Assistance Group in every village, a simplified and multipurpose cooperative of which all inhabitants are members. The groups are set up by a simple majority vote of all villagers over 18, after which membership is compulsory for all inhabitants. The whole character of the system is compulsory. Village cooperatives are financed by shares and subscriptions, which each member is obligated to purchase, and by profits on trading operations and government subsidies and loans. The village council administers the group. Its principal functions are the organization of work in common, improvement of farming methods, sale of products, group purchasing, and the organization of local social and cultural activities. The next stage of cooperative organization is the Associated Rural Group—a federation of village cooperatives to which are assigned the functions of commercialization of products and the execution of projects supposedly of common interest (but in reality proposed at the party's insistence) which are too large for the smaller village units. On the third level of the comprehensive cooperative system are the Mutual Societies for Rural Development. These groups are concentrated in the chief towns of the administrative districts, and perform similar functions on a wider scale. The village cooperatives must associate with the Mutual Societies for Rural Development in order to obtain supplies. All mutual rural development societies in turn are affiliated with a territorial economic activity fund that provides assistance through the organization of markets, search for outlets, and financial and administrative control of the mutual societies. At the head of the entire system is the Institute of Rural Economy, which coordinates the agricultural development programs with the overall Plan.[14] In spite of this neat pyramidal structure, agricultural reorganization in Mali has, at best, been uneven and incomplete. In areas with an active and well-organized Union Soudanaise branch, the villagers have eagerly undertaken the proposed changes. Elsewhere, rural life goes on much as before, little affected by the reforms championed by the party faithful.

In general, the tendency toward a centralized, state-directed agricultural order "in a socialist framework" has been accepted by the peasantry. A move toward greater consolidation and centralization should not arouse popular resistance. Because of an absence of trained organizers and agricultural workers, however, the party has had to be content with rural cooperative reorganization at a generally sluggish pace. The party, through its elaborate hierarchy, has primed the people for reorganization, but adequate leadership is lacking. In time, the party expects the social metamorphosis in rural areas to yield more than economic dividends. By structuring society into village cooperatives, party organizers seek not only to mobilize the people for economic development, but concurrently to manage and control more closely political activity at the grassroots level. In essence, the cooperative movement has added another set of groupings paralleling party organs and assisting the party in its work. Since almost 95 per cent of Mali's population lives in rural areas, agricultural cooperatives would serve the dual purpose of facilitating economic change, and solidifying the Union Soudanaise in political power.

*Industrialization.* Although rural development is regarded as an imperative prerequisite for total economic advancement, it is toward the "future," the industrial future, that some party officials are working. Many facets of the Plan are aimed at projected industrial growth. To speak of Malian industrialization seems ludicrous. Mali's industrial base is rudimentary. There were only about 14 industrial establishments in operation at independence. Compared to Ghana, which has over 500 factories in operation, Mali is indeed underdeveloped. Nevertheless, planned socialism in the Malian context envisions the eventual industrialization of the country. The likelihood of the success of such a program in the decades ahead is, for reasons too numerous to review here, highly doubtful.

The Plan stipulates that the state is either to operate directly or to supervise closely all existing and future industries; but it will apply different methods in the different industrial sectors. Public monopolies will dominate all mining and petroleum enterprises as well as all future heavy industry. Processing industries will be divided into a public and a private sector. The public sector will include several state enterprises authorized in the Plan. New industrial undertakings that are financed by foreign loans and grants will be operated as governmental entities. The private sector will play at best a limited and precarious role. Early in his regime, Modibo Keita asserted that private capital was welcome in Mali as long as it was invested where the government dictated—in industry. In theory, therefore, private investment is not debarred, provided it fits into the framework of the Plan. In order to encourage foreign investment in industrial enterprises, the Code Malien, set forth in May 1962, offers potential investors the free transfer of profits and capital, guarantees against tax increases for specified periods, provision of factory sites at no cost, and a no-strike pledge guaranteed by the Union Syndicale. In return, private enterprises may function as long as they meet the following conditions: (1) "conformity to the Plan," (2) "acceptance of the methods of transferring profits fixed by the government," (3) "acceptance of the government control of its management and sale prices," and (4) "acceptance of a program of technical training of African personnel."[15] Compared with other African investment codes, these are stringent regulations, and little foreign private investment has been attracted to Mali. Still, notwithstanding Mali's backward condition, it is believed that only by industrial diversification of her economy can "real independence" be attained.

If Mali's present policy toward foreign private capital continues to deter investment in the country, the party may alter the Code

Malien in an effort to lure capital. Other African countries—
Guinea, Ghana, and Senegal, for example—have recently amended
investment codes to facilitate taking profits out of the country.*
Faced by this increased competition, Mali may be forced in one
of two possible directions. On the one hand, she might enter into
rivalry to attract capital investments by revising her code. In view
of Mali's sparse human and material resources and relatively defi-
cient infrastructure, she would have a difficult time in the competitive market for foreign capital. On the other hand, she might
choose to socialize or nationalize what limited foreign investment
there is in Mali. A debate on this issue is smoldering within the
ostensibly monolithic Union Soudanaise. Modibo Keita's relatively
moderate faction apparently favors revising the code. The so-called
radical faction, headed by Madeira Keita and Ousman Ba, is pressing for a more militant approach to socialism.

*Finance.* Mali's post-independence budgets reflect ambitious
plans for development. Compared with previous budgets and in relation to the financial resources of the country, they are unrealisti-
cally optimistic. For example, the Ordinary Budget of 1961 called
for the expenditure of about $47 million.[16] This figure represents an
increase of 30 per cent over the 1960 budget. Budgetary funds were
supposed to emanate from four major sources: (1) increased customs receipts, (2) a more stringent income tax, (3) increases in
the rates of numerous minor taxes, and (4) the prompt collection
of Mali's share of the assets of the former Afrique Occidentale
Française. About 53 per cent of all anticipated revenue was to
come either directly or indirectly from commercial transactions.
But the funds were not forthcoming in the amounts envisaged.
Customs receipts, for reasons discussed above, were not as sizable
as expected. Moreover, Mali had to wait until February 1963 before
reaching settlement with Senegal on the outstanding issue of shared
assets in the French West African Federation and the short-lived
Federation of Mali.[17] Consequently, although the government has
not published actual revenue receipts or expenditures for 1960 or
1961, it has been estimated that the deficit on the Ordinary Budget
is about $12 million.[18]

The 1961 Capital Equipment Budget, covering the first year's
investment on the Five-Year Plan, was no less grandiose. About
56 per cent of this approximately $45 million budget was to be

* See Appendix VII of this volume for the changes in Ghana.

devoted to establishing or subsidizing the numerous state enterprises such as the Office du Niger, the Malian Navigation Company, the Transportation Administration, the National Public Works Company, and Air Mali.* It was expected that 65 per cent of the funds for this budget would be supplied in the form of loans, credits, and grants from abroad.

Other measures have been undertaken to raise revenue, such as the establishment of National Bonds and the reorganization of the formerly French-controlled Crédit du Soudan into a Malian People's Bank for Development. The very nature of Mali's subsistence agricultural economy precludes the generation of substantial capital sources from schemes of this sort.

One of the most significant economic and political measures taken by the party was the institution of the *franc Malien*. Almost without warning on July 1, 1962, the government announced both the new fiscal arrangements and its withdrawal from the West African Monetary Union.[19] The immediate results were economically disastrous. The new franc became inconvertible. Few foreigners would accept it, so Malian trade fell sharply. Deprived of their goods, merchants demonstrated against the introduction of the franc and the government countered with repressive measures.

The rationale behind the creation of the independent franc was essentially political and nationalistic. Basic advantages had been anticipated. First, it was to destroy French financial dominance in the country and to reduce Mali's economic dependence on the former metropole. The obligations to consult with France before making major changes in monetary policy were irritating and were regarded as a compromise with national sovereignty. Since at that time there appeared to be a general reduction of commercial relations with France, Mali no longer felt obligated to cater to French sensitivities. With the *franc Malien*, it was felt that Mali could be free to establish any trade relations she wished. To the Malian ruling elite, retaining the French franc constituted a limitation on national freedom and sovereignty; this could not be tolerated. Thus the institution of the new franc can best be understood in the con-

---

* U.S. Department of Commerce, *Economic Developments in the Republic of Mali, 1961* (World Trade Information Service, Economic Reports, Part 1, No. 62-58 [Washington, D.C.: G.P.O., June 1962]), p. 4. The Office du Niger, of course, is a French creation dating from 1932 (the idea goes back even further). In 1961 power was transferred from the semi-autonomous French organism to a Malian Director General representing the new government.

text of the decolonization policy and the quest for "full" independence pledged by party officials in virtually every statement since independence.

*Investissement humain.* In Mali, which suffers from a scarcity of investment capital and skilled labor and a plethora of unemployed manpower, there is need for gainful projects which not only can provide the people with much needed economic and social public works, but can absorb and unite them behind the modernizing elite. One suggested solution is *investissement humain,* or human investment—the use of unpaid, voluntary, collective labor in the construction of public works projects for community welfare.

Mali's program of human investment was largely copied from the program devised by Sékou Touré's regime in neighboring Guinea. It envisions voluntary work parties building schools, bridges, roads, post offices, community centers, athletic fields, and health facilities with only a minimum capital expenditure. Particularly ambitious programs have been planned in the field of education.

In practice, human investment has been relatively successful. All regions of the country have benefited from its tangible accomplishments, especially in rural areas where communal work habits have been traditionally encouraged and have consequently facilitated the organization of community-wide projects. But the concrete results seem meager compared with a less tangible product— the building of a sense of national purpose and confidence among the masses. The projects mean a great deal to almost every participant. They serve to remind him that an economically backward people can, given the determination and leadership, attain a higher standard of living. Such an outlook, of course, serves to strengthen the already well-organized Union Soudanaise and its government. To be sure, human investment is not an economic panacea. But it is a bold and imaginative approach to the problems of underdevelopment and national consciousness, and for these reasons it has served the party well.

### Foreign Aid and Trade Patterns

Approximately two-thirds of the funds for the Five-Year Plan are to be furnished from outside the country in the form of loans, credits, and grants from other governments and international organizations. According to the Plan, the objective of rapid de-

velopment necessitates foreign aid obtained under "favorable conditions." This usually means assistance that is supposedly devoid
of political strings and that does not arouse fears of "neo-colonialism." Ousman Ba's speech to the United Nations General Assembly one month after Mali's independence illustrates such apprehen-
sions.[20] In Ba's view, assistance should not be used as an instrument
of blackmail to influence the uncommitted countries. Therefore,
unless foreign aid is a decisive factor in real economic development,
it is harmful. Similar views, although advanced more tactfully, are
expressed by President Keita.[21] He believes that Western aid
usually implies that the recipient ought to reciprocate by following
a pro-Western foreign policy. However, he contends that aid from
the Communist powers is more immediate and does not offend
the dignity of the recipients. While the Western powers may be
"timidly trying at present to revise their attitude with regard to the
*'tiers monde,'* " they are always outpaced by the countries of the
Eastern bloc. However, current trends in economic and technical
assistance to West African countries tend to contradict Keita's position.* West Africans, particularly in Guinea and Mali, are increasingly looking to the West for aid. In part this is due to Western and Communist reassessments of their respective aid programs,
and a re-evaluation of the character of the aid by the recipient
countries.

Mali's trade pattern does not reflect as significant a Communist
influence as do her sources of assistance.[22] Despite a fear that too
great an economic reliance on one country or group of countries
may tend to subvert Malian independence, Mali remains an associate member of the European Economic Community and still
remains economically dependent on the subsidized French market.

### Conclusions

The theory and practice of "planned socialism" in Mali provide
material for several observations and speculations about the operation of African Socialism in general, and Malian socialism in
particular.

*The gap between theory and practice.* The Malian conception

---

* Among the countries assisting Mali are Bulgaria, Communist China, Cuba, Czecho-
slovakia, East Germany, France, Ghana, Hungary, Israel, North Vietnam, Poland,
USSR, United Arab Republic, United Kingdom, United States, West Germany, and
Yugoslavia.

of socialism is characteristic of the imprecision of political polemics throughout the world. It is loosely defined, varying from time to time and from official to official, but at heart all theories represent a vague attempt at synthesis of the old and the new in African life. Clearly, to view "planned socialism" in a vacuum would be misleading. The test of a political theory is not what is said, but who says it; not how logical or how rational it is, but how in tune it is with reality, and to what extent it is being or has been implemented by the people vying for power in a given political arena. The modernizing elite realizes that to make permanent its role as manager of Mali's future it must seek a more solid basis for its political power. Thus it has undertaken to reorganize the country along "socialist" lines. To increase the state's power automatically enhances the power of the ruling elite. The party has also turned to the masses to solidify its power. In this respect, therefore, it has come to identify its future with the continued support of the masses. To this extent, it appears that the modernizing elite is, in fact, favorably disposed to the interests and wishes of most Malians. Since the elite, to a large extent, shapes the attitudes of the peasantry, the values, goals, and aspirations of the two classes are largely coterminous. Despite tremendous efforts by the elite, Malian society is still highly tradition-bound. The party has found by experience that the peasantry is often apathetic and inert. The party's task is made even more difficult by the high level of illiteracy and the geographical isolation of many regions of the country. The level of educational attainment and economic activity is so low that it will be decades before sufficient momentum can be gathered to transcend the inertia of centuries. In such a setting, "planned socialism" cannot be expected to achieve a social metamorphosis overnight. Theory is as much a product of its environment as it is a producer of environmental change. Theories of African Socialism thus can be expected to be adapted and adjusted to meet diverse territorial conditions.

*The interaction of economic centralization and political dynamics.* By the increased centralization and control of economic life in Mali, the state—more accurately, the governing party—is coming to be recognized as the sole dispenser of benefits and rewards in Malian society. By attempting to decrease the possibility of the formation of competing power centers springing from independent economic foundations, the Union Soudanaise is stabilizing and reinforcing its effective monopoly on political enterprise in the country. The elaborate single-party structure already dominates all organized youth, trade union, and electoral activity. The party is now attempting to add economic prerogatives to these broad powers. In Mali, as elsewhere, there is a profound relationship between the social and economic structure and the political dynamics of the system. Attempting to mold the social order and direct it toward preconceived but vaguely defined ideological norms, the party is approaching the place where it is the exclusive repository of legitimate authority. Increasingly Malians turn to the party with their grievances, problems, and requests. Political action is channeled through the party, and most meaningful political struggle in the country takes place within the party. Control of the party, in turn, yields control of the state machinery.

*The transformation of the popular mood.* There has been an obvious change in the mood of the people of Mali as a result of independence and the expectations associated with "planned socialism." Although the effects of socialism have not yet materially reached down to the mass of the citizenry, the party has managed to create a mystique around the Plan Quinquennal and "planned socialism" as vehicles for change. When socialism is extended to the village level by means of agricultural cooperatives and human investment projects, for example, the villagers enthusiastically participate. They are coming to view the centrally planned economy as an instrument for their own progress rather than for their exploitation. Because of and reflecting this changed attitude, the party leaders have optimistically undertaken a largely unrealistic and overly ambitious development scheme. The Five-Year Plan embodies all the slogans and symbols of anticolonialism, nationalism, and development, and appears to Western observers as little more than an exercise in polemics. The future of socialism in Mali will depend on the extent to which the party can satisfy the expectations it has aroused.

*"Planned socialism" and economic independence.* Obviously Mali's social and economic progress is largely dependent on forces outside the control of the party and the Malian people. Malian socialism must look abroad for the capital necessary to activate and propel the economy. Foreign technical and financial assistance, the continued stability of foreign markets for agricultural products, and the availability of private foreign investment hold the key to

the success of Malian socialism. Increased concentration of power in the hands of the ruling party does not assure economic and social progress. It merely signifies that once capital does enter the country, it will be directed into prescribed channels. Mali, like other African states, is caught on the horns of a dilemma. In order to overcome her essential economic dependence, she must first turn to foreign capital sources for help, thereby magnifying, at least temporarily, her dependence on others.

The objectives that President Keita has expressed are substantially egalitarian and socialistic: "a system where there will be no unemployed, and there will be no multimillionaires . . . a system where there will be no beggars, and where each will eat if hungry."[23] At her present pace it will be years before Mali can even approximate these goals. But Modibo Keita and his compatriots are convinced that their objectives are realizable through the institution of a planned socialist economy.

# Chapter 11

# Tanganyika: The Search for Ujamaa

Fred G. Burke

In April 1962, Tanganyika's Kivukoni College was host to a week-long TANU (Tanganyika African National Union) Study Conference on Pan-African Socialism. This conference provided the occasion for the debut of Dr. Julius Nyerere's political theory in an address entitled "Ujamaa: The Basis of African Socialism."

"Ujamaa" cannot be directly translated into English. Its literal meaning in Swahili varies, but generally it refers to family or brotherhood. For Dr. Nyerere "Ujamaa" signifies a set of ideas and principles that closely approximate what is meant to the English-speaking peoples as "socialism."* However, in common with most political theories, Ujamaa has become associated with many different and often contradictory ideas. In order to clarify this concept, I will first examine the meaning Ujamaa has for Dr. Nyerere and then look at some of the meanings it has acquired as it has been interpreted by various sectors of the Tanganyikan population. Second, it will be viewed from several perspectives: that of a mass ideology, an African brand of socialism, a program of action, and an *ex post facto* justification.

### Dr. Nyerere's Version of Ujamaa

Dr. Nyerere's opening thoughts, "Socialism is an attitude of mind," which inclines men toward a deeply felt sense of obligation for the welfare of their fellow men, sets the tone for his treatise.[1] Unlike European socialism, which grew out of the class struggle, Ujamaa inheres in the very nature of African society, and is an extension of the indigenous belief in responsibility for one's fellow tribesmen. Traditional society, Dr. Nyerere maintains, should serve as a guide to the present not simply because

---

* The problem of language bedevils other aspects of political thought as well. For example, President Nyerere insists that it is incorrect to refer to TANU as a political party, for "there is no proper word in English for the present Tanganyika system" (statement to TANU Annual Delegates' Conference, 1963).

it is indigenous but because it is intrinsically good and has demonstrated that it can provide the essentials, both materially and psychologically, of a good life. Traditional society was basically egalitarian, since everyone contributed to the common pool, and wealth, like the land itself, was held in trust from generation to generation. Hence the present generation, in the use of its heritage, exercises a sacred responsibility to future generations. This basic equality was subverted by European imperialism, which established a stratified system based on racial inequalities. In place of the indigenous ethic of communal responsibility and consensus, the exploitation of the many by the few was introduced. It is generally accepted among Africans that private and national rapacity laid waste the country, alienated the land from its rightful owners, and destroyed indigenous values. Even though the colonizer has left, his legacy remains. Hence, Ujamaa is required to purge all alien ideas inconsistent with it, as well as to revive a way of life, long violated. The people must be reminded of their past egalitarianism. The attitudes that led a chief or an elder to regard his authority as a public responsibility and the people to view the land as a gift of the gods dedicated to the welfare of all must be revived. But to purge society of foreign values and to rediscover pristine virtues are not in themselves sufficient. Ujamaa requires that the traditional attitude of mind (which Dr. Nyerere notes characterizes the extended family) be projected outward to incorporate not only every Tanganyikan but all mankind. Thus the crusade will not only rediscover and revitalize native values but extend these present parochial values to the entire human race. The institution charged with this enormous task is TANU above all, for to TANU is entrusted first of all the construction of a Tanganyikan nation founded on the precepts of Ujamaa.

### Various Interpretations of Ujamaa

Only five years ago most observers felt that Tanganyika would be one of the last territories to receive its independence. Independence came, however, with surprising speed and ease, and without a protracted period of agitation or violence. Perhaps because of this, there emerged no cadre of leaders who, while serving a colonial jail sentence, had had the time and the motivation to formulate a political philosophy.

In these circumstances, the central role of Dr. Nyerere as the political theoretician and philosopher of Tanganyika has been reinforced. Unlike Kenya, which has been both blessed and plagued by many competing leaders, Tanganyika emerged as an independent state with one man at the helm. This is not to say that other Tanganyikans did not contribute energy and skill toward gaining independence or play major roles in the building of the nation. However, aside from Dr. Nyerere, there is an absence of political theorists, men who in formulating the movement's ideology provide a theoretical justification for its premises and goals, and a body of myths, beliefs, and tactics designed to guide its practical operation, as well as an attack upon the existing structure that the movement hopes to change. On the whole, the young and vigorous leaders in the party and government are not of a theoretical turn of mind, but are pragmatic men inclined to action and administration.

Since Ujamaa is neither a call to action nor a program for development but a statement of humanistic ideals, Tanganyika's men of action do not quite know how to regard or use it. On the political hustings and in speeches explaining or justifying their programs, they are inclined to fall back on the slogans and clichés of anti-imperialism and neo-colonialism. Only a few members of Parliament can ever recall Ujamaa being used in debate. The word "Ujamaa" is seldom heard in political and administrative circles in Dar es Salaam or in the up-country regional and area headquarters. On those few occasions where the term is employed, its meaning is vague and imprecise. For example, in a newspaper interview in 1963, J. S. Kasambala, Minister of Cooperatives and Community Development, was reported to have said that his Ministry "had rightfully gained itself the name of Ujamaa—Socialism—because of the immediate direct contact we have with the people of Tanganyika."[2]

I attended several local TANU rallies, particularly during the 1962 presidential campaign, and heard many references to imperialism, neo-colonialism, hard work, and the elimination of certain vices such as prostitution and drunkenness. Rallies were begun, interspersed and concluded with shouts of *Uhuru* (Freedom), *Uhuru na Kazi* (Freedom and Work), *Uhuru na Umoja* (Freedom and Unity), *Uhuru na Jamhuri* (Freedom and the Republic), *Uhuru na Nyerere,* but nothing was heard of Ujamaa or *Uhuru na Ujamaa.* Similarly, in other party activities, little notice is given to Ujamaa. Party correspondence is almost always prefaced by the phrase *Uhuru na Kazi* but never *Uhuru na Ujamaa*. Once in a while, a regional commissioner or minister will lace a speech with ideas that suggest he is familiar with the concept even though he fails to mention it by name. For example, R. S. Wasambura, the commissioner for the Lake Region, frequently speaks of the classless basis of Tanganyikan society and exhorts peasants and students to help build such a society. On the other hand, the Vice-President of Tanganyika, Mr. Kawawa, who rarely employs such an image of the future as a spur to action, characterizes the group of leaders who are primarily concerned with means rather than ends. This energetic group constantly reiterates the need for everyone to work in order to eliminate "ignorance, poverty, and disease."

J. S. Kasambala, Minister for Cooperatives and Community Development, gave the opening address in November 1962 to the Pan-African Cooperative Conference held in Moshi, Tanganyika. Here one might have expected some reference to Ujamaa, the unity of African Socialist societies, or to the critical role that the cooperative movement would play. However, this was not the case, since the Minister chose to emphasize the economics of the cooperative movement.[3] In contrast, President Nyerere on the same day said: "From the start of our national struggle for independence I have recognized the vital role which [the cooperative movement] had to play in giving economic effect to the philosophy of African Socialism."[4] For Dr. Nyerere, Ujamaa is an integral part of his frame of reference comprising the philosophic and ethical foundations of the new society. However, the area and regional commissioners who travel throughout the country inspecting the lower echelons of TANU organization, setting up self-help schemes, and explaining government policy to divisional officials, TANU youth leaders, and local assemblies rarely speak of Ujamaa.

A striking illustration of different interpretations of Ujamaa and how these are linked to an individual's position in the social structure is provided by the example of a deputy secretary and an area chairman of TANU. The deputy secretary is the professional party official at the key area (former district) level. He works closely with the politically appointed area commissioners (who are ex officio TANU secretaries), is relatively well informed, and is in frequent touch with TANU headquarters in Dar es Salaam.

This group is composed, in the main, of young men with less than secondary school education; some have attended courses at Kivukoni College in Dar es Salaam, and nearly all hope some day to be area commissioners, or to be appointed to important positions in one ministry or another. The deputy secretary is a professional party organizer and seldom a local boy. In contrast, the TANU area chairman is almost always a local person who is oriented toward his own constituency. For one deputy secretary, Ujamaa is a national and revolutionary concept. It requires the cooperation of all the people on communal farms and other self-help projects. He thinks of it in terms of nation building, and this brings up images of massive work brigades. Thus, to men like the TANU secretary, Ujamaa is used to describe and justify their own activities, which center around the promotion of self-help schemes, co-operatives, party organization, youth and women's clubs. The area chairman, on the other hand, is inclined to think of Ujamaa (when he thinks of it at all) in local community terms. One specific area chairman said that Ujamaa in his community meant helping one's more unfortunate neighbors, and although he recognized that today it is supposed to include all Tanganyikans, he felt that in reality it probably did not extend beyond one's own village or, at the most, the tribe.

Civil servants in various occupations were questioned as to the meaning of Ujamaa. Even though this stratum is relatively well educated and keeps informed, Ujamaa was not translated as "African Socialism" but rather as "brotherhood." There is an important difference between the sophisticated bureaucrat and the simple peasant. Though both tend to see Ujamaa in terms of familyhood and brotherhood, the bureaucrat is quick to add that today this sense of obligation and consensus is not limited to the parochial unit but incorporates the entire nation. The dictum is to "treat fellow Tanganyikans as members of your family." Only when pressed did they link "Ujamaa" with "African Socialism," and even then they did not give evidence of what the concept actually meant or how one was to go about achieving it. There were two predominating themes: socialism meant "reducing the differences in wealth" and the negation of capitalism, which in turn is usually associated with colonial exploitation.

For a serious discussion of Ujamaa, its philosophical foundations and its significance as a national ideology, one must go to Kivukoni

College. This unique institution, established in 1961, is making an extraordinary contribution to the political life of the nation. Between 50 and 100 men of different age, experience, education and occupation spend from six months to a year at Kivukoni College, where their natural intelligence and curiosity are stimulated by courses in the social sciences. Many of Kivukoni's alumni are today serving in key government and party posts, and although it is difficult to point to specific cases, evidence indicates that these graduates, who are regional and area commissioners, junior ministers, parliamentary secretaries, TANU branch and headquarter officials, are among the few who understand Ujamaa as a national theory and as a guide to action.

Most of Kivukoni's students, sponsored by the government or by TANU, have already demonstrated a high degree of political awareness. In common with many other relatively uneducated political activists, they possess intense though vague and unsophisticated ideas about neo-colonialism, economic exploitation, and capitalism. They tend to interpret Ujamaa in more radical terms than its author. Ujamaa, plus a slight familarity with Marxism, leads some of them to conclude that industries such as TANESCO (Tanganyika Electric Supply Company) and the sisal and sugar estates should be nationalized. Most of these students were early supporters of TANU. They are men particularly sensitive to racial and colonial exploitation, and though Tanganyika is now independent, their personalities bear the marks of real or imagined exploitation. Socialism and Ujamaa are to them one and the same, and are viewed as an antidote to colonialism. Capitalism is odious because it is associated with colonialism and the domination of Africans by Europeans. Or, in the words of a Kivukoni student, "Since capitalism is foreign to us, brought by colonial upheavals, we must not copy it. We must believe in democratic socialism."[5] Socialism to this young man means a sense of brotherhood and economic development by means of the cooperative movement. Ujamaa is more and more likened to the socialism of the Communist bloc. An editorial in the Swahili daily *Uhuru* of September 7, 1963, is indicative. The editor comments that the reasons for official visits to other countries are to secure international assistance, and, just as important, to observe how other nations organize their agriculture and economy. Speaking of the trip to the USSR, Poland, and Czechoslovakia, by Mr. Kahama,

Minister of Trade and Industry, the editor noted that "these are countries that have the politics of Ujamaa. Their economies are run by Ujamaa. Their trade is operated by Ujamaa methods. . . . These are countries which have already prospered under the methods of Ujamaa."[6] From this viewpoint Ujamaa is less a set of general ideas or an "attitude of mind" than the negation of institutions and practices associated with colonial status.* The association of Ujamaa with Soviet-style socialism and with anti-imperialism is sharply posed in the same editorial. Mr. Kahama's visit to the Soviet Union "will bring to a halt the hopes of some great nations, especially those of the [blood] suckers and colonialists who had begun to think that because our ministers had only visited their countries and received aid there, they would be able to put us in their pockets and use us like a slave of theirs."[7] Where Dr. Nyerere emphasizes the natural equality of traditional society, the young men of Kivukoni interpret Ujamaa as calling for an end to Asian domination of the economy and any other legacies of the colonial era. Nyerere's Ujamaa is basically humanistic, while to many of these young men who are now acquiring positions of influence it justifies a policy, as one of them perceptively remarked, of "exploitation of the expropriators."

When a group of secondary school students was questioned about Ujamaa, there was little response. Of 30 students queried, only two indicated they were familiar with the concept. The first described Ujamaa in traditional terms, referring to family obligations, communal planting and harvesting, and home building. The second young man eagerly interrupted to tell his fellow student that he was mistaken and that today Ujamaa meant "socialism." To the query "What is socialism?" most of the boys described it in terms of Ujamaa, that is, community cooperation, the mutual obligations that are an integral part of small-scale kinship societies. When pressed to relate this line of thought to the level of the state, the students seemed confused but suggested that somehow the government would assume responsibility for providing services formerly supplied through the village unit.

Nor did a group of students at the new University College relate Ujamaa to government policy or to the activities of TANU. Simi-

---

* During a parliamentary debate in 1963, Roland Mwanjisi, Parliamentary Secretary to the Ministry of Home Affairs, stated that "English was a capitalist language and Swahili a socialist language" (Tanganyika Parliamentary Debates, February 15, 1963).

larly, the editor of a vernacular newspaper and an elderly local government official quickly replied that Ujamaa meant "African Socialism," but it was evident that the English term had no meaning other than its reference to Ujamaa, and that Ujamaa, in turn, was translated into their own language as helping one's neighbor.

The tendency to conceive of Ujamaa without policy or empirical foundations was notable in every walk of life except for its association with self-help schemes. Seldom was there any agreement with the idea that Ujamaa involved the extension of feelings of brotherhood, obligation, and consensus from the community to the state level. Nevertheless, there exists throughout Tanganyika a surprisingly strong sense of national identity, although it has not necessarily come from indigenous institutions. When a group of secondary students was asked whether they thought traditional societies provided either an inspiration or a model for Ujamaa at the national level, they differed greatly along tribal lines in their replies. Some felt that all traditional social systems were inherently communal and egalitarian and hence appropriate models for the present; others saw in nationalism an escape from a tribalism they found embarrassing either because it was primitive or because its inegalitarianism was inconsistent with Ujamaa.

To dramatize the role of the masses in national development, President Nyerere invented a mythical Tanganyikan whom he called Baba Kabwela. Dr. Nyerere believes that the realization of political and economic goals, regardless of philosophical pronouncements and development plans, depends ultimately on the "attitude of mind" and behavior of Baba Kabwela. His comprehension of Ujamaa is probably most crucial of all. However, the overwhelming majority of peasants appear to be ignorant of the modern meaning or use of Ujamaa. When they are asked its meaning, there is invariably a long hesitation before answering. An experienced community development worker in the Northern Region, who assisted in the questioning of some farmers, concluded, "I had the feeling that this may have been the first time they had ever tried to describe or perhaps think through the significance of Ujamaa." An African community development officer, who had spent considerable time outside of Tanganyika, regarded Ujamaa as a political slogan with no general meaning in its modern connotation for the rural peasant. She felt that it had come to be associated with the necessity of cooperating on self-help schemes and that the only time the peasant heard the word was when it was spoken by politicians at party rallies or mass meetings. On those few occasions where a political speech is translated from Swahili into the local vernacular, the Swahili word Ujamaa is nonetheless used. If the speaker thinks it necessary to explain Ujamaa to his non-Swahili-speaking audience, he employs local terms connoting cooperation, community work, and other such concepts.

The further one moves from the town and from the sophistication of the urban-centered bureaucracy, the less Ujamaa is used or understood. For example, not one of a group of some 20 farmers and town laborers interviewed in the Lake Region recalled ever having heard the term in its modern context. Like political slogans everywhere, Ujamaa tends to mean, to those who have heard it used, the same thing as other contemporary political phrases. Thus there is a tendency to associate Ujamaa with *Ushirika* (partnership, cooperation) and *Umoja* (unity).

A farmer, however, made an important distinction between Ujamaa and *Umoja*. An "Ujamaa" did something, whereas *Umoja* was simply a political term used by those fellows in Dar es Salaam. This, and similar responses, indicate that the word Ujamaa is more likely to bring up concrete though largely traditional referents than such current slogans as *Umoja* and *Jamhuri* (Republic). An action frame of reference tends to be associated with Ujamaa, since it conjures up a vision of people working together on a project. From this perspective, Ujamaa refers to an institution and not an attitude of mind; it can be the family, the cooperative, the age-grade, or any association that is organized for the purposes of mutual assistance. Whereas it is often applied to modern organizations such as cooperatives, voluntary groups, and labor organizations, commercial or profit-making institutions are not regarded as Ujamaa.

The absence of a precise definition of Ujamaa, though useful during a period of rapid social and economic experimentation, is sometimes frustrating even to a sympathetic Tanganyikan observer. In a recent newspaper article entitled "The Policy of Ujamaa Must Be Explained Correctly," this lack of precision is deplored.[8]

A perceptive and experienced interviewer summarized his findings in one region of Tanganyika as follows:

Ujamaa is well understood as a close family-like relationship between all people who would work to improve the well-being of Tanganyika in a material sense. It is usually accepted as government policy, and although it is not explicitly associated with the term socialism (which is not generally known or understood), it is usually considered incompatible with capitalism and is expressed in concrete projects which are undertaken in a traditional work-sharing, profit-sharing way.

Some non-African Tanganyikans insist that Ujamaa, as it is used in the towns, implies a sharp distinction between "them and us," and that it is inconceivable for Ujamaa to refer to Asian or European Tanganyikans. However, among African peasants and laborers there was no reference to race. When asked about the implications of Ujamaa for non-Africans, they tended to include all men in an Ujamaa who identified with and participated in the communal unit. For example, those Europeans and Asians who took part in self-help projects were said to belong to the Ujamaa. An American working with the cooperative movement in Tanganyika was considered to be "within" Ujamaa, as were Europeans and Asians working in the cooperative movement or in other government offices directly related to national development.

For reasons discussed below, "Ujamaa: The Basis of African Socialism," though first delivered as an address in Swahili and subsequently published in English, has had limited circulation in Swahili. This is in contrast to President Nyerere's other two political statements, "Scramble for Africa" and "One Party System."[9] Considerable efforts were made to obtain wide circulation for these two documents and thousands of Swahili translations were distributed. Tanganyika's literacy rate of 10 per cent is low even by African standards, and, since Swahili is the *lingua franca,* the number literate in English is even lower. Thus, with the exception of an infrequent reference to Ujamaa over TBC (Tanganyika Broadcasting Company), there has been almost no attempt to disseminate knowledge about it widely.[10]

From all this, four general meanings of Ujamaa emerge:

1. To President Nyerere, Ujamaa is an attitude of mind inherent in traditional African society, a society corrupted by alien influences that must now be cleansed. Although this concept was developed at the community level, it must now be extended to incorporate the nation and all of mankind.

2. To the few men and women familiar with Ujamaa and socialist theory, Ujamaa provides a basis and a justification for the completion of the African revolution.

3. To the pragmatic men of action—ministers, permanent secretaries, party leaders—Ujamaa is a vague statement of ideals with
little practical significance other than providing a convenient label
or justification for programs and directives required in the struggle
against "ignorance, poverty, and disease."

4. For Baba Kabwela, Ujamaa refers, by and large, to a set of
obligations that he has to other members of his community, defined usually in terms of kinship.

In common with most ideologies, Ujamaa can be viewed as
having a twofold or, to be more exact, a manifold character. Its
pure form, as developed by its originator, is distinct from its popular character, the forms in which it appeals to the masses. Here
it takes the shape of slogans, stereotypes, shibboleths, and folk
arguments, in contrast to the more abstract argument of its founder.

Having discussed the meaning of Ujamaa from the point of
view of different groups in Tanganyikan society, let us turn to an
examination of its origins, its peculiar flavor, and the question of
its applicability to a modern state.

## The Vocabulary of East African Politics

African nationalism in its postwar emergence has contributed its
own colorful dialogue to the language of politics. "Colonialism,"
"racism," "imperialism," "exploitation," and comparable terms
have taken on new urgency and meaning. Although the vocabulary
of politics is basically the same everywhere on the continent, there
are slight but significant variations in emphasis and meaning between East and West Africa. In large part this is the product of
different colonial experiences. The educated African elite is considerably smaller in East than in West Africa, and not only are
there few highly educated leaders in East Africa, but, in contrast
to Ghana or Nigeria, they seem to be less confident and sophisticated. There has been less time for a sizable leadership to evolve
in Tanganyika, and the presence of European and Asian settlers
seems to have retarded the development of energetic self-con-
fidence. East Africa's emergent leaders are men who grew up on
the fringes of an alien European community, where they were
regarded as lacking sufficient intelligence, ambition, and character

to undertake any but the most menial tasks. This experience has had two important effects which today render the language and tone of politics somewhat different in East than in West Africa. East African politics have an intensity and racial bitterness that are relatively absent in West Africa. Note the words of a Kivukoni student in 1962:

When our forefathers were just on the brink of advancing some civilization of their own, these land-hungry wolves from the polar regions stepped in to dismantle the little good that our forefathers had achieved for their posterity . . . the African man lost his freedom and from then onward he was to be reminded that he was inferior . . . an inferiority complex was to be swung around his neck in order to subject him and to reduce him to the lowest dregs of humanity.[11]

Although the vocabulary is the same—"imperialism," "colonialism," and "exploitation"—the words in East Africa express personal embitterment. This is not so much the case in West Africa, where the same language is aimed more against an abstract system than against individual people. The West African has, by and large, escaped the half-century of racial indignities that have been the lot of many Kenyans and Tanganyikans. For East African groups, political independence alone cannot restore a damaged ego or a loss of identity. The continued presence of Europeans and Asians in positions of authority, influence, and affluence is a constant reminder that the African is still regarded with contempt. It is not surprising to find, therefore, that the language of politics is imbued with references to the racial issue and to any remaining symbols of dependence and deference to non-Africans. The political pronouncements of Ghana's leaders, less obsessed with a need to demonstrate racial equality and competence, are bold and are couched in policy and programmatic terms. When Dr. Nkrumah refers to African Socialism he talks about the public ownership of the means of production, basic industrialization, socialist education, and national planning.[12] In contrast, Dr. Nyerere's writings are more a protest against the colonial past than a systematic philosophy for the future. He speaks of "rejecting the capitalist attitude of mind which colonialism brought into Africa."[13] Even his exhortation to work, a major theme in his writings, is phrased in terms deploring the exploitation of African labor and the evils of a leisure "class of parasites."[14]

Dr. Nyerere tries to convince his readers that Ujamaa is unique and indigenous to the African. In a similar vein a TANU branch secretary, when questioned about Ujamaa, said that it was different from socialism in England or the Soviet Union: "It is our own form of socialism, the way we had before you *Wazungu* [Europeans] came and destroyed it. We won't have succeeded until the cooperatives have taken over all the businesses now run by Asians or Europeans." A university student made the point: "Socialism in Europe means to take the wealth and spread it out, but African Socialism is the common effort to create wealth."

There is about Ujamaa, for the reasons already noted, a striking similarity to certain aspects of classical conservatism and even romanticism. Moreover, it contrasts sharply with the more orthodox economics in the writings of Nkrumah. The future must be firmly anchored in the past; new institutions should be based upon the values of the rural parochial village; the model for society should be the family; social organization is a mystic organic phenomenon. In the words of Dr. Nyerere:

We in Africa have no more need of being "converted" to socialism than we have of being "taught" democracy. Both are rooted in our own past —in the traditional society which produced us. Modern African Socialism can draw from its traditional heritage the recognition of "society" as an extension of the basic family unit.[15]

Kenya's Tom Mboya perceives African Socialism in almost Burkean terms:

When I talk of "African Socialism" I refer to those proved codes of conduct in the African societies which have, over the ages, conferred dignity on our people and afforded them security regardless of their station in life. I refer to universal charity . . . and I refer to the African's thought processes and cosmological ideas which regard man, not as a social means, but as an end and entity in society.[16]

The distinction we wish to make here is a subtle one but one that is basic to an understanding of the somewhat defensive, yet utopian, flavor of Ujamaa. Dr. Nyerere's emphasis on the virtue of traditional society and his thesis that Tanganyika's own heritage is sufficiently rich to provide for the future reflect in part the urgent need to establish a sense of pride and dignity so severely weakened by settler-colonialism.

*The Question of Transference*

Dr. Nyerere is not alone in his contention that there is a peculiarly indigenous African form of democracy and socialism. This thesis has been advanced by political spokesmen everywhere on the continent and has been used to justify deviation from an inherited political system as well as to bolster national and cultural identity threatened by a sensitivity to relative backwardness, colonialism, and the alien influences inherent in modernization.

There appears to be an inherent conflict in the logic of Ujamaa. While regarding traditional small-scale societies as the source of simple and egalitarian virtues, there is also a tendency to point with pride to those few traditional sociopolitical systems that were relatively large, powerful, and authoritarian. Despite this duality, frequent reference is made to "traditional society," to which is attributed such common values as egalitarianism, interdependence, communal ownership, and mutual obligation. However, at the same time that customary virtues are extolled, many of the very institutions that gave expression to these virtues are condemned and are being rapidly demolished because they are inconsistent with national unity and the development of a modern state. The new Ministry of National Culture and Youth, a direct outgrowth of Dr. Nyerere's Ujamaa, for example, encourages native dancing, art, and music, while at the same time another new institution, the Rural Settlement Commission, is completing plans to physically relocate millions of Tanganyikans and drastically reorder their social and economic life.

Not only is there a contradiction between the organizational demands of nation building and the revival of traditional culture, but it is questionable whether traditional values are in fact conducive to national development. The attributes of traditional society held by Dr. Nyerere and others to be unique—communal obligations, consensus, democratic decision making, etc.—are characteristic of most small-scale societies. But these societies tend to be highly inflexible and circumscribed. It is evident that a growing number of young Tanganyikans are rejecting communal values which tend to submerge the individual personality within the collectivity and are extolling an individualistic set of values. A Kivukoni student wrote in 1962 that Ujamaa is "mass capitalism"; by this he meant that "the freedom of the individual members of the state is highly observed. Each person on an individual basis should work under his own free will, as hard as he can and as much as he can. The yield of his work is his."[17]

Doubtless some traditional Tanganyikan societies possess certain customary virtues which, if projected to the level of the entire nation, could make a valuable contribution to national unity and development. However, there seems to be little evidence that the "attitude of mind" termed Ujamaa can be extended to the point where it could serve as the underlying ethos for a Tanganyikan nation. In most African societies, kinship is the chief determinant of one's status, role, and hence rights and obligations. Socialism, according to Dr. Nyerere, involves a feeling of responsibility toward one's fellow man in general. However, the nation-state and its subdivisions are territorial units where communal responsibilities and relationships depend not upon kinship groupings but upon a common residential area. While it may be possible to extend a sense of identification with a parochial territory to a more extensive region, it is difficult to see the extension of kinship-based obligations and consensus to a large, spatially defined nation-state. This requires an alteration not in degree but in kind.

In discussions with Tanganyikans, communications became difficult at the point where the transference of Ujamaa from the level of the community to the nation was brought up. Ujamaa among the younger generation in Chaggaland is regarded nostalgically as a respected but somewhat outmoded custom. The sense of community that led one's neighbor or relative to help build a house or cultivate a field is presently not applicable if the individual's project involves the expenditure of money and the use of permanent materials. If cement blocks and lumber are purchased to build a house or to construct a pit latrine, one is expected to hire the necessary labor. The principle of Ujamaa is applicable, however, if a Chagga sets out to build a traditional house of thatching and sticks, or to improve an irrigation furrow.

While many are aware and approve of the attempt to extend Ujamaa from the village to the nation, hardly anyone can suggest how this is to be accomplished. While it is generally agreed that the spirit of Ujamaa should penetrate the entire country, it does not seem likely or possible that this attitude of mind would or could evolve out of tribal custom.

Having questioned the logic of Ujamaa, we hasten to agree with

MacIver that sociopolitical myths are necessary for national iden-tification.[18] The people of Tanganyika are rapidly acquiring a sense of national unity, and there is ample evidence that the society is developing along socialist lines. And even if Ujamaa, as the basis of modern Tanganyikan nationalism and socialism, is a myth, it is nonetheless instrumental to the quest for national unity and modernity. In this stage of its development, Tanganyika needs a national ethos. If such an "attitude of mind" is to be effective, it must have its origins, not from alien ideas and institutions, but from the culture and soil of Tanganyika itself. If traditional soci-eties cannot supply a national ethos, the next best thing is to invent a composite culture than can; and Tanganyika will certainly not be the first country to have done so.

Tanganyika's leaders know the general outlines of the society and polity they would construct, and they realize that a modern state administered in the interests of the vast African majority depends upon a high degree of government initiative and control, not only to engineer development but to employ power to gain control of the economy currently monopolized by Europeans and Asians.

## Ujamaa—From Philosophy to Policy

The previous discussion of the variety of meanings of Ujamaa may lead the reader to conclude that Ujamaa exists only in the realm of words. While the influence of Dr. Nyerere's ideas cannot be exactly determined, it is possible to examine the significance of Ujamaa in government programs involving cooperatives, self-help schemes, "villagization," and land policy. Dr. Nyerere's public statements leave no doubt that he, for one, is guided in his sense of priorities by Ujamaa, and so long as the President of Tanganyika is in a position to direct policy, the country's development will be determined in part by that philosophy.

Let us examine three areas in which it is claimed that Ujamaa provides a guiding and underlying orientation: the cooperatives, self-help, and "villagization" and land policy.

*The cooperative movement.* It is not possible here to describe Tanganyika's cooperative movement in detail. It will suffice to note that producer cooperatives—particularly cotton and coffee—have long played an important role in the economy. In 1963 there were more than 800 societies with a membership exceeding 300,000. In

1962 hundreds of cooperatives and unions joined together to form the Cooperative Union of Tanganyika.

The way in which this multitude of local societies is directly tied to the national capital through the Ministry of Cooperatives and Community Development and the Cooperative Union illustrates the process whereby a form of modern pluralism, hierarchically controlled from the center, is replacing traditional parochial associations. It is at this general level that the strongest case can be made for the importance of Ujamaa in the evolution of modern Tanganyika. A major value implicit in Ujamaa, and one that is appreciated even by the most pragmatic nation builders, is the basic pluralism of customary society. Thus, national unity is being sought not through the systematic destruction of thousands of parochial communities and the imposition of a totalitarian state but through the development of new and nationally oriented forms of community organization which reflect the diffuse rural pluralism of Tanganyika. Tanganyika's leaders are close enough to the *shamba* (farm, countryside) to appreciate the fact that this rich mosaic of local institutions is the very essence of community order and integration. This aspect of nation building is demonstrated by the emphasis placed on cooperative development, local government, local development committees, and the more recent proposals for villagization. But there is a fundamental difference between the new and the old pluralism. Modern local institutions are related in a hierarchical fashion to the national capital, and even though Tankanyika's political system is characterized by considerable devolution of authority, control from the center has been increased. This has been accomplished not only through the concentration of fiscal and regulatory controls within the respective ministries, but also through the systematic employment of TANU in a manner resembling democratic centralism, to provide lateral control at every level. And as government and TANU are rapidly merging into a single political-administrative institution, a unique political system is unfolding.*

Since independence, the cooperative movement has struck out in new directions indicative of the influence of Ujamaa. Under British rule the cooperatives were largely limited to agricultural

---

* Overlapping party, local government, and cooperative society leadership is a common and growing feature of political life in Tanganyika.

marketing and regarded primarily as economic institutions. The post-independence period has witnessed the "nationalization" of the cooperative movement, and its extension to nearly every important sector of the economy. Even more important is a change in the "attitude of mind" regarding the cooperative movement as a social force—as the nation in the garb of producer and consumer. With considerable advice and technical assistance from the Israelis —who were among the first to combine a high degree of central control and planning with an expansion of local institutions and authority—the cooperatives have moved rapidly and vigorously into the wholesale, retail, and import business.*

COSATA (Cooperative Supply Association of Tanganyika) stores and wholesale centers are springing up throughout the country, and the combined coercive force of TANU and the government (frequently exercised by the same person) is employed to ensure the success of this venture. Public and quasi-public bodies are required, for example, to purchase their supplies and materials from COSATA. COSATA's activities are likely to be expanded in the near future to other commercial areas formerly the monopoly of the private sector. The Minister of Cooperatives and Community Development, J. S. Kasambala, visualizes that one day Dar es Salaam's Lumumba Avenue will be "a superhighway of skyscrapers, supermarkets, and banks and the nerve center of the cooperative world."[19] The public sector of Tanganyika's economy will no doubt continue to grow more rapidly than the private, and COSATA will probably emerge as the country's major importer and wholesaler. In 1962 a cooperative bank of Tanganyika was established with a number of regional branches, and in 1963 it established a national insurance company as well. Indications that COSATA would like to gain control of the marketing of Tanganyika's sugar and sisal are already apparent.

The cooperative movement was established in Tanganyika many years ago and reached a high stage of development under the colonial system. It is important to recall that the presence of hundreds of local cooperative societies served as an important and covert base for the extension of TANU organization during the

---

* The Israel Foreign Trade Corporation—Amiran—is both a member of COSATA (Cooperative Supply Association of Tanganyika) and its managing agent. The Tanganyika government invested £150,000 and Amiran £40,000. Local cooperative unions have been "encouraged" to buy shares in COSATA.

middle and late 1950's, and a close association has existed between the two organizations ever since. It would hardly be possible to expand production or initiate far-reaching changes in Tanganyika without the participation and support of the cooperative movement. Even more important is the well-recognized fact that the cooperative movement in East Africa, even under colonial rule, was employed to break the Asian monopoly over the processing of peasant cash crops. To many young Tanganyikans, the significance—in fact, the very purpose—of the current cooperative ventures into import, wholesale and resale, banking and insurance, is to gain control of the economy, to "exploit the expropriators."

*Villagization and self-help.* Acutely aware of the problems and dangers involved in disrupting thousands of relatively isolated, rural communities, Dr. Nyerere also realizes that the development of national identification and economic advancement depends in large part on the mobilization of the peasantry. TANU, the only association with a mass membership and an authority structure linking the capital city to every village, has to assume the major responsibility for prying the masses loose from parochial concerns and involving them in the processes of nation building. It was with these thoughts in mind that Dr. Nyerere in January 1962 resigned from the office of Prime Minister to give his full attention to the rejuvenation of TANU in order to prepare it for a task which he believed to be even more crucial than the attainment of independence.

It is difficult to analyze the way this problem was approached, for it has involved simultaneous changes in a variety of institutions. The authority and skill of the government were requisite but could accomplish nothing without the grass-roots organization and political support that only TANU could provide. The problem of cooperation was solved, in part at least, by the politicalization of the administration. The entire provincial and district administration was revamped, with TANU officials replacing expatriate administrators. Local government was reorganized along party lines and tightly controlled by the relevant Central Government Ministry and by the TANU-Government Area Commissioner.*

At the lower level of government chiefs, some of whom were

---

* The Area Commissioner is the ex officio TANU Area Secretary. It is expected that the marriage of TANU and the administration will be completed soon, when the TANU office is moved directly to the administrative headquarters.

also traditional rulers, there occurred the most fundamental change of all. Chieftaincy, which many observers thought to be an organic and inviolate aspect of the customary political system, was abolished almost overnight. Today there are no official chiefs in Tanganyika; they have been replaced by divisional executive officers who, in effect, are responsible to the merged TANU-government administration. Local headmen who formerly were recruited primarily by the chiefs are now elected on a TANU ticket, and in this manner the linkage of party and administration necessary for mass participation has been completed to the grass-roots level.

This new structure was assigned the task of relating local development need to national planning. Self-help schemes were launched by local party functionaries and government administrators in cooperation with community development and local government officials. Village development committees are being established in every village in Tanganyika. These committees, composed of the local TANU leader, Youth League and women representatives, and other local dignitaries, meet in newly completed community centers, which often double as TANU headquarters. A combination of traditional sanctions and TANU coercion is employed to ensure a high level of involvement. In theory each village prepares a plan, which is submitted to the area (former district) development committee for coordination and then sent on to the regional development committee and eventually to the Ministry for Development Planning. Approval for local projects is required from the area development committees (in practice, the Area Commissioner). Everyone is "asked" to work on a given day for a certain number of hours. Funds and materials not locally available but necessary to a self-help project are provided by the government.

It is not our purpose here to evaluate Tanganyika's famous self-help program. Suffice to say that despite many examples of bad planning and lack of coordination, the contribution of millions of peasants has been extraordinary.* What we are concerned with is the extent to which this mass participation is a spontaneous expression of Ujamaa. Here too we must conclude that the answer is not clear. There exists a long history of participation in communal

---

* In Njombe District alone, for example, 28 new roads of 572 miles were completed in 1962, as well as eight dispensaries, 17 schools, 58 community centers, and 151 wells.

projects. But this is based more upon a half-century of colonial experience than on indigenous native custom. Large self-help projects in which thousands of persons contributed labor to the construction of major community amenities are not new in Tanganyika, and, though it is not possible here to compare the results accurately, it is likely that communal work projects initiated before independence were of a comparable magnitude to current self-help schemes. Tanganyika's landscape, for example, is dotted with huge earth dams constructed by the people over the past 50 years. Some societies such as the Chagga possess a highly developed customary system of communal labor necessitated in large part by the complex irrigation system on the slopes of Mt. Kilimanjaro. In most societies, however, obligation for communal assistance was narrowly defined and usually involved an immediate reward in the form of food and drink.

A study of traditional Tanganyikan societies reveals few institutions wherein extensive and voluntary communal labor was undertaken without some promise of an immediate return, and though little physical coercion was employed, communal labor during the colonial era was certainly not based upon voluntary participation. Having said all this, one still cannot deny the fact that at any given moment during the day there are somewhere in Tanganyika thousands of men, women, and children swinging *jembes* (hoes) and carrying rocks and earth. Why? Two answers—neither wholly accurate and both somewhat naïve—are frequently advanced. The proponents of Ujamaa say that mass participation is the natural expression of customary obligation extended to the level of the state—in short, customary Ujamaa is expressed as modern nationalism. The critics claim that participation is based in part upon habit built up during the colonial era and even more on the application of coercion by TANU. Examples of severe coercion do exist, and an important problem has been to curb the overenthusiastic zeal of local TANU leaders who would build Tanganyika in a day. Also, people are accustomed to turning out when requested, even if coercion is neither threatened nor implied, for to many simple peasants it nonetheless lingers in the background. Furthermore, the power of TANU to command participation is supported by the authority of local governments, which can apply official sanctions if need be. It is also true that there is a somewhat less enthusiastic participation than one might be led to believe from the effective propaganda emanating from the government and

TANU. Many projects, launched with great fanfare and gusto, with flashbulbs popping as hundreds of peasants led by a Minister or Regional Commissioner sing as they wield *jembes*, remain uncompleted as enthusiasm and participation wane. However, it is just as evident that mass participation depends upon something more than traditional custom, colonial habit, and party coercion. Nationalism—an identification with the spirit or "attitude of mind" —pervades the country, and there is an obviously voluntary and enthusiastic element in self-help participation.

Villagization is the most recent as well as the most daring and ambitious program designed to maintain a high level of mass involvement while spectacularly improving the peasants' standard of living. A fundamental decision to regroup the people of Tanganyika into hundreds of new village units was made late in 1962. The program is based on the belief that, given the limited resources, sparse population, and difficult communication system, the only way to provide education, electricity, medical services, water, and other modern amenities for Tanganyika's millions is to bring them together into sizable villages. Pilot schemes in two areas are already under way. Though it is too soon to make any judgments, it is evident that Tanganyika will not be spared the human problems that have plagued every effort to redistribute and reorder the lives and habits of people, even though it be in their own interest. Villagization will involve fundamental alterations in customary institutions, and though similar revolutionary policies characterize other socialist societies, it is difficult to see how villagization is derived from or is consistent with Ujamaa. One major alteration that is needed concerns land use and tenure.

*Ujamaa and the land.* In 1962 the Tanganyika Agricultural Corporation (TAC) launched a program involving the granting of 80-acre holdings to individual farmers, with the intention of developing large-scale African commercial agriculture. This program was later shelved for fear that it would be contrary to a classless society, communal agriculture, and agricultural cooperatives.

Dr. Nyerere's statement on African Socialism, though couched in general humanistic terms, deals quite precisely with the question of land use and ownership, an important and controversial issue in Tanganyika.

And in rejecting the capitalist attitude of mind which colonialism brought into Africa, we must reject also the capitalist methods which go with it. One of these is the individual ownership of land. To us

in Africa, land was always recognized as belonging to the community.
. . . The TANU government must go back to the traditional African
custom of landholding.[20]

The land tenure proposals of the government that subsequently
developed are implicit in Dr. Nyerere's Ujamaa, and there can be
little doubt that, in this case, policy flowed directly from philosophy. The government's proposals on land were advanced almost
simultaneously with the publication of "Ujamaa."[21]

The 1963 legislation based on the 1962 White Paper, which in
turn, was previewed in "Ujamaa," effectively abolished all freehold titles and set out procedures for conversion to leasehold, as
well as outlining the obligations for development that the new
forms of tenure implied. However, this policy deliberately did not
apply to land held by Africans "under native law and custom," and
hence not regarded as freehold. The policy was designed to return
to the people of Tanganyika—with the government as their agent
—land that had been alienated by Europeans and Asians, and to
enable the government to require the leasers to develop the land
in conformity with the interests of the African majority.

Although opposition came primarily from Europeans and
Asians, who had the most to lose, there was some criticism from
African quarters as well. The lack of African unanimity on this
issue reflects the absence of a homogeneous traditional culture.
Although communal holding of land is customary in most African
societies, a wide range of variation exists with respect to land use,
security of tenure, and the loci of authority. But more important
than customary differences is the emergence over the past 50 years
of new and modern attitudes and practices. Among the coffee-
growing Haya and Chagga, the two wealthiest and most highly
developed societies in Tanganyika, individual ownership and
transfer are common. Dr. Nyerere's statements in "Ujamaa" that
freehold ownership of land must be abolished and that Tanganyika
must return to customary practices were not well received, and
many prosperous coffee growers went so far as to threaten to quit
TANU over this issue. There is some suggestion that the underlying reason why "Ujamaa" was not widely circulated or published in Swahili was fear of political consequences.

Underlying Dr. Nyerere's concerns for the maintenance of communal landownership is the desire to avoid the creation of a class
of rich farmers working privately owned lands. This notion fits
in well with the idea of a classless society, embodied in "Ujamaa."

However, attitudes toward variations in wealth and social standing differ considerably. When asked about Ujamaa, a peasant from a large tribe characterized by a relatively equalitarian social system, replied that "Ujamaa may take riches away from those outside the Ujamaa who have been using them badly and transfer them to those who have been used badly." On the other hand, Chagga and Haya respondents, possibly because of a relatively more sophisticated and hierarchical social system, or because of modern values associated with their comparative wealth and educational standards, did not feel that Ujamaa necessarily excluded social or economic differentiation. One mature, educated, and relatively wealthy respondent suggested that Ujamaa, in its modern application, is simply a way in which the poorer people who are not able to assist nation building through taxation can make their contribution. But it does not require, he added, that everyone contribute through communal labor.

In the case of land we have a situation where government policy grew directly out of Dr. Nyerere's philosophy of African Socialism. Little effective opposition was generated by the application of these principles to alienated land held by Europeans and Asians. However, the inference that these same principles might apply to Africans' holdings conflicted with deeply institutionalized but nonetheless modern attitudes toward land tenure and use.

## Some Concluding Observations

The sacrifices that Dr. Nyerere and others have made to win independence for Tanganyika were undertaken neither to enhance their own personal power nor simply to raise the living standards of the masses. The driving force behind Tanganyika's nationalism was the refusal of a rising elite, once aware of its subjugation, to tolerate a continued state of degradation for themselves and their fellow Africans. Political independence was but the first step by Africans to provide a framework with which to refashion society to achieve a higher level of material existence consistent with human dignity and imperative to the establishment of a free people.

An examination of Ujamaa in practice reveals a number of basic inconsistencies. The democratic and communal virtues of small-scale societies found throughout the world are attributed to what is considered to be a single entity, the extremely diverse and heterogeneous societies of Tanganyika. At the same time that their rustic values are acclaimed as the basis for a modern, purely African political philosophy, development programs are proceeding to dismantle the very institutions within which these pristine virtues are expressed.

These contradictions, though important, should not be permitted to conceal the real significance of Ujamaa. For it is the persistence within the new nation of Tanganyika of diverse institutions, values, and attitudes that necessitates the development of a unifying national ethos. An attempt is being made to employ Ujamaa in all its diverse meanings to effectively tap the universal spring of human strength and emotion—the desire for self-respect. *Uhuru* promised Tanganyikan Africans the self-respect that only a free people responsible for their own destiny could possess. When enthusiasm and identification began to wane, once the green and black flag had replaced the Union Jack, TANU launched a campaign of *Uhuru na Jamhuri* (Freedom and the Republic) to elicit the support of the people for removing the last vestiges of alien political control.* *Uhuru na Kazi* (Freedom and Work) to build Ujamaa was subsequently employed to involve the masses in a struggle against "ignorance, poverty, and disease." Whether or not movement toward national unity and economic development can be maintained depends upon continuing a high level of mass involvement and participation. The policy of government and party has been to fire enthusiasm with new programs and slogans at the moment that enthusiasm or emotion seems to lag. Nor is it only national development that is at stake, since, as many of the existing elite are acutely aware, TANU's very legitimacy is also in jeopardy. Unless enthusiasm and participation are maintained, disillusionment, opposition, and parochialism will likely set in. Dr. Nyerere and others are increasingly aware of the necessity of providing concrete evidence that *Uhuru na Kazi* is worthwhile— for it is apparent that without results it will be impossible to maintain present levels of involvement and participation.

To ponder at length whether Ujamaa is to be employed as a blueprint for the future or as justification and explanation for policies requisite to rapid modernization is to miss the main point, for both processes are simultaneously under way. It is possible on the basis of the style of nation building already demonstrated and

---

* The lack of enthusiasm over *Jamhuri* and the subsequent presidential election indicate that this source of involvement had about run dry.

the related "attitudes of minds" implicit in Ujamaa to make some concluding generalizations.

Ujamaa, because it is essentially a metaphysical statement of humanistic values and a condemnation of human exploitation, is sufficiently imprecise and flexible to provide justification or explanation for almost any government policy. It is unlikely that Ujamaa will confine nation building in any way to a predetermined path.

The traditional roots of Ujamaa, emphasizing face-to-face association, cooperation, brotherhood, mutual obligation, and consensus, will tend to promote the development of local institutions, and we can anticipate more rather than less pluralism in modern Tanganyika. However, the activity of the modern institutions of Ujamaa—cooperative societies, local government, TANU branches, and youth leaders—must be directed and channeled according to national needs as determined in Dar es Salaam. The nation, like the extended family, expects everyone to contribute to the general welfare, and though all members are to share in the harvest there should be no doubt as to the loci of authority.

The frequent insistence that theirs is a classless society also finds expression in Ujamaa. The inference is not that there should be no status distinctions but, rather, that society—like the extended family—is classless in that all members employ their special skills, various resources, and talents to promote the fortunes of the national community.

The philosophy of a single-party democracy can also be said to be implicit in Ujamaa. The two-party system, according to Dr. Nyerere, evolved in the West in response to competition between socioeconomic classes. But as African society is essentially classless, there is no basis for two parties. A political theory drawing its sustenance from traditional soil would require that controversy and differences as to how the general welfare might best be served be reconciled within the Ujamaa.

Ujamaa is more the product of an attitude of mind growing out of a colonial experience than it is an indigenous fountainhead of contemporary political theory. Nonetheless, it has supplied a convenient and powerful ideology which is evolving into a comprehensible, flexible, and dignified ethos for programs and policies that spring from the complex physical and psychological needs of an emergent and dynamic people.

# Appendixes

Appendix I

# A Guide to Pan-African Socialism

George Padmore

[The class struggle arises out of private ownership of the means of production. Exploitation through the utilization of the means of production did not always exist.]

Marx pointed out that the basis of all primitive social systems, such as the Greeks and Romans, at the dawn of history was common property in what was at the time the essential means of living on the land. The same is observable in all African societies prior to European penetration and the introduction of the law of real property. And because every social unit among Africans had equal rights in the soil or, to put it more correctly, no individual right in land existed, there were no distinct class privileges. Such primitive societies were, therefore, not divided into economic classes as we know them today. There were no employers or wage workers because the common ownership of land afforded to each an opportunity to gain a livelihood without selling his labor power. The social relations were for this reason those of social equality. The whole African social system arising out of and resting upon the basis of the tribal communal, or common ownership in the means of living— the land—shaped itself in agreement with that basis into a form of "primitive communism."

Social differences only appear when a people lose their communal control of the land and society begins gradually to divide into

George Padmore provided much of the organizational basis for the Pan-African movement when his home in London was an open house for African students studying abroad. Active for many years in the Communist movement, Padmore broke with it when he became convinced that the Communists sought to use colored peoples for their own ends. This essay is an edited version of an unpublished manuscript on the origins of socialism written in 1959, just prior to his death. Over two-thirds of the essay, which was addressed to Africans, was devoted to a historical sketch of Marx's thinking and to the Russian Revolution of 1917 and events afterward. We have eliminated much of this material, and present here only those sections of the original manuscript that are relevant to Africa. Some headings and synopses have been added in brackets.

classes based on property ownership, bringing about a fundamental change in social relations. . . .

[Although man's conquest of technology has permitted the development of productive forces that could solve the problem of scarcity, these forces have not been fully unleashed. Instead, the social class of capitalists exploits workers, giving rise to the class struggle.]

It is this possibility of abundance which has sharpened the struggle between the "haves" and the "have nots" throughout the world. The common people of Asia and Africa and other under-developed areas are demanding a share in the good things of life. The socialist objective, which is combined with the nationalistic awakening in these Asian and African countries, constitutes forces whose dynamism is changing the destinies of the hitherto forgotten peoples of color throughout the world. . . .

### The Anti-Imperialist Struggle

The struggle for national liberation in the colonial and dependent countries is a part of the world-wide struggle for the assertion of the exploited and dispossessed against the status quo. It can per-haps be qualified as a manifestation of the class struggle in its acutest form, since the colonial masses are the "oppressed of the oppressed"; and they instinctively see that it is only by liberating themselves from colonialism and imperialism that there will be any chance at all for them to assert their own African personality and their right to share in the abundance which the present level of economic and technological development has made possible for all to enjoy.

Even in his day, when modern imperialism was young and it was difficult to foresee the vast monopolistic form which it would take, Karl Marx already commented upon the malevolent work-ings of the colonial system and intimated that a struggle would eventually involve the millions of the darker races of Asia and Africa.

Marx predicted, too, that the struggle between the classes within European society would not by any means be a straight one, but that sometimes the working class would gain the upper hand, and at other times, the capitalist class. But the struggle was inevitable because of the economic contradictions within capitalism and the conflicting interests between the "haves" (the capitalists and imperialists) and the "have nots" (the workers in the European countries and the masses of the workers and peasants in Asia and Africa), which are irreconcilable within the existing social order. Yet, however long it might last, Marx was so confident of the ultimate victory of the working class and the colonial peoples that dogmatic emphasis upon its inevitability permeated his writings. . . .

[The Russian Revolution provides an example to Africans because so much was accomplished by it. While Africans should study the Revolution, this does not mean that we must apply information uncritically.]

It was during the years of crisis (of the civil war and foreign intervention) that the Bolshevik leaders discovered who were their real friends and allies. The expected revolution in the Western European countries, such as Germany, France, and Britain, which Marx had predicted, failed to materialize. The failure of the Western European proletariat to fulfill the Marxist expectations and thereby come to the rescue of the Russians, who had, as it were, "beaten the gun" at a time when the young struggling Soviet Republic most needed aid from outside, caused the Russian Communists to reconsider their relationship with the Socialists of the West.

[*The Russian Revolution and the Colonial Question*]

Left to consolidate the Revolution and undertake the industrialization of their bankrupt country out of their own resources and amidst the encirclement of a hostile capitalist Europe, the Russian Communists turned to Asia in the hope of undermining Western imperialism through the encouragement of colonial revolutions among the darker races from whose exploitation the European powers derived their strength.

This orientation toward Asia and Africa was a violent departure from orthodox Marxist strategy, which affirmed that the proletarian revolution which was to usher in communism would first occur in the highly developed countries of Europe and America, where there existed the economic and social prerequisites as well as an educated and cultured industrial working class who would be the architects of socialism. Never for one moment had Marx conceived that the colonial peoples in the backward countries of Asia and Africa would be more revolutionary than the white workers of Europe. . . .

Russian and Chinese practitioners of Marxism number over 800 million human beings. They make communism a force to be reckoned with seriously. It is therefore essential for us in Africa to understand the workings and objectives of Marxist philosophy so that we may see what there is in it which we may be able to adopt and bend to our own economic and social needs without accepting it wholesale as dogma. We, Africans, must not allow Western propaganda to prejudice us against the positive scientific achievements of the Russians. We may reject their political system, but we cannot ignore their scientific and technological contribution if we are to emerge from our present stagnation and backwardness. . . .

Here we are only concerned with the political consequences of Lenin's national and colonial policy as it applied to the colored races of Asia and Africa. His grand gesture of offering self-determination to the non-Russian nationalities had a tremendous psychological effect upon the backward peoples not only in Asiatic Russia but throughout the Orient. It inspired confidence in the Bolsheviks at a time when the supporters of the former regime were conducting a bitter civil war and using the territories of the Middle East in the hope of restoring Czarist power. It rallied millions of the newly emancipated colored peoples of the Asiatic borderlands of "Mother Russia" to the side of the Red Army and the young Soviet government against the White Guard aristocrats, who were receiving financial and military aid from the British and French governments in the attempt to defeat the Bolsheviks. . . .

The actual revolution had been accomplished with the minimum loss of life and bloodshed. It was only with the ensuing civil war, inspired by the counterrevolutionary aristocrats and capitalists, in which all the European nations united to crush the Revolution, that so much blood was let loose.

But all the efforts of the counterrevolution to destroy the young Soviet power and put back the Czar failed, largely because Lenin's bold anticolonial strategy paid such rich dividends. It was Stalin himself, an Asian colonial born in Georgia, who declared that but for the contributions made by the non-Russian nationalities, the Bolsheviks might not have been able to hold out against the overwhelming capitalist forces which were ringing around them, especially the foreign armies of intervention.

"It need hardly be shown," wrote Stalin, "that the Russian workers could not have gained the sympathies of their comrades of other nationalities in the West and the East if, having assumed power, they had not proclaimed the rights of the peoples, if they had not renounced their 'rights,' let us say, to Finland (1917), if they had not renounced all claims to certain parts of Mongolia and China, and so on and so forth. . . . "

It is for us, Africans, to subject Marxism to our own critical examination and see what there is in it which can be usefully applied to the conditions facing us in Africa in general and Ghana in particular.

The great mistake which so many so-called Marxists have made is to turn their master's teachings into dogma instead of using it as an intellectual instrument for understanding the evolution of human society and a guide to chart the course of future social development. No less a Marxist than the Chinese Communist leader, Mao Tse-tung, has warned his countrymen against becoming the slaves of Marxist dogmatism. "There are people who think that Marxism is a kind of magic truth with which one can cure any disease. We should tell them that dogmas are more useless than cow dung. Dung can be used as fertilizer." We, Africans, can well endorse this wise Chinese observation. . . .

[The Russian Revolution opened up enormous possibilities for the people of Russia. Present-day leaders such as Zhukov and Voroshilov came from the common people, from peasant and worker backgrounds.]

There is no need to suppose that only the so-called intellectuals and college graduates can administer the state or run an army or direct foreign affairs. Indeed, the trust that the early Communist leaders placed in the working class has been more than well rewarded forty years after the Revolution. Sputniks are concrete testimony to the quality of Russian scientists, physicists, engineers, administrators, and others, the vast majority of whom have sprung from the working class and peasant background. Russia has more than caught up with the countries of Western Europe. She has actually surpassed Britain, France, and Germany in technological advance and lags only behind the U.S.A. in certain fields of production, though the European countries had a lead of more than one hundred years in industrial development. And even the existing gap between them and the Americans, the Russian leaders claim, will be closed within the next ten years provided there is no atomic war.

The Russians also claim that this phenomenal advance could never have been achieved without socialist planning and the mobilization of the country's natural resources and labor power. The key, of course, to Russia's tremendous advancement has been electrification. Without an abundance of cheap power, the rate of industrialization and mechanization of agriculture could not have been so marked. . . .

[Padmore briefly discusses the single-party system found in the Soviet countries.]

The emergence of the Communists as the only party in Russia was largely accidental. . . .

If defection had not occurred among the anticapitalist, anti-Czarist parties of the left, following an attempt on the life of Lenin by Fanny Kaplan, a member of the Social Revolutionary Party, on August 30, 1918, it is possible that Russia might now have had a multiparty type of government in place of the present one-party system. In other words, the one-party form of state is not inherent in socialism. In fact, under true socialism, Marx asserted that the people, especially those who work by hand and brain, are supposed to be not less but much more free than under the rule of capitalism. . . .

### [The Communists and Africa]

In Africa, there are no well-organized Communist parties. On this continent, the successful nationalist movements have the support of the masses, and because of this, communism in Africa is of considerably less threat than it is in Asia, since these African nationalist movements, expressing as they do the aspirations of the indigenous populations, have cut the ground from under the Communist feet.

Communism is regarded by most Africans as just another foreign ideology emanating from Europe, a continent which has preyed upon Africa for centuries. On the other hand, Africans have had no direct contact with Russians, since Russia never owned colonies in Africa, so that all they know about the Russians and communism is through Western propaganda, which they distrust.

The revolution taking place in Africa is threefold. First, there is the struggle for national independence. The second is the social revolution, which follows the achievement of independence and self-determination. And third, Africans are seeking some form of regional unity as the forerunner of a United States of Africa. However, until the first is achieved, the energies of the people cannot be mobilized for the attainment of the second and third stages, which are even more difficult than the first. For it means the total elimination of the economic and social heritage of colonialism, such as bribery and corruption, ignorance, poverty, disease, and the construction of a society in consonance with the aspirations of the people for a welfare state with their well-being at heart.

### [What Is Socialism?]

The socialist objective is not, as certain of its opponents have made out, the leveling down of living standards, but rather their raising up, so that the majority, rather than just a minority as at present, will enjoy the benefits of the abundance which machine techniques and modern science have made possible.

Nor does socialism, as has also been contended, mean merely taking from the rich to give to the poor, for a mere redivision of the present available wealth in the hands of individuals will not satisfy to any appreciable extent the gap which now exists between the "haves" and the "have nots." The socialist objective means the scientific planning of production and distribution, through the common ownership of the basic means of production and services, so that ultimately all people regardless of race, color, creed, or social origin will be able to enjoy exactly what they want to fill their needs. But this stage, according to Marx, will not be reached until socialism evolves into full-fledged communism, which will correspond to the attainment of the classless society. At such a stage there is no privileged class which exploits others by exercising exclusive ownership over the means of production.

[Although there are many forms of socialism, there is a general philosophy that can be summarized as follows:]

1. *From each citizen according to his ability.*

2. *To each citizen according to his needs.*

3. *Equal opportunity for all citizens to give of their best to their country.*

4. *Democratically elected government of the people, by the people, for the people.*

[*The Need for an African Socialism*]

Just as the various schools of European socialism aspire to bring about on earth the good life, whereby each shall contribute according to his ability and each shall share according to his needs, we must evolve our own form of African Socialism, suited to our own conditions and historical background, so as to serve best the needs of the people of Ghana. In other words, we must not follow blindly the socialistic lines of approach which have occurred either in Western Europe or in Soviet Russia, where conditions are entirely different from those in Africa. Lenin, the architect of the first socialist state, and his party did not blindly follow Marxism in creating the instruments best suited to Russian conditions. Similarly, the African approach to socialism must be based on a policy of adaptation, while keeping constantly in mind our goal—the peaceful advance to African Socialism, which should have the following principal aims and objectives:

1. *Politically,* African Socialism shall strive to promote and safeguard popular democracy based upon universal adult suffrage (one individual, one vote, regardless of race, color, creed, or sex), fundamental human rights, social justice, and the rule of law.

2. *Economically,* African Socialism shall seek to promote and safeguard the people's well-being through the common ownership and control of the essential means of production and distribution, and ultimately the abolition of power to live by rent, interest, and profit.

3. *Socially,* African Socialism shall seek to promote and safeguard full employment by the state and performance by all citizens of work of social value according to their ability, while all citizens will share in the common resources of the nation according to their needs. Equal opportunity shall be given to all, regardless of race, tribe, color, class, or creed. Talent and character shall be the only criteria of merit in public life.

In Ghana, unlike Russia, the Convention People's Party (CPP) government have already laid the solid foundation of political democracy based upon parliamentary government, universal adult suffrage, freedom of assembly, speech, and press, as well as the rule of law. It is now up to the Ghana government to reinforce political democracy with economic democracy. This calls for planning, as it is only through planning that the CPP will be able to fulfill its election promises to the people and eradicate the main social evils facing the country—unemployment, disease, poverty, illiteracy.

But to carry out our plans in order to attain the objective of the welfare state means not only a change in the economic structure of society. The approach to planning and the carrying out of that planning call for fundamental changes in the customs, habits, and institutions of the people as well as an overhauling of their mode of thinking. All the planning in the world will not carry us forward to the "New Jerusalem" as long as those responsible for the implementation of those plans do not have a socialist approach. Thus, it is only with changes in thought and customs and approach that it will be possible to create the social mechanisms and human means which socialism and its building call for. In other words, you cannot build socialism without socialists.

It cannot be too firmly stressed that socialism is more than an economic system. It is a social arrangement whereby the people hold in common the means of production and share according to their needs in the fruits of their collective labor, that is, the goods and services which they together fashion from the productive means. In contradistinction to the capitalist system, in which each individual is out for himself only, the socialist system demands the maximum cooperation between all the members of the society, because it is this cooperation alone which will bring that abundance which will make the good life available for all in Ghana.

### [A Program of African Socialism for Ghana]

Our starting point in economic reconstruction must be the *land*, with its communal ownership and production and its element of cooperative self-help. This is the foundation stone on which we must build the new socialist pattern of society in Ghana. We may borrow ideas from America, China, India, Yugoslavia, Israel, Sudan, and elsewhere, but the actual pattern must be founded upon the African base. The agricultural sector, which is already largely in the hands of the Africans, must be raised to such a level that the condition of the farmer not only is advanced from its present subsistence level, but must be made to produce a surplus of wealth to provide the accumulation of capital necessary to pay for the importation of the machinery and technical "know-how" required for the industrial sector.

The primary aim of agriculture must be diversification to relieve the country's reliance upon its present single-crop economy—cocoa. Emphasis must first of all be upon food production, with a greater variety of foods for home consumption, so as to do away with the considerable importation of foodstuffs, which are at present such a drain on our foreign exchange resources, which could otherwise be employed for development purposes. Animal husbandry and dairy farming must be included in our agricultural planning. Increased availability of foodstuffs from our land will be effective in holding down the cost of living, which reflects positively upon the general cost of our development. For we shall not have to meet constant demands for increased wages to meet inflationary living costs.

As far as the farmer himself is concerned, he must be assured of markets for his product at agreed price levels; otherwise he will have no incentive in increasing his output. In addition to taking care of domestic needs, agricultural production must sustain our industrial development. Market research should show the way to increase our agricultural exports.

To meet these objectives, we may find that the existing agricultural and rural pattern can be adapted to more than one productive form. There is, for instance, large-scale cooperative farming like the Gezira scheme, which has been so successful in the Sudan. The United Ghana Farmers Council could here take the initiative in getting villages to clear stool lands and put them under cultivation, while the Agricultural Development Corporation (ADC) would assist with loans and technical management until the farmers are able to take over and run the enterprise themselves.

Producers' cooperatives should also enter upon the scene as the marketing entrepreneur. Another form could be that of individual farm production linked to the cooperative village center, which will be the point of collection for farm products and their subsequent distribution by the cooperative societies in the towns and other urban communities.

But whatever form is adopted, it is necessary that the village shall be the focal point of the surrounding farming community, and shall provide the social and cultural amenities which will bring town life to the countryside and thereby save the drift away from the land and the rural areas, since our industrial development must, at least for the time being, be toward small-scale rather than large-scale enterprises.

Industries must first aim at meeting domestic requirements to save importations. Where it is possible, surpluses can be provided for export to pay for welfare necessities. Ancillary industries should be linked to the products of agriculture and mining.

Because of lack of capital resources by Ghanaians and the deficiencies in technical and managerial experience, it will be necessary for government or semipublic institutions like the Industrial Development Corporation (IDC) and ADC in many cases to initiate and carry out singly or jointly with private enterprise and the cooperatives the major industrialization projects and the modernization of large-scale agricultural and husbandry schemes where these will be advantageous.

The whole aim of our economic program, agricultural and industrial, must be to move away from a trading economy to an industrial economy. African businessmen today are too tied up with merchandising; they are too concerned with distributing foreign importations instead of busying themselves with the production of consumer goods in Ghana. We want to encourage manufacturing capitalists and not wholesale and retail trading capitalists. For as long as African businessmen continue to think only in terms of selling other people's goods we shall not alter the old imperialist pattern of our economy. Only to the extent that we are able to transform the present economic structure from trade to manufacture shall we be able to progress along the socialist road to self-sufficiency and prosperity. Therefore, while government should give every encouragement to Ghanaians to enter the fields of producing essential goods and adopt positive measures to protect them from unfair competition by foreign imports, no assistance should be given to them for purely shopkeeping and trading operations.

Apart from economic planning as such, there must be technical planning. And for this, it is necessary to have a whole new educational system which, apart from the traditional educational subjects having an African perspective, will provide the human instruments for the carrying through of socialist planning. The educational system must provide more statisticians, bookkeepers, accountants, auditors, commercial legal experts, technical experts at all levels and in all branches, scientists, engineers, managers, administrators, and the rest. In this respect, we can learn much from the Russians, who have revolutionized their educational system to meet the demands of our scientific and technological age.

Moreover, the new education must be geared to producing a different kind of citizen from the one we know: one who will know his history, his background and his socialist future; his need to live in cooperation with his neighbors and to give unselfish service to his country; and the need for his country to live in unity and amity with other countries. The new citizen must be made aware of the new socialist planning and understand his part and place in the new scheme of things.

There must be capital. Nothing is possible without capital. Socialists are, in effect, the manipulators of capital free of capitalist aims; that is, they want to invest capital for social ends rather than for private profit and the exploitation of man by man. Society cannot be built without capital, but capital can be accumulated without capitalists. Ghana is rich in capital.

Ghana is rich in capital which consists of her natural resources plus her labor power. Yet we cannot escape a period of austerity in order to harness this capital for constructing our socialist pattern of society. But how to attain this austerity? We must forgo those things which are not essential by imposing heavy taxation on luxury goods. Let those who want them pay for their ostentation.

The government must use all the powers vested in it to accelerate this process of industrialization. This calls for bold planning on all fronts of our national life. It involves the complete reorganization not only of the basic foundations of our society, but of the ideas, the mental outlook, and the social habits of the people. Many prejudices and social attitudes will have to be abandoned, wasteful expenditure on funerals and weddings, and the giving and taking of "dash." The youth will have to be taught the dignity of labor. Older people will have to be taught thrift—the need to save and invest their savings in productive undertakings. Idleness will have to be condemned as a social evil. The spirit of self-help and cooperation will have to be encouraged. Bribery and corruption must be harshly punished and examples made of the most important transgressors by long terms of imprisonment and the confiscation of their property, especially in cases involving theft of state funds and property. For these are crimes against society as a whole and not just an individual.

As the first independent African nation to embark upon a program of economic planning, we must make a conscious effort to evolve new forms of socialist techniques applicable to our African environment and historical background, which may serve as a guide to other African countries when they, too, attain independence. It is, therefore, important to have convinced and dedicated socialists responsible for our socialist planning. Only through such a realistic approach will we be able to achieve our social objectives and make socialism a reality for the people of Ghana and an example to the rest of Africa.

Since the government and public corporations will have to shoulder the major responsibility for industrialization, they will need the active support and cooperation of the Ghana Trades Union Congress, the United Ghana Farmers Council, and the Cooperative Movement, representing the two most important social classes in Ghana—the industrial workers and the peasant farmers. This alliance between the real producers of the nation's wealth will enable the government, through the political guidance of the socialist-committed CPP, to mobilize the enthusiasm and dynamism of the whole people in the carrying out of the Five-Year Plan.

On the other hand, national planning must be flexible enough to draw in the participation of local as well as foreign capital interests. But these antisocialist elements must not control or direct our march toward Pan-African Socialism. Accordingly, the following sectors will have their definite functions within the Plan:

1. *State and semipublic sector*, i.e., rail, road, sea, and air transport, electricity, port authorities, etc., will represent the main socialist sector.

2. *Cooperative sector*. This will represent the semisocialist sector and should receive special assistance in order to broaden and strengthen the cooperative character of the national economy. The cooperative movement must become the main economic instrument to combat and contain the expansion of private capitalists and middlemen seeking to monopolize trade and commerce.

3. *African business sector* will aim to assist Africans in promoting industrial, agricultural, and commercial undertakings that will benefit the general national economy.

4. *Free enterprise sector*. While foreign capitalists should be encouraged to participate in productive undertakings or in providing essential services of a socioeconomic nature as will benefit the general national economy, they must be rigidly controlled and kept strictly within their allotted sector. All business dealings in usury and stock market speculation must be forbidden.

5. *Mixed state and private sector*. This mixed state-capitalist eco-

nomic sector will cover joint enterprise of government-subsidized corporations and private capital (local and foreign) under such conditions as will ultimately strengthen and broaden the socialist sector of the national economy. (The Puerto Rican government has used this form of mixed economy most successfully.)

It is only out of the wealth derived from industrialization and increased agricultural productivity that we shall be able to pay for the social services and other amenities which the CPP and the CPP government have pledged to the people. These amenities— water, electricity, roads, telecommunications, houses, hospitals and health centers, and schools—must take top priority in our next Five-Year Plan. For politics cannot be divorced from economics; as a socialist political party we must, if we want to retain the support of the masses and thereby political power, meet the immediate basic needs of the voters before the next general election.

### The Role of the Party in Development

The CPP has not only to explain the government's policy and plan to the masses. It has the task, above all, to mobilize the support of its main allies, the Trade Union Congress and the United Ghana Farmers Council, the youth, and the working women to back the economic revolution at which we are aiming, just as it did in carrying through the national revolution which has brought us independence. Both revolutions—the national revolution and the economic revolution—are interrelated, the second being dependent upon the first.

Political power has given us the possibility of planning the country's economic emancipation. Without political power, no planning would have been possible, as we know from our period of colonial dependence. But to have achieved political independence and to fail to carry the national revolution into the economic revolution would be to betray the interests of the common people and the trust which they have placed in our party. Our failure in this connection would, moreover, leave our political independence open to perpetual threat from outside imperialist pressures.

The colonialists, having been forced to concede the political power which automatically gave them control over the economic resources of our country, are concentrating upon the economic counterrevolution in an effort to restore their absolute control over us by economic means. It is for us, therefore, not only to be vigilant but to reinforce our strength by building up our economy on a socialist basis, firmly keeping under state control the basic means of production. This alone will enable us to withstand the pressures which foreign capitalists will, by all means, increasingly try to force upon us.

We must have no illusions about this battle for economic freedom, which will be even more difficult than the struggle for political freedom, since it will be more subtly and covertly carried on. Moreover, while the imperialists were able to enlist only a few reactionaries in opposing our struggle for independence, there are many Africans who are ready to assist them in keeping us economically enslaved as long as they personally get a few crumbs from the overladen table of foreign capitalism. Black capitalists are as much our enemies as white capitalists.

Our aim is economic independence on a socialist pattern, and to carry out our plan there should be in command Africans with a socialist perspective. We cannot afford to jeopardize our economic freedom by leaving its direction, and even some of its planning, in the hands of antisocialist expatriates. The first loyalty of such expatriates is to their own imperialist country and only secondarily to the government which employs them. While we may have to rely upon foreign technicians and experts until we are able to provide sufficient of our own, they will be employed just to do a specific job and not to plan and direct our economic future.

We must also be on our guard against anti-Convention People's Party African capitalist elements infiltrating into our party and using it merely as a means of enriching themselves at public expense and of corrupting our socialist ideology and distorting our economic program.

With the new Five-Year Plan which the government has recently made public, we shall be embarking upon a new epoch, the outcome of which will decide the future of Ghana and the hope of Africa. Our party, the CPP, under the leadership of Kwame Nkrumah, must be the standard-bearer of Pan-African Socialism.

Appendix II

# Ujamaa: The Basis of African Socialism

Julius K. Nyerere

Socialism—like democracy—is an attitude of mind. In a socialist society it is the socialist attitude of mind, and not the rigid adherence to a standard political pattern, which is needed to ensure that the people care for each other's welfare.

The purpose of this paper is to examine that attitude. It is not intended to define the institutions which may be required to embody it in a modern society.

In the individual, as in the society, it is an attitude of mind which distinguishes the socialist from the nonsocialist. It has nothing to do with the possession or nonpossession of wealth. Destitute people can be potential capitalists—exploiters of their fellow human beings. A millionaire can equally well be a socialist; he may value his wealth only because it can be used in the service of his fellow men. But the man who uses wealth for the purpose of dominating any of his fellows is a capitalist. So is the man who would if he could!

I have said that a millionaire can be a good socialist. But a socialist millionaire is a rare phenomenon. Indeed he is almost a contradiction in terms. The appearance of millionaires in any society is no proof of its affluence; they can be produced by very poor countries like Tanganyika just as well as by rich countries like the United States of America. For it is not efficiency of production, or the amount of wealth in a country, which makes millionaires; it is the uneven distribution of what is produced. The basic difference between a socialist society and a capitalist society does not lie in their methods of producing wealth, but in the way that wealth is distributed. While, therefore, a millionaire could be a good socialist, he could hardly be the product of a socialist society.

Originally an address by the President of Tanganyika to a conference on African Socialism held at Kivukoni College in Dar es Salaam, "Ujamaa: The Basis of African Socialism" was published in April 1962 by the Tanganyika African National Union, of which Mr. Nyerere is president.

Since the appearance of millionaires in a society does not depend
on its affluence, sociologists may find it interesting to try to find out
why our societies in Africa did not, in fact, produce any millionaires—for we certainly had enough wealth to create a few. I think
they would discover that it was because the organization of traditional African society—its distribution of the wealth it produced—
was such that there was hardly any room for parasitism. They
might also say, of course, that as a result of this Africa could not
produce a leisured class of landowners, and therefore there was
nobody to produce the works of art or science which capitalist
societies can boast. But works of art and the achievements of science are products of the intellect, which, like land, is one of God's
gifts to man. And I cannot believe that God is so careless as to
have made the use of one of His gifts depend on the misuse of
another!

Defenders of capitalism claim that the millionaire's wealth is
the just reward for his ability or enterprise. But this claim is not
borne out by the facts. The wealth of the millionaire depends as
little on the enterprise or abilities of the millionaire himself as the
power of a feudal monarch depended on his own efforts, enterprise, or brain. Both are users, exploiters, of the abilities and enterprise of other people. Even when you have an exceptionally intelligent and hard-working millionaire, the difference between his
intelligence, his enterprise, his hard work, and those of other members of society cannot possibly be proportionate to the difference
between their "rewards." There must be something wrong in a
society where one man, however hard-working or clever he may
be, can acquire as great a "reward" as a thousand of his fellows
can acquire between them.

Acquisitiveness for the purpose of gaining power and prestige
is unsocialist. In an acquisitive society wealth tends to corrupt those
who possess it. It tends to breed in them a desire to live more com-
fortably than their fellows, to dress better, and in every way to
outdo them. They begin to feel they must climb as far above their
neighbors as they can. The visible contrast between their own comfort and the comparative discomfort of the rest of society becomes
almost essential to the enjoyment of their wealth, and this sets off
the spiral of personal competition—which is then antisocial.

Apart from the antisocial effects of the accumulation of personal
wealth, the very desire to accumulate it must be interpreted as a
vote of "no confidence" in the social system. For when a society

is so organized that it cares about its individuals, then, provided he is willing to work, no individual within that society should worry about what will happen to him tomorrow if he does not hoard wealth today. Society itself should look after him, or his widow, or his orphans. This is exactly what traditional African society succeeded in doing. Both the "rich" and the "poor" individual were completely secure in African society. Natural catastrophe brought famine, but it brought famine to everybody—"poor" or "rich." Nobody starved, either of food or of human dignity, because he lacked personal wealth; he could depend on the wealth possessed by the community of which he was a member. That was socialism. That is socialism. There can be no such thing as acquisitive socialism, for that would be another contradiction in terms. Socialism is essentially distributive. Its concern is to see that those who sow reap a fair share of what they sow.

The production of wealth, whether by primitive or modern methods, requires three things. First, land. God has given us the land, and it is from the land that we get the raw materials which we reshape to meet our needs. Second, tools. We have found by simple experience that tools do help! So we make the hoe, the axe, or the modern factory or tractor, to help us to produce wealth —the goods we need. And, third, human exertion—or labor. We don't need to read Karl Marx or Adam Smith to find out that neither the land nor the hoe actually produces wealth.

And we don't need to take degrees in economics to know that neither the worker nor the landlord produces land. Land is God's gift to man—it is always there. But we do know, still without degrees in economics, that the axe and the plow were produced by the laborer. Some of our more sophisticated friends apparently have to undergo the most rigorous intellectual training simply in order to discover that stone axes were produced by that ancient gentleman "Early Man" to make it easier for him to skin the impala he had just killed with a club, which he had also made for himself!

In traditional African society everybody was a worker. There was no other way of earning a living for the community. Even the Elder, who appeared to be enjoying himself without doing any work and for whom everybody else appeared to be working, had, in fact, worked hard all his younger days. The wealth he now appeared to possess was not his, personally; it was only "his" as the Elder of the group which had produced it. He was its guardian. The wealth itself gave him neither power nor prestige. The respect paid to him by the young was his because he was older than they, and had served his community longer; and the "poor" Elder enjoyed as much respect in our society as the "rich" Elder.

When I say that in traditional African society everybody was a worker, I do not use the word "worker" simply as opposed to "employer" but also as opposed to "loiterer" or "idler." One of the most socialistic achievements of our society was the sense of security it gave to its members, and the universal hospitality on which they could rely. But it is too often forgotten, nowadays, that the basis of this great socialistic achievement was this: that it was taken for granted that every member of society—barring only the children and the infirm—contributed his fair share of effort toward the production of its wealth. Not only was the capitalist, or the landed exploiter, unknown to traditional African society, but we did not have that other form of modern parasite—the loiterer, or idler, who accepts the hospitality of society as his "right" but gives nothing in return! Capitalistic exploitation was impossible. Loitering was an unthinkable disgrace.

Those of us who talk about the African Way of Life, and, quite rightly, take a pride in maintaining the tradition of hospitality which is so great a part of it, might do well to remember the Swahili saying, *Mgeni siku mbili; siku ya tatu mpe jembe*—or in English, "Treat your guest as a guest for two days; on the third day give him a hoe!" In actual fact, the guest was likely to ask for the hoe even before his host had to give him one—for he knew what was expected of him, and would have been ashamed to remain idle any longer. Thus, working was part and parcel, was indeed the very basis and justification, of this socialist achievement of which we are so justly proud.

There is no such thing as socialism without work. A society which fails to give its individuals the means to work, or, having given them the means to work, prevents them from getting a fair share of the products of their own sweat and toil, needs putting right. Similarly, an individual who can work—and is provided by society with the means to work—but does not do so, is equally wrong. He has no right to expect anything from society because he contributes nothing to society.

The other use of the word "worker," in its specialized sense of "employee" as opposed to "employer," reflects a capitalist attitude of mind which was introduced into Africa with the coming of colonialism and is totally foreign to our own way of thinking. In the old days the African had never aspired to the possession of personal wealth for the purpose of dominating any of his fellows. He had never had laborers or "factory hands" to do his work for him. But then came the foreign capitalists. They were wealthy. They were powerful. And the African naturally started wanting to be wealthy too. There is nothing wrong in our wanting to be wealthy; nor it is a bad thing for us to want to acquire the power which wealth brings with it. But it most certainly is wrong if we want the wealth and the power so that we can dominate somebody else. Unfortunately there are some of us who have already learned to covet wealth for that purpose—and who would like to use the methods which the capitalist uses in acquiring it. That is to say, some of us would like to use, or exploit, our brothers for the purpose of building up our own personal power and prestige. This is completely foreign to us, and it is incompatible with the socialist society we want to build here.

Our first step, therefore, must be to re-educate ourselves; to regain our former attitude of mind. In our traditional African society we were individuals within a community. We took care of the community, and the community took care of us. We neither needed nor wished to exploit our fellow men.

And in rejecting the capitalist attitude of mind which colonialism brought into Africa, we must reject also the capitalist methods which go with it. One of these is the individual ownership of land. To us in Africa, land was always recognized as belonging to the community. Each individual within our society had a right to the use of land, because otherwise he could not earn his living, and one cannot have the right to life without also having the right to some means of maintaining life. But the African's right to land was simply the right to use it; he had no other right to it, nor did it occur to him to try and claim one.

The foreigner introduced a completely different concept—the concept of land as a marketable commodity. According to this system, a person could claim a piece of land as his own private property whether he intended to use it or not. I could take a few square miles of land, call them "mine," and then go off to the moon. All I had to do to gain a living from "my" land was to charge a rent to the people who wanted to use it. If this piece of land was in an urban area I had no need to develop it at all; I could leave it to the fools who were prepared to develop all the other pieces of land surrounding "my" piece, and in doing so automatically to raise the market value of mine. Then I could come down from the moon and demand that these fools pay me through their noses for the high value of "my" land: a value which they themselves had created for me while I was enjoying myself on the moon! Such a system is not only foreign to us, it is completely wrong. Landlords, in a society which recognizes individual ownership of land, can be—and they usually are—in the same class as the loiterers I was talking about: the class of parasites.

We must not allow the growth of parasites here in Tanganyika. The TANU government must go back to the traditional African custom of landholding. That is to say, a member of society will be entitled to a piece of land on condition that he uses it. Unconditional, or "freehold," ownership of land (which leads to speculation and parasitism) must be abolished. We must, as I have said, regain our former attitude of mind—our traditional African Socialism—and apply it to the new societies we are building today. TANU has pledged itself to make socialism the basis of its policy in every field. The people of Tanganyika have given us their mandate to carry out that policy, by electing a TANU government to lead them. So the government can be relied upon to introduce only legislation which is in harmony with socialist principles.

But, as I said at the beginning, true socialism is an attitude of mind. It is, therefore, up to the people of Tanganyika—the peasants, the wage earners, the students, the leaders, all of us—to make sure that this socialist attitude of mind is not lost through the temptations to personal gain (or to the abuse of positions of authority) which may come our way as individuals, or through the temptation to look on the good of the whole community as of secondary importance to the interests of our own particular group.

Just as the Elder, in our former society, was respected for his age and his service to the community, so, in our modern society, this respect for age and service will be preserved. And in the same way as the "rich" Elder's apparent wealth was really only held by him in trust for his people, so, today, the apparent extra wealth which certain positions of leadership may bring to the individuals who fill them can be theirs only insofar as it is a necessary aid to the carrying out of their duties. It is a "tool" entrusted to them for the benefit of the people they serve. It is not "theirs" personally; and they may not use any part of it as a means of accumulating more for their own benefit, or as an "insurance" against the day when they no longer hold the same positions. That would be to betray the people who entrusted it to them. If they serve the community while they can, the community must look after them when they are no longer able to do so.

In tribal society, the individuals or the families within a tribe were "rich" or "poor" according to whether the whole tribe was rich or poor. If the tribe prospered, all the members of the tribe shared in its prosperity. Tanganyika, today, is a poor country. The standard of living of the masses of our people is shamefully low. But if every man and woman in the country takes up the challenge and works to the limit of his or her ability for the good of the whole society, Tanganyika will prosper; and that prosperity will be shared by all her people.

But it must be shared. The true socialist may not exploit his fellows. So that if the members of any group within our society are going to argue that, because they happen to be contributing more to the national income than some other groups, they must therefore take for themselves a greater share of the profits of their own industry than they actually need; and if they insist on this in spite of the fact that it would mean reducing their group's contribution to the general income and thus slowing down the rate at which the whole community can benefit, then that group is exploiting (or trying to exploit) its fellow human beings. It is displaying a capitalist attitude of mind.

There are bound to be certain groups which, by virtue of the "market value" of their particular industry's products, will contribute more to the nation's income than others. But the others may actually be producing goods or services which are of equal, or greater, intrinsic value although they do not happen to command such a high artificial value. For example, the food produced by the peasant farmer is of greater social value than the diamonds mined at Mwadui. But the mineworkers of Mwadui could claim, quite correctly, that their labor was yielding greater financial profits to the community than that of the farmers. If, however, they went on to demand that they should therefore be given most of that extra profit for themselves, and that no share of it should be spent on helping the farmers, they would be potential capitalists!

This is exactly where the attitude of mind comes in. It is one of the purposes of trade unions to ensure for the workers a fair share of the profits of their labor. But a "fair" share must be fair in relation to the whole society. If it is greater than the country can afford without having to penalize some other section of society, then it is not a fair share. Trade union leaders and their followers, as long as they are true socialists, will not need to be coerced by the government into keeping their demands within the limits imposed by the needs of society as a whole. Only if there are potential capitalists among them will the socialist government have to step in and prevent them from putting their capitalist ideas into practice!

As with groups, so with individuals. There are certain skills, certain qualifications, which, for good reasons, command a higher rate of salary for their possessors than others. But here again, the true socialist will demand only that return for his skilled work which he knows to be a fair one in proportion to the wealth or poverty of the whole society to which he belongs. He will not, unless he is a would-be capitalist, attempt to blackmail the community by demanding a salary equal to that paid to his counterpart in some far wealthier society.

European socialism was born of the Agrarian Revolution and the Industrial Revolution which followed it. The former created the "landed" and the "landless" classes in society; the latter produced the modern capitalist and the industrial proletariat.

These two revolutions planted the seeds of conflict within society, and not only was European socialism born of that conflict, but its apostles sanctified the conflict itself into a philosophy. Civil war was no longer looked upon as something evil, or something unfortunate, but as something good and necessary. As prayer is to Christianity or to Islam, so civil war (which they call "class war") is to the European version of socialism—a means inseparable from the end. Each becomes the basis of a whole way of life. The European socialist cannot think of his socialism without its father—capitalism!

Brought up in tribal socialism, I must say I find this contradiction quite intolerable. It gives capitalism a philosophical status which capitalism neither claims nor deserves. For it virtually says, "Without capitalism, and the conflict which capitalism creates within society, there can be no socialism"! This glorification of capitalism by the doctrinaire European socialists, I repeat, I find intolerable.

African Socialism, on the other hand, did not have the "benefit" of the Agrarian Revolution or the Industrial Revolution. It did not start from the existence of conflicting "classes" in society. Indeed, I doubt if the equivalent for the word "class" exists in any indigenous African language; for language describes the ideas of those who speak it, and the idea of "class" or "caste" was non-existent in African society.

The foundation, and the objective, of African Socialism is the extended family. The true African Socialist does not look on one class of men as his brethren and another as his natural enemies. He does not form an alliance with the "brethren" for the extermination of the "nonbrethren." He rather regards all men as his brethren—as members of his ever extending family. That is why the first article of TANU's creed is: *Binadamu wote ni ndugu zangu. Na Afrika ni moja.* If this had been originally put in English, it would have been: "I believe in human brotherhood and the unity of Africa."

"*Ujamaa,*" then, or "familyhood," describes our Socialism. It is opposed to capitalism, which seeks to build a happy society on the basis of the exploitation of man by man; and it is equally opposed to doctrinaire socialism which seeks to build its happy society on a philosophy of inevitable conflict between man and man.

We, in Africa, have no more need of being "converted" to socialism than we have of being "taught" democracy. Both are rooted in our own past—in the traditional society which produced us. Modern African Socialism can draw from its traditional heritage the recognition of "society" as an extension of the basic family unit. But it can no longer confine the idea of the social family within the limits of the tribe, or, indeed, of the nation. For no true African Socialist can look at a line drawn on a map and say, "The people on this side of that line are my brothers, but those who happen to live on the other side of it can have no claim on me"; every individual on this continent is his brother.

It was in the struggle to break the grip of colonialism that we learned the need for unity. We came to recognize that the same socialist attitude of mind which, in the tribal days, gave to every individual the security that comes of belonging to a widely extended family must be preserved within the still wider society of the nation. But we should not stop there. Our recognition of the family to which we all belong must be extended yet further— beyond the tribe, the community, the nation, or even the continent —to embrace the whole society of mankind. This is the only logical conclusion for true Socialism.

## Appendix III

# African Socialism

## Mamadou Dia

After a year of direct experience of independence during a particularly difficult period in world history, we are able to define our attitude to certain problems.

As regards the problem of doctrine, we can now say with certainty that our ideology is that of African Socialism.

At this stage of development, in view of our efforts and our reflections, we can attempt, in a first synthesis, a definition of African Socialism, of the African road to socialism, the outline of which should now be discerned and the need for which should be affirmed. . . .

How . . . do we see African Socialism?

First of all, we wish to fit our ideological problem into a world context. As I had occasion to affirm at the U.N. General Assembly, it is within our vision of a harmonious world that we shall seek to build African Socialism, in order that it may satisfy man's present needs and his future aspirations. To be more specific, we believe that since Africa is not going to be committed to any bloc, a synthesis will be possible between individualistic and socialistic values, harmony between them being achieved in the complete human personality. This synthesis of a true socialism and a true humanism, which will rest on African reality and African values while not rejecting the enriching contributions of other cultures, will be genuinely African but will at the same time have universal importance.

Our ideology, being truly socialist, is concerned with giving back their meaning to certain fundamental principles: First of all, the requirements of the common good, which are binding on all

Extracts from a speech made by the former president of the Council of Ministers of the Republic of Senegal on April 4, 1961, at Dakar at the National Assembly on the occasion of the anniversary of Independence Day. (*Socialist International Information* [London], XI, No. 18 [May 6, 1961], 276–77.)

members of a group—the freedom to fulfill these requirements, which means that the members of the group choose to be collectively responsible for the development of their community.

Second, our ideology implies the complete development of the human personality within the group, that is, a fundamental humanism.

Our road, being that of genuine African Socialism, leads us toward the realization of this socialist society by infusing into it our African values.

We shall build our communities with the aim of promoting the common good and in the light of the lessons to be learned from our sociological structure, which abounds in healthy forms of community life, forms which we are in process of adapting to the organizational needs of our modern state.

In these communities in which our freedom, in conformity with the African genius, acquires strength and value through discussion and debate, we aim at developing a new type of man, inspired by an awareness of the world and also by a sense of the spiritual values of the forces of life whose rhythm forms our aesthetic valuation. Is this not a stirring promise of a new humanism, faithful both to Africa and to man's calling and hence the meaning of the universe? This spiritual humanism will be in harmony with the Christian as well as the Moslem way of life, for we are in a profound sense a people of believers. Our vision of the world implies the view that all believers, faced with this genuine choice, are especially called upon to argue in a fraternal spirit, in order to give the support of spiritual values to our African Socialism which is not a scholastic theory but a vital challenge and hence also an ethic and an obligation.

We for our part can discern that, within this new synthesis, the old categories of idealism—Marxism, materialism, and liberalism—lose their meaning and their interest.

Thus our Negro blood is for us no longer the banner of revolt: it now enriches our revolution.

Appendix IV

# African Socialism

Tom Mboya

The word "socialism" is so much in current use that it is worth pausing a little while to inquire what this popular word means. Here in Africa we have states and statesmen wedded to the idea of "African Socialism" as the goals of the economic and social policies of their governments. President Nkrumah of Ghana has declared that the establishment of "African Socialism" is the target of his government. Over in Asia the ruling Indian Congress is pledged to establish a "Socialistic Pattern of Society" in India.

What is socialism and what is African Socialism and what does it mean to us in terms of our short- and long-term objectives in economics and politics?

Before answering these questions I would like to take a short detour and examine the basic facts about the current African political situation. I am doing this because I am convinced that only by putting it in its temporal context will it be possible for us to understand fully the nature and significance of this term "African Socialism."

Today Africa is experiencing a critical social, political, and economic transition. We are emerging from colonial rule to political independence; we are immersed in a massive transition in which we are seeking new identities at personal, national, and international levels. Africans are struggling to build new societies and a new Africa and we need a new political philosophy—a philosophy of our own—that will explain, validify, and help to cement our experience. In and around the world today there are millions of people and hundreds of nations engaged in a similar venture; the aims they have in view are not very different from our own, but we differ in tradition and background; their position and perspective vis-à-vis the challenge to be faced is not the same as we have.

This article, written when Mr. Mboya was Minister of Labor of Kenya, is reprinted from *Transition*, VIII (March 1963), and may not be reproduced in any other form without prior permission.

We are thus cast for our own role, and we either live up to it or not.

We have already made very positive beginnings, for in the concept of Pan-Africanism, with its insistence on African brotherhood, nonalignment vis-à-vis ideological power blocs, the African personality, democracy, etc., we have a set of values and beliefs which give meaning and direction to our political demands and objectives.

You all know that Pan-Africanism is a movement based on our common experience under the yoke of colonialism and is fostered by our sense of common destiny and the presence of traditional brotherhood. I strongly believe that in the field of economic relations we can similarly be guided by the traditional presence of socialist ideas and attitudes in the African mental make-up. When I talk of socialist attitudes those of us who have grown up under the intellectual climate of the Western world will no doubt be thinking of socialism of the Western type. There are, of course, others who will be thinking in terms of a Marxian brand of socialism. As a matter of fact, there is such a tragic orgy of confusion in parts of this continent over this and other concepts that I do wish our people would sit back and think for themselves a little bit. We have Africans who call themselves socialists—"African Socialists"— but if you scrutinize their thought processes you discover that they are so blindly steeped in foreign thought mechanics that in their actions they adopt standards which do great violence to the concept of African brotherhood. These so-called "socialists" peddle and parrot foreign slogans and allow themselves to be swept away by emotions which have nothing to do with the noble aspirations of our people. It appears to me that although Africa is getting rid of Western colonialism and is still fighting against its hangover, known as neo-colonialism, there is yet another fight to be waged— the fight against intellectual imperialism. This fight must be waged now, side by side with the fight for economic independence. It is because of this stark reality that I value the concept of "African Socialism" so much.

When I talk of "African Socialism" I refer to those proved codes of conduct in the African societies which have, over the ages, conferred dignity on our people and afforded them security regardless of their station in life. I refer to universal charity which characterized our societies and I refer to the African's thought processes and cosmological ideas which regard man, not as a social means, but as an end and entity in the society.

### The Organic Tradition

It might be argued from what I have just said that African Social-ism stands in a class by itself. This is not true. The basic tenets of socialism are universal and we are either socialists by these basic principles or not at all. I have said earlier that socialism is a mental conditioning or an attitude of mind established in order to achieve rational relationship and harmony in the society. In the Western socialist tradition, this mental attitude has taken roots from the thoughts and experiences of the people dating back to ancient times. It began with Aristotle's dictum that man is a social (politi-cal) animal which has no potency and no life outside the society. From this dictum has risen a host of economic, social, and political thoughts. For example, because man is a social animal his eco-nomic plight and destiny are bound up with the functions of the society in which he lives. Therefore every member of a society has certain obligations to the society in which he finds himself, and conversely, every society has certain responsibilities toward its members. Also, it occurred to those people that the society is an organic thing with individuals playing the role of cells in the organism. From this premise the interdependence of members of the society has been inferred. Thus in the society the rich are rich mainly because the society has made it possible; similarly the poor are poor mainly because the society has made it possible. Therefore if, in any society, a group of individuals control the land, capital, skills, and other means by which members of the society make a living, and if they use these means to achieve selfish ends, then an abnormal situation develops in the social organism. The society being an organic thing, if any groups own and control the means by which the others live, the latter literally become slaves, for "he owns me who owns the means by which I live." Furthermore, by constitution, the society is organic and no member of it is inde-pendent enough to stand on his own—as a matter of fact "no man is good enough to be another man's master." Therefore, the best and the most rational way of running a society is to do so in such a way that there is equality of sacrifice in all walks of life, and in such a way as to give to each according to his needs and take from each according to his ability.

This is why in the general concept socialism stands for equality of opportunity, security of income and employment, equality before the law, the rule of law, individual freedom, universal franchise, state regulation of economic life, state control of vital means of production and distribution, etc.

## Sons of the Soil

In the African tradition we find an attitude of mind which very closely approximates these which I have just mentioned, though they spring from a different stimulation and premise. In Africa the belief that "we are all sons (and daughters) of the soil" has exercised tremendous influence on our social, economic, and political relationships. Arising from this belief are the logic and practice of equality because "we are sons (and daughters) of the soil." Also, arising from the same belief is the practice of communal ownership of the vital means of life—the land. The hoe became the symbol of work, every able-bodied male and female worked. Laziness was not tolerated and there were appropriate social sanctions and ethics to encourage hard work and industriousness. Poverty existed but it was not due to man exploiting man. The social, cultural, and economic gap between the rich and the poor was not great, partly because wealth *per se* did not confer, as such, social and political power on the wealthy people as it does under Western society, and because the operation of kinship helped to spread out the income of the wealthy. There was equality of opportunity—everyone had land and hoe at the start of life. The acquisitive instinct, which is largely responsible for the vicious excesses and exploitation under the capitalist system, was tempered by a sense of togetherness and rejection of graft and meanness. When I think of African Socialism I also have in mind those ideals and attitudes of mind in our tradition which have regulated the conduct of our people with the social weal as the objective. I think it is worth while emphasizing the fact that these ideals and attitudes are indigenous, and that they spring from the basic experience of our people here in Africa and even here in Kenya. It was not difficult to learn and practice them because they were expressed in the language of the soil, which our people understood, and not in foreign slogans. They represented an honest attempt to do and practice what was in the best interests of the African.

What, then, is the significance of these attitudes vis-à-vis our aims in the economic and political fields in Kenya?

### The Kenya Destiny

In Kenya, as in the other East African countries, we are committed to one economic destiny, based on an East African Common Market, harmonized financial, fiscal, and social policies, etc. The objective of the common approach of the policies themselves is the achievement and maintenance of the highest possible rate of increase in the standard of living of all our people, the creation of the necessary conditions to this end and the enhancement of freedom and maintenance of order. I would like to submit that without basic loyalty to Kenya and East Africa, the achievement of these objectives can be an impossible proposition. In this respect I would like to point out that the positive attitudes I have just mentioned provide the best mental and human framework in relation to these aims. If we have accepted the challenge of development it would be a contradiction if we adopted conflicting attitudes.

Under the guidance of our socialist tradition I would like to see the Kenya of today transform itself along the following lines.

Since over three-quarters of Kenya's population depends on agriculture and since agriculture is the largest single contributor to Kenya's gross domestic product, the expansion and modernization of agriculture and relative production must be given priority with three aims in view—first, to expand the employment base and provide more food for the country's population; second, to diversify our export crops and expand their production to enable the country to earn more foreign exchange, as it is these earnings which will determine to a large extent the volume of imports which can be made available for economic development in other sectors; third, to accelerate rural development; fourth, to lay the foundation for industrialization by expanding the domestic market through processing, for export, most of the primary products which we now export in the raw state and through manufacturing for the East African market.

Up to now Kenya's agriculture has depended mainly on European settler capital, skill, and enterprise based on unequitable land tenure. We must rapidly move away from this type of development. Our current experience shows that this concentration on European agriculture (and on the few Asian-owned plantations), together with the concentration of primary industries in Nairobi and in the settled areas, is responsible for the serious problems we are facing today. Today Kenya is facing balance-of-payment difficulties; the employment structure of our country is unequal and unstable; urbanization is growing apace and there is haphazard human movement in the country; the discrepancies in the living standards of urban and rural people are widening and there is widespread frustration and social dislocation. We must do something immediately to harmonize the progress of various sectors of our economy and to involve the bulk of our working force in the task of economic and social development. We must stop the present underutilization of our rural labor; the present low land and labor productivity prevailing in our rural areas has to be done away with and our rural folk must be helped to live decently. There are several measures we must adopt to achieve these goals—we must encourage better farming methods to start with; we must promote and finance greater investments in agriculture to achieve more rapid progress; we must invest in irrigation, flood control, land reclamation, provision of agricultural machinery and equipment, research, and improved communication. The devastating droughts and floods of last year have taught us a lesson for they hit our poor rural people harder than anybody else. Side by side with the above measures all efforts must be made to extend vocational training to our agricultural labor force. Agricultural cooperatives must be encouraged, and land reforms, aiming at increasing efficiency of agriculture, to secure social justice and promote economic development must be launched. In doing all this we must exploit to the full the experience and knowledge already in the hands of our farming communities and augment it with all kinds of agricultural research.

Agricultural development alone is not enough. The development of trade and industry must be accorded second highest priority and the aims of our policy in this respect must be to encourage the establishment and growth of industries which would contribute directly and materially to economic growth and to enable our people to participate increasingly in the ownership, direction, and management of our industry and trade.

There are various ways in which we can achieve these aims; our government should participate directly in the vital industrial undertakings; it should provide funds for training local entrepreneurs and to enable them to participate in industry. Our government should establish a Development Bank to offer loans to industries and to organize the flow of foreign capital. The government should provide services—research, etc.—to industries. Last, through fiscal policies, social legislation, and appropriate monetary policies, the government should stimulate private investment while at the same time offering the wage earners and primary producers security of income and employment.

In order that agriculture, industry, and trade may bear fruit, we must have a transport system which coordinates their functions. To begin with, our investment in transport must aim at eliminating wasteful arguments between road transport and railway, etc. Second, roads should be realigned in pursuance of a policy of balanced regional development. The educational policy should aim at two targets—first, to expand the rate of literacy and deepen the sense of our Kenya and East African citizenship; second, to provide and improve the quality of manpower needed for rapid development. This calls for the expansion of educational facilities at all levels—primary, secondary, and technical education, teacher-training and university education. In the fields of health we should tackle the problem in various directions. Health education should be promoted, more doctors and nurses should be trained; there should be more collaboration with the other East African countries in the field of research. Of course, more capital will have to be spent on putting up more hospitals and clinics. Each district should have a well-equipped hospital to help reduce overcrowding in the major hospitals. Mobile health teams for the rural areas should be established, and so on.

### Group Responsibilities

There is no end to what our government can do to promote rapid development. But government alone cannot be entrusted with this heavy task. I have pointed out that in African Socialism the society has an obligation too. In the African society of today (and tomorrow) there are several groups of people, i.e., intellectuals, businessmen, journalists, cooperatives, trade unions, etc. These groups can and should play their part in the development of the country. I have already outlined elsewhere what I think should be the role of the press and journalists in a developing country like Kenya.* I have a few words to say about the other groups. I begin with the intellectuals. Our intellectuals face a grave challenge; I hope they

* See *Transition*, IV.

realize it. I have already pointed out that foreign orientation—Eastern or Western—is artificial; we have a tradition and a human base on which to build a philosophy of life. I have already pointed to the socialist outlook in our tradition. Will the intellectuals pick up the threads and help us defeat intellectual imperialism? The challenge of developing Kenya needs well-trained intellectuals and technicians who are also interested in politics whatever their professional expertise; it needs shrewd economists and sharp-witted, actively inquiring minds with a sense of responsibility—people who can help us to separate the realities of development from the wild dreams of men in travail—men with practical acumen and a strong devotion to the well-being of our country, which stops short of doctrinarianism and fanaticism. Will these be forthcoming?

Now for our businessmen. This group of people are needed to share in the task of development as industrialists and in commerce both in the rural and urban areas. But will they evolve business ethics suitable to this situation while at the same time adhering to the standards of efficiency, initiative, and thrift which will enable them as a group to help Kenya make the maximum use of its resources in the context of economic planning? Will they contribute toward the establishment of industrial democracy?

The trade unions have a duty too. The wage earner has a vital stake in the whole development of Kenya, and the desire of organized workers of Kenya to play a decisive role in the economic development of the country is worthy of encouragement. Workers as workers know best where the shoe pinches; our trade unions should be independent enough and should enjoy freedom of association to defend the interests of their members. But as we are committed to economic planning, our unions must perform their functions while observing certain obligations. In this context the cooperation of the trade unions should be called for to accelerate the process of capital formation and to lay the foundations of industrial development. The crucial factor is leadership. If our unions are led by patriotic, intelligent, and dedicated men who understand the long- and short-term economic implications of the policies of the unions, then all will be well. I know that trade union leadership, like political leadership, confers power on the leaders, but in the context of African Socialism power—all power—must be used for the good of the society.

To return to my thesis, I would like to submit that the challenge we face demands one loyalty and a unified approach. In view of this I would like to remind you of the superiority of traditional African Socialism. It gave members of the society a secure and relatively adequate livelihood, and it gave them a full opportunity to share in the making of the conditions upon which their happiness depended. Each member of the society was able, by his own and by collective efforts, to produce for himself the means of self-fulfillment. I commend it to you and to our people in our search for means of rationalizing and humanizing our efforts to plan our society for economic and social growth.

Let us go abroad to ask for loans and technical skills, not for ideals and ideologies. We must come forward ready to build from our own resources, energy, and sweat the Africa of our own vision and dreams, and not the blueprints of the West or the East.

Appendix V

# Some Aspects of Socialism in Africa

Kwame Nkrumah

The paramount task before the newly independent nations of Africa is the raising of an equitable and progressive social order which will provide food, clothing, and shelter to meet the needs of the people in accordance with their means; a social order that will reflect a higher standard of living in the happiness of our people.

Economically, this means full employment, good housing, and equal opportunity for educational and cultural advancement up to the highest level possible for all the people. In concrete facts, it means *that the real income of all types of workers, farmers, and peasants must rise; that prices of goods must not overleap wages; that house rentals must be within the means of all groups; that educational and cultural amenities must be available to all the people.*

If ability to pay is the passport to the good life, then at this time most of the people of Africa are precluded from it.

## War on Poverty

Unless those of us who have responsibility for leading the people make good our economic and social program, then most of the African people are doomed to perpetual exclusion from the good life, and the purpose of our effort is defeated.

In this tremendous task of bringing our peoples forward out of poverty, the whole of our nation—civil servants, all types of workers, teachers, farmers, peasants—indeed, all able-bodied men and women, must stand together as one man.

*How are we to achieve our goal within the shortest possible time?*

My assertion is that socialism is the only pattern that can within the shortest possible time bring the good life to the people. For

Reprinted from an article by the President of Ghana in *Pan Africa* (Nairobi), April 19, 1963, pp. 13–14.

socialism assumes the public ownership of the means of production—the land and its resources—and the use of those means for production that will bring benefit to the people.

### Socialist Production

Socialist production is production of goods and services in fulfillment of the people's needs. It is not production for individual private profit, which deprives such a large section of the people of the goods and services produced, while their needs and wants remain unsatisfied.

One point, however, we have to get clear. Here in Africa, not only do the people as yet not own all the major means of production and distribution, but we have to lay the actual foundations upon which socialism can be built, namely, the complete industrialization of our continent.

*All talk of socialism, of economic and social reconstruction, is just empty words if we do not seriously address ourselves to the question of basic industrialization and agricultural revolution, just as much as we must concentrate on socialist education.*

Secondary industries are vitally necessary, for it must be one of our principal aims to replace imports of foreign goods by home-produced goods.

Moreover, secondary industries must be planned to take up the production of our agriculture and to widen the outlets for the output of our farmers and peasants.

But secondary industries, important as they are to making us economically independent, will still leave us heavily reliant upon outside sources and skill unless we build up those heavy industries which alone provide the fundamental basis of industrialization.

Such projects as the steel-producing plant, the oil refinery, and the machine tool plant which we are planning in Ghana, as well as the Volta and Bui electrification schemes, are capital projects in the real sense of the term.

### Energy Is the Key

Energy is an indispensable element in industrialization. Without energy we cannot lay the foundations of industrialization. Industrialization presupposes electrification. Indeed, it is our lack of vital sources of energy that has been preventing us from carrying into effect so many of our ideas and plans for reconstruction. We could not even talk about a steel plant until we could envisage energy for working it.

Hence our preoccupation in Ghana with the Volta River Project and other schemes that will provide water power both for electricity and for irrigation of regions that are starved of water at certain periods of the year. These schemes and projects are an essential key to our industrial progress, the basis upon which we may build up our heavy industries, our machine-tool factories, and our ancillary manufactures.

As long as we are unable to make our own machine tools, the instruments for the manufacture of all the myriad commodities, large and small, we at present import, we shall continue to be at the mercy of outside sources of supply. We shall continue to be economically dependent and all talk of socialist progress will be so much empty chatter.

### Basic Development

To implement our objective of basic economic reconstruction, we must earmark a much larger proportion of our revenue to the erection of basic industries and the multiplication of our agricultural products. We must try and establish factories in large numbers at great speed and see to it that there is a quick development of electricity and water supplies.

And here a revolution is needed in our approach to planning. Unfortunately, too much planning has been largely piecemeal and unpurposeful. It has not been linked in an organized manner. Too many governmental and semigovernmental bodies and departments have been concerned in the drawing up and executing of plans. What we need are not reports, but plans of action.

### Take Stock of All Resources

If our planning is to be a revitalizing force, increasing our productivity and progress toward the socialist objective, it must take stock of all our human and natural resources; it must count our economic assets. We must make an inventory of our natural, mineral, and agricultural heritage; we must number our manpower and our actual and potential reservoir of skills.

This means that everything we do must be related to an overall plan. Educational, social welfare, and health programs, for example, cannot be devised in isolation. They must be planned in rela-

tion to the needs of our health development and the enhancement
of the lives of the people. Plans for these sectors must be coor-
dinated with plans for the economic sphere. For economic expansion needs urgently the output of the schools, the technical institutes, and the universities.

*Above all, our economic advancement must be the foundation
upon which to erect an equitable and happy society.*

Our planning must aim at a twofold purpose: to increase productivity and to accumulate capital for the expansion of industrialization. Development should be financed more and more from
production, which should be targeted, and less and less from taxes
and dues, which make heavy demands on those sections of the
community least able to afford them.

Our increased productivity can give surpluses for reinvestment
in further production and in this way increase real wealth.

To raise wages without securing higher rates of productivity is
to set in motion the vicious circle of a great volume of money
chasing scarce goods and resulting in inflation. Increased productivity, coupled with socialist planning, will permit the control of
prices and the circulation of goods in the community interests.

It does not mean that every advance in productivity will lead
to an immediate enhancement of standards of living. This is especially the case in the early stages of industrialization, when the
need to plow back capital achieved out of greater productivity is
of paramount importance more to the strengthening of the economic base than to consumer goods.

### A Question of Priorities

The socialist objective implies the overall good of all the community and in the interests of that socialist objective it may be necessary for everyone to forgo some small immediate personal benefit
for the greater benefit a bit later on. Social services in the interest
of the community, for instance, confer more advantages upon a
great number than would increased wages for certain groups of
workers.

But as productivity rises appreciably and the socialist base of the
economy extends through the increasing public ownership of the
means of production—the land and its natural resources, the factories and their production—a government not only can mobilize
greater surpluses of capital in the best interests of the country, but

can also reach a position from which it can reward labor for its greater exertions by increased wages.

## New Outlook Necessary

And because the government, through its planning, can at the same time operate controls upon commodity prices, labor will feel a double benefit in a wage increase which will not be eaten up in higher prices as under a capitalist economy.

*If this new economic and industrial policy is to succeed, there must be a change of outlook in those who are responsible for running our affairs. They must acquire a socialist perspective and a socialist drive keyed to the socialist needs and demands. They must not remain the servants of a limping bureaucracy.*

The executives of our public and statutory organizations must achieve a new attitude toward their jobs, which they owe to the struggles of the people and the labor of the farmers and workers.

In Africa, too many public corporations, such as industrial and agricultural development corporations, are at present being subsidized instead of producing profit for further capital investment.

This state of affairs must be reversed. For no economy, least of all the young economies of Africa, struggling to find a stable economic base, can afford to drain its resources in subsidizing unproductive ventures from which only well-paid executives profit.

Moreover, we cannot afford to waste our resources in men and materials in this way, but must use them wisely in pursuit of our aim of socialist benefit for all the people.

We must educate our men of affairs in their responsibilities in the conduct of the establishments to which they have been assigned.

## This Is the Next Battle

Our task does not end with political independence. Independence requires a new approach to economic and industrial development, and every avenue of information and education must be used to stir the political consciousness of the people and make them alive to the new objectives.

Without the support of the masses of the people, our plans can fail. The people need to be stirred to a new awareness of their role in carrying forward the socialist reconstruction. They must be inspired with the same spirit which swept them into the battle for political emancipation which brought them into independence.

## Appendix VI

# African-Style Socialism

## Léopold Senghor

Among the values of Europe, we have no intention of retaining capitalism, not in its nineteenth-century form at least. Of course, private capitalism was, in its early days, one of the factors of progress, just as feudalism was in its time, and even colonization. . . .

Today it is an out-of-date social and economic system—like federalism, like colonization. And, I would add, like the imperialism in which it found its expression. Why? Because if, with its specializations, the collectivization of work constitutes a critical step toward *socialization*, the defense or, more exactly, the extension of private property does not lead in this direction. Just as serious is the alienation, in the material realm and the realm of the spirit, of which capitalism is guilty. Because capitalism works only for the well-being of a minority. Because, whenever state intervention and working-class pressure have forced it to reform itself, it has conceded only the minimum standard of living, when no less than the maximum would do. Because it holds out no prospect of a fuller being beyond material well-being. . . .

But our socialism is not that of Europe. It is neither atheistic communism nor, quite, the democratic socialism of the Second International. We have modestly called it the *African Mode of Socialism* . . . Mr. Potekhin, the Director of the African Institute in Moscow, in his book entitled *Africa Looks Ahead*, gives the following definition of the fundamental traits of the socialist society. The state's power is vested in the workers. All means of production are collective property, there are no exploiting classes, nor does one man exploit his fellow; the economy is planned, and its essential aim is to afford the maximum satisfaction of man's material and spiritual needs. Obviously we cannot withhold our support from this ideal society, this earthly paradise. But it still has

Extracts from a lecture the Senegalese President delivered in 1961 at Oxford. Reprinted from *West Africa*, November 11, 1961.

to come about; the exploitation of man by his fellow has yet to be stamped out in reality; the satisfaction of the spiritual needs which transcend our material needs has to be achieved. This has not yet happened in any European or American form of civilization, neither in the West nor in the East. For this reason we are forced to seek our own original mode, a Negro-African mode, of attaining these objectives, paying special attention to the two elements I have just stressed: *economic democracy and spiritual freedom.*

With this prospect before us, we have decided to borrow from the socialist experiments—both theoretical and practical—only certain elements, certain scientific and technical values, which we have grafted like scions onto the wild stock of Negritude. For this latter, as a complex of civilized values, is traditionally *socialist* in character in this sense; that our Negro-African society is a classless society, which is not the same as saying that it has no hierarchy or division of labor. It is a *community-based society*, in which the hierarchy—and therefore power—is founded on spiritual and democratic values: on the law of primogeniture and election; in which decisions of all kinds are deliberated in a Palaver, after the ancestral gods have been consulted; in which work is shared out among the sexes and among technico-professional groups, based on religion . . .

Thus, in the working out of our African Mode of Socialism, the problem is not how to put an end to the exploitation of man by his fellow, but to prevent it ever happening, by bringing political and economic democracy back to life; our problem is not how to satisfy spiritual, that is cultural needs, but how to keep the fervor of the black soul alive . . .

Scientific research, planning, and cooperation sum up exactly the program which my country, Senegal, has just put into action, the moving force being Monsieur Mamadou Dia, the Prime Minister. Our first four-year plan is under way with its research institutes, its state banks, its state enterprises, its produce marketing boards, its cooperatives, which now comprise 80 per cent of the peasants, who themselves form 70 per cent of the total population. All this was preceded by a social and economic survey, which took more than 18 months to complete.

And yet we have not legally suppressed private capitalism which is foreign to our country; we have not even nationalized anything. Above all, we have not shed a single drop of blood. Why? Because we began by analyzing our situation as an underdeveloped and colonized country. The essential task was to win back our national independence. Next we had to eliminate the flaws of colonial rule while preserving its positive contributions, such as the economic and technical infrastructure and the French education system. Finally, these positive contributions had to be rooted in Negritude, and fertilized at the same time by the socialist spirit to make them bear fruit. They had to be rooted in Negritude by a series of comparisons between existing systems. Where private capitalism comes into peaceful competition with socialism, the latter must, I feel sure, emerge triumphant, provided that it transcends the goal of mere well-being, and does not secrete hatred. In the meantime, we need capital, even from private sources. Our aim is to fit it into the development plan, by controlling its use.

At this point we part company with the socialist experiments of Eastern Europe, with Communist experiments, while taking over their positive achievements. I spoke earlier of the living experience of a re-won freedom. To the list of needs which the plan must satisfy, I might have added leisure. This is how research, planning, and cooperation transcend, in their essence, the objective of material well-being. Science, by which I mean the quest for truth, is already a spiritual need. As is that rapture of the heart, of the soul, which art expresses, art which itself is only the expression of love. These spiritual needs, which weigh so heavy in Negro-African hearts, were touched on by Marx, as by Mr. Potekhin; but Marx did not stress them, nor did he fully define them.

Appendix VII

# Documents on Socialism and Private Enterprise in Ghana

## 1. *The Socialist Basis for Ghana's Seven-Year Plan*\*

Ghana has chosen the socialist form of society as the objective of her social and economic development. This choice is based on the belief that only a socialist form of society can assure Ghana a rapid rate of economic progress without destroying that social justice, that freedom and equality, which are a central feature of our traditional way of life.

Our socialist policy is based on certain fundamentals, which include the following:

(i) The economy must be developed rapidly and efficiently so that it shall, within the shortest time possible, assure a high rate of productivity and a high standard of living for each citizen based on gainful employment.

(ii) The income from our physical assets and from the labor of our people applied to these assets year by year must be utilized for socially purposeful ends. Never must public want and private affluence be allowed to coexist in Ghana. And among the most important ends that the community must provide for out of its incomes should be the education and welfare of its children, and the continued expansion of the economy itself.

(iii) The community through its government must play a major role in the economy, thus enabling it to assure the maintenance of a high level of economic activity, the provision of adequate employment opportunities, the equitable distribution of the nation's output, and the availability of the means of satisfying overriding social ends.

The building of a socialist society is not an easy task. In other

\* Extracts from Ghana, *First Seven Year Development Plan* (Accra: Office of the Planning Commission, 1962), pp. 1–4.

countries the progress toward socialism has not been smooth or rapid—even the pioneers in this enterprise are still in the process of building socialism. The path that Ghana chooses toward socialism must be one that will lead us at the end to a prosperous and just society.

In order to ensure that Ghana's progress in the construction of a socialist form of society shall be as speedy and efficient as possible, the correct transitional arrangements must be made based upon objective consideration. Government has therefore decided as follows:

(i) During the transition to a socialist form of society the economy of the country will remain a mixed economy, in which public and private enterprise will each have a legitimate, recognizable, and very important contribution to make toward economic growth. In this and subsequent development plans separate tasks will be clearly assigned to public and private capital in the field of both productive and nonproductive investment.

(ii) Under the mixed economy system conditions must be preserved in which both public and private investment can fulfill their assigned tasks. The plans for national economic development will assign tasks which must be fulfilled by each sector if the momentum of progress toward the ultimate objective of a prosperous Ghana is to be maintained. Any suggestion that vigorous state and private sectors within the same economy are incompatible is historically incorrect. Ghana's policies will be so designed as to obtain the maximum contribution from each sector toward the overall growth of the economy.

(iii) The government will actively encourage the voluntary association in cooperative societies of farmers and those engaged in small-scale manufacturing and service industries. In this way they will be able to have access to capital resources and technical assistance much more readily than will be possible if they continue as individual operators.

The building of socialism imposes especially heavy responsibilities on the state in the field of economic policy and development. In order to ensure that Ghana makes significant progress toward building a just and prosperous socialist economy during the next twenty years the government will observe certain constants in its expenditure pattern:

(i) The financial resources of government will be used conscientiously for the provision of employment opportunities through productive investment as they are used for the provision of social services and other items of public consumption. As the state finances each year out of budget surpluses a large proportion of the productive investments made in the country, the economy will become progressively socialized until by the end of the transition period the state will be controlling on behalf of the community the dominant share of the economy. This would have been accomplished without our ever having to resort to such expedients as nationalization, which, if carried out with full compensation, would only change the ownership of the means of production without adding to productive capacity or employment opportunities, and, if carried out without such compensation, would inevitably incur such a large measure of hostility as to make our development plans very much more difficult to achieve.

(ii) These productive investments of the state must be concentrated on the most strategic sectors of industry and agriculture, thus giving the state control over essential supplies and the vital springs of economic activity while at the same time laying foundations for the further growth of the economy.

(iii) The projects chosen for state investment must contain in large proportion those with high rates of return and short payoff periods. Only thus can we ensure that the investable resources in the hands of the state will grow rapidly, thereby enabling the state to extend further its participation in economic activity without having to impose intolerable increases in the burden of taxation falling on the people.

(iv) State enterprises will be expected to make a contribution to the public revenues within a reasonable time, and they should not be allowed to become a permanent liability to the economy: enterprises which make losses indefinitely represent a waste of both capital and current labor resources. Successful enterprises can only be run by competent managements and disciplined labor force.

(v) The state's economic activities must never take such a form as to hinder the citizens' own efforts to help themselves. In the provision of communal services, of housing, and of employment opportunities, the more individual or local efforts that are successful the less need will there be for the state to borrow money or to increase the levels of taxation for the same purpose and the less social tension will be generated. Such enterprise whenever possible will be directed through collective and cooperative channels. Individual and cooperative effort of this sort is an integral part of the Ghanaian way of life and is compatible with our socialist principles. Government will devise a system of taxation to prevent excessive inequalities in society. This ceiling will be low enough to rule out undue affluence without being so low as to discourage individual effort. The more private investment in Ghana is contributed by our own people the less will Ghana be indebted to, or dependent upon, foreigners of all sorts, and consequently the greater the degree of her real independence will be.

## 2. The Five Sectors of the Economy*

In planning our industrial expansion, more and more emphasis will be placed on developing rural industries in such a way that factories can be planned as near to the available raw materials as possible, and so give the same opportunities for employment to the people who live in the rural areas as in the big towns. So great has been the pace of development in Ghana that our five-year plan has had to be abandoned, because it failed to meet our urgent needs and aspirations. We are now engaged in preparing a new and comprehensive seven-year plan for the economic, industrial, agricultural, and technological development of the country. We hope to inaugurate this plan in January 1963. Thus by 1970 the completion of the plan will coincide with the tenth anniversary of our Republic.

May I now draw your attention to an important matter. The direct participation of the government in industry appears to have created doubts about government's intentions in regard to the part that can be played by overseas capital and investments in the development of Ghana.

With the conclusion of the Volta Loan Agreement, the government has received a large number of inquiries from business and financial interests from overseas which demonstrate keenness to participate, to an increasing degree, in the development of the country's economy. It is appropriate, therefore, that I should take this opportunity to redefine the government's policy in regard to private enterprise and investment in general.

* Extract from a speech by Dr. Nkrumah laying the foundation stone of the City Hotel in Kumasi, March 24, 1962. From *Osagyefo in Kumasi* (four speeches of Dr. Nkrumah, Accra: Ministry of Information and Broadcasting, 1962).

It is the declared policy of the government to build a society in which the principles of social justice will be paramount. Toward this end it will maintain its policy of economic planning and increasing participation in the nation's economic activity.

We have decided, therefore, that in no sector of the economy will exclusive rights of operation in respect of any commodity be conferred on any single person, company, or establishment; all enterprises are expected to accept the economic policy of the government as the basis of their activity and to operate within the framework of the laws of the nation.

The government recognizes five sectors, all operating side by side in the nation's economy. These sectors are: (1) state enterprises; (2) enterprises owned by foreign private interests; (3) enterprises jointly owned by the state and foreign private interests; (4) cooperatives; and (5) small-scale Ghanaian private enterprises.

State enterprises are the enterprises completely owned and operated by the state, and will include all enterprises managed under the direction of the competent governmental organs. The main aims of operating state enterprises are:

Firstly, to ensure an ever-growing and steady employment for the people.

Secondly, to increase national income and the revenues of the state in order to raise the living standards of the people, to expand and improve both education and health services.

Thirdly, to have at the command of the state significant and growing stocks of commodities in order to be able to influence the market, this influence being aimed at the stabilization of the price level and that of currency.

Lastly, to supply those services which the private sector does not wish or is not allowed to supply.

The government accepts the operation in the country of large-scale enterprises by foreign interests, provided that they accept the following conditions: firstly that foreign private enterprises give the government the first option to buy their shares, whenever it is intended to sell all or part of the equity capital; and secondly that foreign private enterprises and enterprises jointly owned by the state and foreign private interests be required to reinvest 60 per cent of their net profits in Ghana.

Enterprises jointly owned by the state and foreign private interests will be operated jointly by government and private foreign interests, whose respective shares in the equity capital shall be agreed by both parties.

Government will support and encourage the formation of co-operative enterprises of producers both in agriculture and in trade and industry.

In order to encourage and utilize personal initiative and skill, Ghanaians can undertake small-scale enterprises, provided that they are not nominees or sleeping partners of foreign interests.

In future the private small-scale personal enterprise sector will be exclusively reserved for Ghanaians. Foreign concerns already established in this sector will be allowed to continue operation, on condition that they do not expand their present establishment and scale of operations. In future, therefore, there will be no room for overseas interests in the small-scale enterprises sector in Ghana.

Our aim is to build up Ghana into a strong and progressive nation, economically, industrially, and technologically, and foreign private interests are invited to share in this development.

We want to see that every citizen of Ghana has the opportunity to develop his or her abilities to the fullest extent, in order to make maximum contribution to the country's development. We must realize that the strength and character of a nation depend on the quality of its citizens. It must be our aim, therefore, to build a state which will be universally acknowledged as honest and incorruptible. The state organizations and factories which we are daily establishing represent a great challenge to the energy and integrity of our people, whether they are in direct charge of such organizations or whether they are ordinary employees in the enterprises.

### 3. *"Ghana's Socialism Creates 'Happy Atmosphere' for Private Capital"**

I am happy to say that as a result of the sacrifice made by the people of Ghana, by the government and by you, the members of the business community, the financial situation has now stabilized. There has been a radical improvement in our balance of international trade, and the country's reserves have shown a healthy recovery. But this does not mean that the time has come for us to relax. Our economic position needs to be still further improved, particularly

---

* Extracts from a speech by President Kwame Nkrumah at a dinner for businessmen at Flagstaff House, the Presidential residence, Accra, February 22, 1963. From Press Release No. 2/63, Ghana Information Services, New York City, April 3, 1963.

in the new period of development which we are about to enter with our Seven Year Plan.

In the past year or so, while we have adopted these vigorous measures to protect Ghana's economy we have had to experiment with a number of devices in order to achieve our aim. I am fully aware of the difficulties which some of us have encountered owing to the changes that have to be made from time to time.

I would like to say, however, that the Government of Ghana stands by the principles which I enumerated at the last Budget with regard to investment, and which I repeat here:

The government will continue to encourage private investors to establish and operate in Ghana.

Our government has no plans whatever to take over industries in the private sector; it is neither its wish to do so nor its aim of policy. When private investors enter into fields where state enterprises operate, they will compete on absolutely equal terms without discrimination.

Gentlemen, we must be frank and honest about our intentions and motives. There should be no secret doubts in the relations between us. We can only coexist on the basis of absolute frankness. We, on our part, welcome every honest investor who wants to work for his equitable profits, but we shall not tolerate anyone who seeks to direct what political course we should follow. Any government, or, for that matter, any organization which invests in, or gives a loan or assistance to, another country like our own, must on no account interfere directly or indirectly in the internal or external affairs of that country. If any such attempt is made on the strength of such credit, loan, aid, or assistance to interfere in the political, social, economic, cultural, and military affairs of our country, then we shall consider that the motives underlying such activities and operations have a neo-colonialist character.

Perhaps between the theory and practice, there may have been some mistakes made in the application of the rules and regulations. I wish to say, therefore, that if any such mistakes have been made, they have been made in good faith and with the best of intentions.

In order that such mistakes may not be repeated, I have instructed that the rules and regulations should now be put on a firm and clear-cut basis. You all know what is required of you, and I am confident that you will accept these in fairness and good spirit, and thereby contribute to the economic growth of Ghana. I am happy to say that an Investment Bill is nearing completion and is expected to be introduced shortly in Parliament. This bill, when it becomes law, will provide legal backing to government policy with regard to investment and also, at the same time, define the nature of concessions which the government proposes to make to investors.

Gentlemen, perhaps it will be a good thing for me at this juncture to say something about our hopes of the future. We are in the process of establishing a society in which men and women will have no anxiety about work, food, and shelter; where poverty and illiteracy no longer exist and where disease is brought under control; where our educational facilities provide our children with the best possible opportunities for learning; where every person uses his talents to their fullest capacity and contributes to the general well-being of the nation.

In order to attain these objectives, we have accepted the socialist pattern of society, believing that at a certain level of economic growth of a less developed country such as Ghana, state enterprise can coexist with private business interests, provided certain rules are observed on both sides.

I have stated elsewhere:

There are circumstances in which the import of foreign capital is of benefit to the importing country, especially in the case of the emerging developing country where large-scale sources of capital accumulation are small and not so easy to mobilize. Foreign capital is thus useful and helpful if it takes the form of a loan or credit to enable the borrowing country to buy what it needs from whatever sources it likes, and at the same time to retain the control of the assets to be developed.

One of the worst things that can happen to less developed and emerging countries is to receive foreign aid with political and economic strings attached. These aids are very often wrapped up in financial terms that are not easily discernible.

Foreign investment made in an emerging and developing country by a foreign company in order that such company can make a profit has nothing to do with *aid*. This does not mean that a developing country may not find it advantageous to make a contract with a foreign company for the setting up of, say, a factory or an industry.

Real aid is something quite different. It consists of direct gifts or loans that are given on favorable terms and without strings attached.

The problem, therefore, is how to obtain capital investment and still keep under sufficient control to prevent undue exploitation, and how to preserve integrity and sovereignty without crippling economic or political ties to *any* country, bloc, or system. In other words, can state enterprise and private enterprise exist in a less developed country? I say yes, *provided they both conform to the general framework of the overall plan made by the state.*

As I have said already, our ideas of socialism can coexist with private enterprises. I also believe that private capital, and private investment capital in particular, has a recognized and legitimate part to play in Ghana's economic development. We are consistent in these ideas. I have never made any secrets of my faith in socialist principles, but I have always tried to make it quite clear that Ghana's socialism is not incompatible with the existence and growth of a vigorous private sector in the economy.

Gentlemen, I need hardly say that Ghana expects you—indeed, Ghana invites you—businessmen, industrialists, bankers, manufacturers, and investors, to play a significant role in this economic growth and development.

Let me end by saying—and I say this with emphasis and sincerity—that those of you who will be investing in Ghana will be investing in a very stable country; a country united; a country determined to make progress; a country determined to industrialize; a country determined to mechanize and diversify its agriculture; a country dynamic and honest in its intentions and consistent in its policies.

Look around the country for yourselves. Invite your business friends to come here and see with their own eyes the happy atmosphere pervading everything we do; the stability we rightly boast of; the buoyance of our economy and the happy relationships existing between all races who live here. There can be no better assurance to investors than these. Tell them not to be taken in by the mischief of a section of the press in Europe and America.

4. *Extracts from the Capital Investment Act, April 19, 1963\**

AN ACT to encourage the investment of foreign capital and other purposes connected therewith. . . .

PART I—CAPITAL INVESTMENTS BOARD

1. (1) There is hereby established for the purposes of this Act a Capital Investments Board. . . .

---

\* Extracts from copy obtained from the Commercial Attaché, Ghana Trade and Investment Office, New York City.

2. (1) The functions of the Board shall be
   (a) to initiate and organize activities for the encourage-
       ment of investment of foreign capital and to provide
       for the creation of the conditions required therefor;
   (b) to grant approval for capital investments;
   (c) to maintain liaison between investors and govern-
       ment departments, agencies, and other authorities
       concerned, to give and disseminate information in
       matters of capital investments in Ghana, and to assist
       investors in the implementation of their projects;
   (d) to recommend to any competent authority to grant,
       within the scope of the enactments which apply in
       its sphere of competence or with the implementation
       of which it is charged, any exemption, reduction, fa-
       cility, or license in respect of any enterprise, property,
       investment, or loan likely to assist in the attainment
       of the objects of this Act; and
   (e) to do all acts as are incidental or conducive to the at-
       tainment of the purposes of this Act. . . .

PART II—OBLIGATIONS OF INVESTORS

4. (1) Any person who has invested, or intends to invest, capital
   in any sector of the national economy and wishing to enjoy
   any benefit conferred by this Act shall submit to the Board
   the particulars of a project containing a detailed description of the enterprise carried on or intended to be carried
   on. . . .
5. Approval for capital investments under this Act may be granted
   for the purpose of contributing to the attainment of
   (a) the development of the productive capacity of the national
       economy through the efficient utilization of its resources
       and economic potential;
   (b) the full utilization and expansion of the productive ca-
       pacity of existing enterprises;
   (c) the saving on imports, the increase of exports, and the im-
       provement of services which will assist the strengthening
       of the payments position of the country; or
   (d) a high level of employment and the impartation of techni-
       cal skill to persons who are citizens of Ghana.
6. Any person to whom an approval has been granted under this
   Act shall,

(a) during the continuance in force of the agreement . . . , institute arrangements for the training of persons who are citizens of Ghana in administrative, technical, managerial, and other capacities, with a view to securing the benefit of their knowledge and experience in the conduct of the project concerned; and

(b) provide adequate facilities for the benefit and enjoyment of employees. . . .

PART III—PROTECTION OF INVESTMENTS

8. (1) Subject to the provisions of this section, no investment under this Act shall be subject to expropriation by the government.

(2) Where, however, in exceptional circumstances an approved project is taken over in the public interest, the government shall pay fair compensation for the takeover, in the currency in which the investment was originally made.

(3) Where there is a dispute as to the amount of compensation payable under this section, the matter shall be referred to an arbitrator appointed by the parties and, failing such appointment, to arbitration through the agency of the International Bank for Reconstruction and Development.

9. Notwithstanding the provisions of any other enactment,

(a) there shall be no restriction

(i) on the remittance of capital, including appreciation, to the country of origin of an investment under this Act, in the event of a sale or the liquidation of the approved project;

(ii) on the transfer of profits to the country of origin of the investment after the payment of any tax due in respect of the investment;

(iii) on the transfer of payments in respect of principal, interest, and other financial charges where a loan has been granted to a project by a nonresident for the purposes of the project in accordance with the approved conditions of the loan;

(b) reasonable facilities shall be provided by the Minister to expatriate personnel employed or engaged in an approved project under this Act for making remittances abroad in respect of the maintenance of their families and other contractual obligations such as insurance premiums and contributions to provident and pension funds:

Provided that the Minister may, in order to safeguard the external payments position, impose temporary restrictions.

PART IV—INCENTIVES FOR INVESTORS, INCOME TAX BENEFITS

10. (1) Notwithstanding the provisions of any other enactment a company granted an approval under this Act shall, during the continuance in force of the agreement . . . , and subject to the other provisions of this Act, be exempt for a period of five years or for such longer period not exceeding ten years beginning from the date of production from the payment of income tax. . . .

11. Capital allowances shall be granted in respect of buildings, plant, machinery, structures, roads, furniture, fixtures, and fittings used for the purposes of an approved project in accordance with the Schedule to this Act, after the period of exemption specified in the immediately preceding section.

12. In determining the chargeable income of a person who has incurred a capital expenditure on scientific research for the purposes of the development or advancement of an approved project, there shall be deducted from that income, every year for five years beginning with the year in which he incurred the said expenditure, an amount equal to twenty per centum of such expenditure. . . .

PART V—MISCELLANEOUS

21. A project, part of which is an approved project and part of which is not an approved project, whether the unapproved part was established before the grant of the approval or thereafter but outside the scope of the approved project, shall be entitled to the benefits conferred by this Act in respect of the approved part only.

22. Any investment not approved for the purposes of this Act or in respect of which no application has been made to the Board under Section 4 of this Act may be allowed to repatriate capital, interest, and other financial charges subject to the provisions of the Exchange Control Act, 1961 (Act 71). . . .

# Notes

## Introduction

1. Philip Selznick, *TVA and the Grass Roots: A Study in the Sociology of Formal Organization* (Berkeley: University of California Press, 1953).
2. D. K. Chisiza, *Africa—What Lies Ahead* (New York: African American Institute, 1962).

## William H. Friedland: Basic Social Trends

1. Kwame Nkrumah, speech at the opening of the hall of trade unions, July 9, 1960, Accra.
2. Julius Nyerere, "Ujamaa," speech made at a Tanganyika African National Union (TANU) conference on socialism, Dar es Salaam, April 1962. See Appendix II in this volume, pp. 240–41.
3. "To the Greeks, work was a curse and nothing else." (Adriano Tilgher, *Work* [New York: Harcourt, Brace, 1930], p. 3.)
4. It will be recalled that when Adam and Eve lived in the Garden of Eden, work was unnecessary. When they ate of the tree of knowledge, God drove them from the Garden and placed on man the injunction to labor, saying: "In the sweat of thy brow, shalt thou earn thy bread." This was hardly a view that saw work as a blessing.
5. Max Weber, *The Protestant Ethic and the Spirit of Capitalism* (London: Allen & Unwin, 1956).
6. In Soviet Russia, work was first seen as a moral obligation. Originally, the socialist slogan was "From each, according to his ability; to each, according to his need." When a high level of production was not achieved, action was taken to enforce the obligation to labor. This included not only coercion but the installation of piecework systems. Thus, the slogan was changed and became "To each, according to his production."
7. John Tettegah, *A New Chapter for Ghana Labour* (pamphlet, Accra, 1958), p. 26. It is possible to take another view of the Ghanaian situation and interpret Tettegah's role as an agent of party control of the unions. Cf. Lester N. Trachtman, "The Labor Movement in

Ghana: A Study in Political Unionism" (Cornell University: unpublished master's thesis, 1960).

8. I am summarizing, for lack of space, a complex conflict between the TFL and the TANU government. The split has also been reflected within the TFL itself. One wing of the unions, the most significant in terms of its place in the country's economy, is concerned with continuing the pattern of activities developed during the course of the drive for independence. These include continual demands for wage increases. The leaders of TANU wish to place limits on the consumption activities of organized workers. This has brought the government and TANU into conflict with some of the recalcitrant union leaders. In the course of this battle, one wing of the unions has supported TANU. The strategy of the TANU government in dealing with the unions has been borrowed from Ghana. Thus, recent legislation has provided for dues checkoffs and the economic security of the unions. Accompanying this were provisions that seriously impede the right to strike and give to the Minister of Labor considerable powers to settle labor-management disputes. This legislation has not sat well with the major wing of the TFL.

(Since writing the above, the issue was resolved following the January 1964 mutiny, by the passage of legislation that dissolved the TFL and its constituent unions. A single new union, the National Union of Tanganyikan Workers, has been created in its place. By this legislation, the President of Tanganyika is given the right to appoint the general secretary and the deputy general secretary of the Union. These officials serve at the pleasure of the President. The Minister of Labor, Michael Kamaliza, was appointed as the first general secretary.)

9. Mr. Nyerere discusses this idea at some length in an article, "The Task Ahead of Our African Trade Unions," *Labour* (Ghana Trades Union Congress publication), June 1961. In this article, Mr. Nyerere chides the British trade unions for continuing to be suspicious of government after the British Labour Party came to power. This he attributes to habits built up in a class society over a long period of time.

10. It is not possible here to examine in detail the debate that took place at the 1921 Congress, during which three distinct views of the role of unions came to the fore. The debate is reviewed by Isaac Deutscher, *Soviet Trade Unions* (London: Royal Institute of International Affairs, 1950), chap. 2. None of the Communists felt that, in a fully developed socialist society, independent institutions of the working class were necessary to defend workers at their work place.

Parenthetically, it might be noted that the situation of the unions in Russia was entirely different from that in Africa. The Russian unions were significant because of their role in re-establishing the economy, which was in a state of collapse following the revolution. The unions undertook crucial productionist activities to get the economy functioning. In the case of the African unions, most economies were operating fairly well when independence was achieved. Thus, the turn toward productionism is more dramatic in Africa than in Russia.

11. Léopold Senghor, *African Socialism* (New York: American Society for African Culture, 1959), p. 38; emphasis in original.

12. Quoted by Alan Rake, "Mr. Ivory Coast," *Africa Report*, VII (April 1962), 4. Mr. Rake obtained this quote from *L'Afrique Noire*, December 6, 1951.

13. Quoted by Ruth Schachter, "Trade Unions Seek Autonomy," *West Africa*, January 26, 1957, p. 81. See also Thomas Hodgkin, "A Note on the Language of African Nationalism," in Kenneth Kirkwood, ed., *African Affairs: Number One* (St. Antony's Papers, No. 10; London: Chatto & Windus, 1961), p. 37.

14. Hodgkin, "A Note on the Language of African Nationalism," pp. 37–38.

15. Nyerere, "Ujamaa," Appendix II, pp. 240–41.

16. *Ibid.*, pp. 244–45.

17. Senghor, *African Socialism*, p. 38.

18. Nyerere, speech at the awarding of an honorary degree at Makerere College, April 9, 1962.

19. *Sunday News* (Dar es Salaam), July 29, 1962.

20. In the Congo (Leopoldville), the unions have issued ultimatums to the government demanding that salaries of legislators be cut or the unions would strike for wage increases. See the report on the Third Congress of the Union of Congolese Workers, Leopoldville, December 11–15, 1961, in the *International Labour Review*, LXXXV (1962), 529.

21. In India, for example, the government is confronted by difficulties in keeping educated personnel from migrating to other countries where economic benefits are higher. I am indebted to Sagar Jain for calling this fact to my attention.

22. Nkrumah, speech at the laying of the foundation stone of the TUC Hall of Trade Unions, October 17, 1959.

23. Nyerere, "The Task Ahead of Our African Trade Unions." There is a striking similarity here to Catholic views of society: "From John of Salisbury to Dante and Occam and Nicholas Cusanus, no point of fancied analogy between the parts and members of the body and the various functions of Church and State was left unexploited" (Henry Osborn Taylor, *The Medieval Mind*, Vol. II, 4th American ed. [London: Macmillan, 1927], p. 305). The imagery of likeness between units of society and the human body was utilized in "Rerum Novarum" by Pope Leo XIII: "The great mistake . . . is to possess oneself of the

idea that class is naturally hostile to class; that rich and poor are intended by nature to live at war with one another. . . . The exact contrary is the truth. Just as the symmetry of the body is the result of the disposition of the members of the body, so in a State it is ordained by nature that these two classes should exist in harmony, and agreement, and should, as it were, fit into one another, so as to maintain the equilibrium of the body politic. Each requires the other; capital cannot do without labor, nor labor without capital." See the Encyclical Letter of Pope Leo XIII, "Rerum Novarum: The Condition of Labor," May 1891. I am grateful to Maurice Neufeld for calling my attention to the similarities discussed here.

24. Senghor, *African Socialism,* p. 38.

25. Cf. Ruth Schachter, "Single-Party Systems in West Africa," *American Political Science Review,* LV (1961), 294–307.

26. L. Gray Cowan, "Guinea," in Gwendolen M. Carter, ed., *African One-Party States* (Ithaca, N.Y.: Cornell University Press, 1962), pp. 149–236.

27. *Ibid.,* p. 183.

28. See my paper "Some Sources of Traditionalism among Modern African Elites," read at the 1962 meeting of the International Sociological Association, Washington, D.C.

29. While the discussion here has been limited to Africa, we are dealing with tendencies that are world-wide. Peronism in Argentina, Ataturkism in Turkey, the mass party systems of the totalitarian countries, all represent trends toward the creation of focal institutional societies. In this respect, the discussion of the African situation should be integrated with the continuing discussion in sociology and political science on the character of mass society.

30. For the basic arguments see K. Davis and W. E. Moore, "Some Principles of Stratification," *American Sociological Review,* X (1945), 242–49; M. W. Tumin, "Some Principles of Stratification: A Critical Analysis," *American Sociological Review,* XVIII (1953), 387–94, with replies by Davis and Moore following.

31. See, for example, John B. George, "How Stable Is Tanganyika?" *Africa Report,* VIII (March 1963), 5.

*Chandler Morse: Economics of African Socialism*

1. Julius Nyerere, "Ujamaa"; see Appendix II, p. 238.

2. Fernand Gigon, *Guinée: Etat-Pilote* (Paris: Librairie Plon, 1959), pp. 23, 26.

3. Elliot Berg, commenting on the resolution on doctrine passed in November 1956 at the Conakry conference of the Confédération Géné-

rale du Travail Africain (CGTA), says: "The resolution proclaims the need to work out an ideology which is specifically African. It rejects essential elements of traditional Marxism, denying the existence of the class struggle in contemporary Africa and stressing the inapplicability, because of the colonial situation, of other basic Marxist tenets." One tenet, however, was rejected on grounds unrelated to colonial status. Thus, the resolution "questions collectivization of the means of production 'as a result of current political developments, particularly in Eastern Europe.'" See "French West Africa" in W. Galenson, ed., *Labor and Economic Development* (New York: Wiley, 1959), p. 217 and fn. 67.

4. See the comments of Mamadou Dia as reported in *Africa Report,* VI (October 1961), 10. However, according to Fenner Brockway, *African Socialism* (London: Bodley Head, 1964), p. 39, the underlying reason for the political events that led to Dia's dismissal in December 1962 and subsequent imprisonment was his espousal of more radical steps toward socialism, following a visit to Russia.

5. D. K. Chisiza, *Africa—What Lies Ahead* (New York: African-American Institute, 1962), p. 28. For some of the factors making for a pragmatic dilution of socialism in some African Socialist countries, see William J. Foltz, "The Radical Left in French-speaking West Africa," in William H. Lewis, ed., *Emerging Africa* (Washington, D.C.: Public Affairs Press, 1963).

6. *Ghana: Seven-Year Development Plan* (Accra: Office of the Planning Commission, January 1964).

7. See *Ghana: Second Development Plan, 1959–64* (Accra: Government Printer), p. 18; "Economic Notes: Nationalization in Ghana?" in *Africa Report, V* (November 1960), p. 7; also see Léopold Senghor, *African Socialism* (New York: American Society for African Culture, 1959), p. 41; "Economic Notes: Guinea Government Relaxes Code for Foreign Investors" in *Africa Report,* VII (April 1962), 17. For more details on the code, which provided certain guarantees against expropriation, authorized tax remissions, and assured repatriation of 20 per cent of profits, see Victor D. DuBois, *Reorganization of the Guinean Economy* (American Universities Field Staff, Reports Service, West Africa Series, Vol. VI, No. 1 [February 1963]), p. 19; and for the text of the code see *Révue du Développement Economique,* No. 1, January 1964 (Conakry: Ministère du Développement Economique). Also see Fernand Gigon, *Guinée,* p. 69; "News Review: Guinea Moves Slowly to Nationalize Utilities" in *Africa Report,* VI (March 1961), 11, and "News Review: Guinea Nationalizes Remaining Private Bank" in *Africa Report,* VII, No. 3 (March 1962), 11. Note also that the United States has concluded an investment guarantee agreement with Guinea,

the ninth African state to reach such an accord. See "Economic Notes: United States and Guinea Sign Investment and Aid Agreements" in *Africa Report,* VII (June 1962), 9. See also *Africa Report,* VII (April 1962), 17, and John Hatch, "Nkrumah's Ghana: A Positive View" in *Africa Report,* VII (August 1962), 10, for references to restrictive provisions in Guinea and Ghana. Also see *The Three-Monthly Economic Review* (London: The Economist Intelligence Unit), "Ghana, Nigeria, Sierra Leone, Gambia," No. 38 (June 1962), pp. 2–5; and "Former French Tropical Africa and Liberia," No. 9 (May 1962), p. 12; No. 6, July 1961, pp. 13–14. Ghanaian policy has now been embodied in the Capital Investments Act of April 19, 1963. This Act sets up an Investment Board, a procedure for facilitating the financing of proposals meeting certain requirements, and tax relief for approved projects. It also removes all restrictions on the repatriation of foreign capital invested in approved projects and permits the unrestricted transfer of interest and earnings on foreign investments in such projects. Reinvestment of 60 per cent of all foreign earnings had previously been required (and may continue to be on investments other than those approved under this Act). However, the 1963 budget provided for higher taxes on remitted profits (13 shillings in the pound) than on profits retained (9 shillings). Also see speech of F. K. D. Goka, Minister of Finance and Trade, on October 8, 1962, to the Ghana Parliament (Supplement, *Ghana Today,* October 10, 1962). On Tanganyika, see Rashidi Kawawa, as reported in "Finance: Economic Revolution" in *The Reporter,* August 4, 1962, p. 16. The operational provisions of the new law, referred to in the text, are those that assure transferability of profits and original foreign investment in "approved" projects, and that guarantee compensation at "full and fair value," to be determined by arbitration if necessary, whenever approved foreign investment may be "compulsorily acquired." See Suppl. No. 1 to *Tanganyika Gazette,* XLIV, No. 50, September 20, 1963. Tanganyika also concluded a standard form of investment guarantee agreement with the United States. See *Tanganyika Standard,* November 15, 1963.

8. See note 7 above, and references therein.

9. René Dumont, *L'Afrique noire est mal partie* (Paris: Seuil, 1962), p. 227; also *Horoya* (Organ of the Parti Démocratique de Guinée), No. 316 (October 17, 1963). See also Nos. 314 (October 10, 1963) and 315 (October 12, 1963).

10. *Ghana: Second Development Plan,* p. 17.

11. *Ghana: Seven-Year Development Plan,* chap. 1, p. 2. However, the 1962 Program of the Convention People's Party, which set the policy framework for the Plan, specified five sectors, as follows: (1) state enterprises, (2) enterprises owned by foreign interests, (3) enter-

prises owned jointly by the state and foreign private interests, (4) co-operatives, (5) small-scale Ghanaian enterprises. See Appendix VII, pp. 270–72 of this volume.

12. Senghor, *African Socialism*, p. 41.

13. *Ghana: Second Development Plan*, p. 17.

14. Senghor, *African Socialism*, pp. 40, 41.

15. Gigon, *Guinée*, p. 27.

16. "Economic Notes: Soviet Union Will Help Ghana State Farms," *Africa Report*, VII (July 1962), 11; also "Cabinet Information Paper by the Minister of Agriculture, Review of the Operation of State Agricultural Enterprises" (mimeo., 1963), and "Ghana State Farms Corporation Cropping Programme: 1964" (mimeo.); *Ghana: Second Development Plan*, chap. 2, *passim*. Note also the following reference to cooperative and state farms in President Nkrumah's Sessional Address to Parliament, October 2, 1962 (published in Supplement to *Ghana Today*, October 10, 1962): "Considerable progress has already been made on these farms, which employ modern techniques of mechanization and fertilization. Dams and irrigation works are being built in many parts of the country, and already the response of the people to the new challenge has been most encouraging. Agricultural Production Drive Committees have been formed throughout the country to coordinate the efforts of the agricultural cooperatives, of the United Ghana Farmers' Cooperatives, the state farms, and the agricultural wing of the Workers' Brigade." Since then, a Young Farmers' League has also organized nearly 50 "resettlement farms" for people in the 17–25 age group who have left middle school, and resettlement has begun of 80,000 persons whose lands and villages (roughly 700) will be inundated by the new Volta Lake, in over 50 modernized and cooperatively organized agricultural villages (*Some Facts about Resettlement* and *Power for Progress* [Accra: Volta River Authority, 1963]). Also see *Ghana: Seven-Year Development Plan*, chap. 4.

17. It is also worth noting in this connection that upwards of 200 trade unionists, according to official announcement, were "detained" following the mutiny of the Tanganyika Rifles in January 1964. See *Tanganyika Standard* (Dar es Salaam), January 28, 1964.

18. Senghor, *African Socialism*, p. 37.

19. Nyerere, "Ujamaa," Appendix II, p. 243.

20. *Tanganyika Standard* (Dar es Salaam), February 27, 1964.

21. See chap. 6 in Neil J. Smelser, *The Sociology of Economic Life* (Englewood Cliffs, N.J.: Prentice-Hall, 1963), for a discussion of differentiation and integration in developing areas.

22. See the analysis of the Dakar Colloquium on African Socialism by Aristide Zolberg in the present volume.

23. See K. M. Panikkar, *Revolution in Africa* (London: Asia Publishing House, 1961), p. 61; Gigon, *Guinée,* pp. 26–27; and Kawawa in *The Reporter,* August 4, 1962, p. 16. But compare Berg ("French West Africa," p. 214): "The African civil servants and clerks, then, form a class which combines many of the qualities of an intelligentsia with those of the rising middle class."

24. Mamadou Dia, *The African Nations and World Solidarity* (New York: Praeger, 1961), pp. 95–96.

25. Senghor, *African Socialism,* p. 40.

26. Press release No. 2/63 (April 3, 1963): "Ghana's Socialism Creates 'Happy Atmosphere' for Private Capital" (Ghana Information Services, New York City). See Appendix VII, pp. 272–75.

27. Berg ("French West Africa," p. 223), referring to the increased autonomy that preceded independence, and anticipating fuller autonomy, said: "Responsibility is now in the hands of African political leaders, and they will have hard decisions to make; budgetary considerations, for example, are sure to lead to resistance to union demands by the new African governments. Hence the classic conflicts in the relations between governing party and trade unionists may be expected to arise in AOF [Afrique Occidentale Française] as they have inevitably arisen elsewhere." But Gigon (*Guinée,* p. 69) cites Irving Brown, the American international labor union operator, whom he met in Conakry, as expressing the postindependence view that "the Guinean labor unions are among the most politically conscious in the world, and constitute the lance's point of the Democratic Party." For an informative discussion of recent developments in a formerly British country, see Lester N. Trachtman, "The Labor Movement in Ghana: A Study in Political Unionism," *Economic Development and Culture Change, 10,* No. 2 (January 1962). Trachtman concluded the main part of his analysis with the statement that a labor movement in an underdeveloped area "cannot be judged solely by the standards used for Western unions, but must also be evaluated by its contribution to national development. Against this must be weighed its responsibility for the welfare of the workers." Then, after the 19-day strike of port workers in September 1961, he added a postscript, which began with the observation, "Events since the foregoing analysis was written have demonstrated one of the potential pitfalls of political unionism, namely, a revolt by the rank and file."

28. Nyerere, "Ujamaa," Appendix II, p. 243.

29. John Maynard, *The Russian Peasant and Other Essays* (2 vols. London: Victor Gollancz, 1942), pp. 8–9 and *passim.*

30. The Gezira scheme in the Sudan is an interesting example of successful agricultural development carried out by effectively coupling

state enterprise to private incentives. A pragmatic concern with results rather than a doctrinaire devotion to a single form of economic organization guided the British colonial administrators who were responsible. See Arthur Gaitskell, "Planned Regional Development in Underdeveloped Countries: Reflections from Experience in the Gezira Scheme in the Sudan," in H.R.H. the Duke of Edinburgh's *Study Conference on Human Problems in Industry, 1956* (Background papers, V. II. London: Oxford University Press, 1957).

31. In this connection, it is interesting to note that at least one writer has suggested that cooperatives may be insufficiently dynamic for Tanganyika. See Clyde Sanger, "The Changing Face of Tanganyika," *Africa Report,* VII (July 1962), 4. *The Three-Monthly Economic Review* contains frequent reports on the progress of cooperatives, state farms, and agricultural developments generally in the African Socialist countries. Also see René Dumont, *L'Afrique noire est mal partie,* chap. 15, for a useful discussion of the interplay between technical and organizational problems of agricultural modernization in countries with socialist aims.

32. Julius K. Nyerere, "Africa's Place in the World," in *Symposium on Africa* (Wellesley, Mass.: Wellesley College, 1960), p. 158.

33. Kwame Nkrumah, *I Speak of Freedom* (New York: Praeger, 1961), p. 163.

34. See "Mixed Economic Development in Ghana" (reprinted from *The Times* [London], February 8, 1961) in *Africa Report,* VI (March 1961), 16.

*Igor Kopytoff: Traditional African Societies*

1. See, for example, numerous statements by African leaders quoted in the special issue on African Socialism of *Africa Report,* VIII (May 1963).

2. Léopold Sédar Senghor, *African Socialism* (New York: American Society for African Culture, 1959), p. 32.

3. Katherine George, "The Civilized West Looks at Primitive Africa: 1400–1800. A Study in Ethnocentrism," *Isis,* XLIX (1958), 62–72.

4. St. Clair Drake, "An Approach to the Evaluation of African Societies" in John A. Davis, ed., *Africa Seen by American Negroes* (Paris: Présence Africaine, 1958).

5. Melville J. Herskovits, *The Human Factor in Changing Africa* (New York: Knopf, 1963), pp. 137ff, 451ff.

6. Senghor, *African Socialism,* p. 31.

7. Julius K. Nyerere, "Africa's Place in the World," in *Symposium on Africa* (Wellesley, Mass.: Wellesley College, 1960), p. 158.

8. Cf. Aidan Southall, ed., *Social Change in Modern Africa* (London: Oxford University Press for International African Institute, 1961), pp. 31ff and *passim*.

9. See, for example, L. Baeck, "An Expenditure Study of the Congolese *Evolués* of Leopoldville, Belgian Congo," *ibid.*, p. 168.

10. W. E. Abraham, *The Mind of Africa* (Chicago: University of Chicago Press, 1962), p. 114.

11. Placide Tempels, *La Philosophie bantoue* (Paris: Présence Africaine, 1948).

12. See, for example, the various interpretations given to Pueblo culture as examined by John W. Bennett, "The Interpretation of Pueblo Culture: A Question of Values," *Southwestern Journal of Anthropology*, II (1946), 361–74.

*Dorothy Nelkin: Socialist Sources of Pan-African Ideology*

1. George Padmore, *Pan-Africanism or Communism?* (London: Dobson, 1956), pp. 21–22.

2. W. E. B. DuBois, *Dusk of Dawn* (New York: Harcourt, Brace, 1940), pp. 88–89.

3. Francis L. Broderick, *W. E. B. DuBois, Negro Leader in a Time of Crisis* (Stanford, Calif.: Stanford University Press, 1959), p. 86, quoting DuBois in *Horizon*, I (1907).

4. *Crisis* (NAACP, New York), XVIII (January 1919), 112.

5. DuBois, *Dusk of Dawn*, p. 279.

6. Padmore, *Pan-Africanism or Communism?*, p. 133.

7. *Crisis*, XXVII (January 1924), 120.

8. Colin Legum, *Pan-Africanism—a Short Political Guide* (London: Pall Mall Press, 1962), p. 30.

9. *Crisis*, XXIII (April 1922), 247.

10. *Crisis*, XXII (May 1921), 8.

11. *Crisis*, XXXIII (November 1926), 8.

12. *Crisis*, XXXIII (February 1927), 189.

13. *Crisis*, XXXIV (October 1927), 264.

14. DuBois, *Dusk of Dawn*, p. 298.

15. W. E. B. DuBois, "Marxism and the Negro Factor," *Crisis*, XL (May 1933), 104. See also *Crisis*, XXII (August 1921), 151–52, and XXXIX (July 1932), 234.

16. W. E. B. DuBois, *The Negro* (New York: Holt, 1915), p. 242.

17. DuBois, *Dusk of Dawn*, p. 135.

18. *Ibid.*, p. 188.

19. *Ibid.*, p. 301.

20. Broderick, *W. E. B. DuBois*, p. 144.

21. George Padmore, "An Open Letter to Earl Browder," *Crisis*, XLII (October 1935), 302.

22. Joseph Stalin, *Marxism and the National Question* (New York: International Publishers, 1942), p. 183.

23. V. I. Lenin, *Selected Works* (New York: International Publishers, 1943), X, 236.

24. *Ibid.*, V, 284.

25. Legum, *Pan-Africanism*, p. 31, refers to him as Otto Makonnen, "now director of the African Affairs Centre in Accra."

26. Padmore, *Pan-Africanism or Communism?*, p. 148.

27. *Ibid.*, p. 149.

28. *Ibid.*, p. 150.

29. W. E. B. DuBois, *Color and Democracy: Colonies and Peace* (New York: Harcourt, Brace, 1945), pp. 116–17.

30. Padmore, *Pan-Africanism or Communism?*, p. 161.

31. *Ibid.*, p. 181 (quoted from the Fifth Congress Resolutions).

32. *Ibid.*, p. 172 (quoted from the Fifth Congress Resolutions).

33. Padmore, *Pan-Africanism or Communism?*, p. 18.

34. Nkrumah, *The Autobiography of Kwame Nkrumah* (Edinburgh: T. Nelson, 1957), p. 60.

35. *Ibid.*, pp. 52–53.

36. *Ibid.*, p. 53.

37. Alexander Dallin, "The Soviet Union: Political Activity," in Zbigniew Brzezinski, ed., *Africa and the Communist World* (Stanford, Calif.: Stanford University Press, 1963), p. 10.

38. *World Marxist Review*, November 1961, p. 45. Quoted in Dallin, "The Soviet Union," p. 36.

39. Zbigniew Brzezinski, "Conclusion: The African Challenge," in Brzezinski, ed., *Africa and the Communist World*, p. 210.

40. Quoted by Paul-Marc Henry, "Pan Africanism: A Dream Come True," *Foreign Affairs*, 1959, p. 442.

41. St. Clair Drake, "Hide My Face?," in Herbert Hill, ed., *Soon One Morning* (New York: Knopf, 1963), pp. 78–105.

42. L. S. Senghor, "Negritude and African Socialism," in Kenneth Kirkwood, ed., *African Affairs: Number Two* (St. Antony's Papers, No. 15; London: Chatto & Windus, 1963), p. 11.

43. Kwame Nkrumah, *Hands off Africa!* (Accra: Kwabena Owosu-Akyem, 1961), p. 23.

44. "Africa and the EEC," *Africa Report*, VI (August 1961), 11.

45. Nkrumah, *Hands off Africa!*, p. 30.

46. *Ibid.*, p. 28.

47. "People's Conference Plans Permanent Body," *Africa Report*, IV (February 1959), 7.

48. Nkrumah, *Hands Off Africa!*, p. 32.

49. Legum, *Pan-Africanism*, p. 82.

50. Quoted from Azikiwe's opening speech to the Lagos Conference, by Joseph L. Sterne, "The Lagos Conference," *Africa Report*, VII (February 1962), 4–6.

51. Gerald Howson, "A Visit with Dr. Okpara," *Africa Report*, VII (November 1962), 24, 26.

52. Alan Rake, "Mr. Ivory Coast," *Africa Report*, VII (April 1962), 3–4.

53. Quoted from an article by Houphouët-Boigny in *Afrique Nouvelle*, March 22, 1961, in Gwendolen Carter, ed., *African One-Party States* (Ithaca, N.Y.: Cornell University Press, 1962), p. 311.

54. L. Senghor, *African Socialism* (New York: American Society of African Culture, 1959), p. 46.

55. Joseph S. Nye, Jr., "From Common Market to Federation," *Africa Report*, VIII (August 1963), 4.

56. J. K. Nyerere, "Africa's Place in the World," in *Symposium on Africa* (Wellesley, Mass.: Wellesley College, 1960).

57. Mamadou Dia, "Closing Speech at Dakar Colloquium," *Africa Report*, VIII (May 1963), 17–18.

*Margaret Roberts: A Socialist Looks at African Socialism*

1. C. A. R. Crosland, *The Conservative Enemy* (New York: Schocken Books, 1962), p. 122; emphasis added.

2. I. I. Potekhin, *Afrika smotrit v budushchee* (Africa Looks Ahead; Moscow: Oriental Languages Publishing House, 1960).

3. Habib Bourguiba, "Neo-Destourian Socialism," address delivered June 24, 1961. Published by the Tunisia Government.

4. A. Fenner Brockway, *African Socialism* (London: Bodley Head, 1963).

5. Kwame Nkrumah, address to the Convention People's Party, May 5, 1962.

6. Pierre Kanoute, "Le Socialisme africain: Expression de l'humanisme africain," *Afrique Nouvelle*, November 30–December 6, 1962.

7. Julius K. Nyerere, "Africa's Place in the World," in *Symposium on Africa* (Wellesley, Mass.: Wellesley College, 1960), p. 157.

8. Julius K. Nyerere, "Scramble for Africa," *Spearhead*, I, No. 4 (1962), 15.

9. G. F. Kim, in *Narody Azii i Afriki*, V, 1962.

10. Dr. Seydou Badian Kouyate, paper delivered at the Dakar Colloquium.

11. President Sékou Touré, quoted by a Guinean delegate at the Dakar Colloquium, *Africa Report*, VIII (May 1963), 26.

12. Kwame Nkrumah, *Dawn Broadcast*, April 8, 1961.

13. Ahmed Ben Bella, speech to the National Assembly, December 4, 1962.

14. President Tsiranana, reported in *Bulletin de Madagascar*, May 1962.

15. President Maga, reported in *Le Temps du Niger*, August 2, 1962.

16. Quoted in *Le Temps du Niger*, September 23, 1962.

17. Ahmed Ben Salah, radio broadcast, August 6, 1962.

18. Editorial, *The Spark* (Bureau of African Affairs, Accra), March 1963.

19. Julius Nyerere, "The Task Ahead of Our African Trade Unions," *Labour* (Ghana TUC publication), June 1961.

20. Mamady Kaba, president of the National Confederation of Guinean Workers, in a speech to a trade union conference at Bamako in January 1960.

21. Sékou Touré, *La Guinée et l'émancipation africaine* (Paris: Présence Africaine, 1959), p. 233.

22. Kwame Nkrumah, *I Speak of Freedom* (New York: Praeger, 1961), p. 163.

23. Kweku Folson, in *Venture* (London), October 1963.

24. D. K. Chisiza, *Africa—What Lies Ahead* (New York: African-American Institute, 1962), p. 28.


*Aristide R. Zolberg: The Dakar Colloquium*

1. *Afrique Nouvelle* (Dakar), No. 801 (December 14–20, 1962), p. 3.

2. *Ibid.*, No. 800 (December 7–13, 1962), p. 11.

3. M. Boubou Hama, President of the National Assembly of Niger, as reported in *Jeune Afrique* (Tunis), No. 113 (December 17–23, 1962), p. 7.

4. For a survey of recent developments in this sphere, see the reports by Victor D. DuBois in American Universities Field Staff, Reports Service, West Africa Series, Vol. V, No. 4 (1962), and Vol. VI, No. 2 (1963).

5. *Afrique Nouvelle*, No. 800, p. 11.

6. *Jeune Afrique*, No. 113, p. 6.

7. The contributions of non-African participants will not be discussed here. For a summary, see *Afrique Nouvelle*, No. 801, pp. 8–9.

8. *Ibid.*, p. 3.

9. Quoted in *Africa Report,* VIII (May 1963), 18.

10. *Jeune Afrique,* No. 113, p. 6.

11. *West Africa,* December 29, 1962, p. 1449.

12. Thomas Hodgkin, "A Note on the Language of African Nationalism," in Kenneth Kirkwood, ed., *African Affairs: Number One* (St. Antony's Papers, No. 10, London: Chatto & Windus, 1961), p. 22.

13. The discussion that follows is based upon the mimeographed texts of some of the contributions to the colloquium and on accounts of the others in *Afrique Nouvelle,* Nos. 800 and 801, *Africa Report,* VIII (May 1962), *West Africa,* December 29, 1962, and *Jeune Afrique,* No. 113. All translations from the French are my own.

14. M. Otabela (Cameroun), Mimeographed Colloquium Paper, p. 4.

15. Dr. Biobaku (Nigeria), Mimeographed Colloquium Paper, p. 5.

16. Assefa Demisse (Ethiopia), Mimeographed Colloquium Paper, p. 5.

17. M. Chaker (Tunisia), Mimeographed Colloquium Paper, p. 6.

18. El Moktar Marouf (Mauritania), Mimeographed Colloquium Paper, p. 6.

19. See F. X. Sutton, "Planning and Rationality in the Newly Independent States in Africa," *Economic Development and Cultural Change,* X (1961), 42–50.

20. M. Chaker, p. 5.

21. Mamadou Dia (Senegal), in *Afrique Nouvelle,* No. 801, p. 16.

22. See the contributions of Guinea, Sierra Leone, and Ethiopia to the colloquium.

23. Mamadou Dia, in *Afrique Nouvelle,* No. 801, p. 16.

24. Assefa Demisse, p. 2.

25. M. Adoum (Chad), Mimeographed Colloquium Paper, p. 2.

26. L. S. Senghor, in *West Africa,* December 29, 1962, p. 1449.

27. Chabi Mama (Dahomey), Mimeographed Colloquium Paper, p. 9.

28. Mamadou Dia, in *Afrique Nouvelle,* No. 801, p. 15.

29. Chabi Mama, p. 9.

30. Mamadou Dia, in *Afrique Nouvelle,* No. 801, p. 15.

31. M. Adoum, p. 2.

32. Dr. Kouyate (Mali), in *Afrique Nouvelle,* No. 801, p. 8.

33. L. S. Senghor, in *Afrique Nouvelle,* No. 800, p. 11.

34. M. Adoum, p. 4.

35. Hodgkin, p. 39.

36. M. Anguile (Gabon), in *Afrique Nouvelle,* No. 801, p. 8.

37. Chabi Mama, p. 12.

38. Dr. Biobaku, p. 5.

39. M. Chaker, p. 6.

40. Dr. Kouyate, in *Afrique Nouvelle,* No. 801, p. 8.

41. L. S. Senghor, in *West Africa,* December 29, 1962, p. 1449.

42. A. Kithima (Congo-Leopoldville), Mimeographed Colloquium Paper, pp. 2, 5.

43. Ruth Schachter Morgenthau, "African Socialism: Declaration of Ideological Independence," *Africa Report,* VIII (May 1963), 20–21.

44. Congo (Leopoldville) delegate, Mimeographed Colloquium Paper, pp. 20–21.

45. Chabi Mama, p. 12.

46. Dr. Biobaku, p. 4.

47. M. Chaker, p. 8.

48. Mamadou Dia, in *Afrique Nouvelle,* No. 801, p. 15.

49. Dr. Biobaku, p. 4.

50. M. Chaker, p. 12.

51. As quoted in *Afrique Nouvelle,* No. 801, p. 9.

52. Dr. Kouyate, in *Afrique Nouvelle,* No. 801, p. 8.

53. L. S. Senghor, in *Afrique Nouvelle,* No. 800, p. 11.

54. M. Rabemananjara (Malagasy Republic), in *Afrique Nouvelle,* No. 801, p. 9.

55. M. Adoum, p. 4.

56. El Moktar Marouf, p. 9.

57. Ruth Schachter Morgenthau, p. 4.

58. Mamadou Dia, in *Afrique Nouvelle,* No. 801, p. 16.

59. L. S. Senghor, in *Afrique Nouvelle,* No. 800, p. 11.

60. Chabi Mama, pp. 12–13.

61. Dr. Kouyate, in *Afrique Nouvelle,* No. 801, p. 8.

62. Chabi Mama, p. 4.

63. M. Rabemananjara, p. 9.

64. Bakary Coulibaly, as quoted in *Jeune Afrique,* No. 113, p. 7.

65. Dr. Biobaku, p. 2.

*Colin Legum: Ghana*

1. Kwame Nkrumah, *Address to CPP Study Group in Flagstaff House* (Accra, 1961).

2. Nkrumah, *Africa Must Unite* (New York: Praeger, 1963), p. 119.

3. *Ibid.,* p. 130.

4. *Ibid.,* p. 53.

5. Program of the Convention People's Party, *Work and Happiness* (Accra, 1962).

6. Nkrumah, *I Speak of Freedom* (London: Heinemann, 1961), p. 163.

7. Nkrumah, *The Autobiography of Kwame Nkrumah* (Edinburgh: Nelson, 1957), p. 45.

8. Nkrumah, *Towards Colonial Freedom* (London, 1962).

9. The document known as "The Circle" appears in Nkrumah, *Autobiography,* Appendix B, pp. 303–4. The quotes that follow, pertaining to "The Circle," are from this document unless otherwise noted.

10. Nkrumah, *Laying of the Foundation Stone of the Winneba Ideological Institute, 1961* (Accra, February 18, 1961. Also see statements on this goal in Nkrumah, *Africa Must Unite,* pp. 52ff.

11. *Ibid.*

12. For a description of one of these meetings see Nkrumah, *Address to CPP Study Group.*

13. Nkrumah, *I Speak of Freedom,* p. 164.

14. Tawia Adamafio, "The New Party Structure," *The Party* (Accra), September 1960.

15. CPP Revised Constitution, 1962, Part Four.

16. Nkrumah, *Winneba Address.*

17. Nkrumah, *I Speak of Freedom,* pp. 163ff.

18. *The Party,* July 1959.

19. Mr. Kofi Baako's lectures were reproduced in *The Ghanaian Times* (Accra), January 24, 25, 26, 28, 29, 1961.

20. Nkrumah, *African Must Unite,* p. 119.

21. *The Spark* (Accra), April 3, 1964.

22. Program of the Convention People's Party, *Work and Happiness* (Accra, 1962).

23. Report by Dr. Joseph Bognor to President Nkrumah, February 1962 (unpublished).

24. Ghana, *First Seven Year Development Plan* (Accra: Office of the Planning Commission, March 1962).

25. *Ibid.*

26. The preceding quotes are from Nkrumah, *Laying of the Foundation Stone.*

27. Nkrumah, *The Noble Task of Teaching* (Accra: Ghana Government Printer, April 8, 1961).

28. The following quotes are from Nkrumah, *Dawn Broadcast* (Accra: Ghana Government Printer, April 8, 1961).

29. Nkrumah, *Building a Socialist State* (Accra: Ghana Government Printer, April 22, 1961).

30. *Evening News* (Accra), April 6, 1962.

31. *The Guardian* (London), May 22, 1961.

32. *Ibid.*

33. *The Spark,* December 11, 1963.

34. *Ibid.*

35. George Padmore, *Pan-Africanism or Communism?* (London: Dobson, 1956), pp. 341–42.

36. *The Spark, April* 19, 1963.

37. *Ibid.*

38. *The Spark,* March 1, 8, 15, 22, 29; April 5, 12, 19, 1963.

39. *The Spark,* April 19, 1963.

40. *The Ghanaian Times,* October 16, 1962.

41. *The Spark,* February 22, 1963.

42. *The Spark,* August 9, 1963.

43. Nkrumah, *Autobiography,* p. 12.

44. Nkrumah, *The Old and the New: Law in Africa,* Address to the Ghana Law School (Accra: Ministry of Information and Broadcasting, January 4, 1962).

45. The following quotes are all from Nkrumah, *Consciencism* (London: Heinemann, 1964).

46. *The Spark,* March 26, 1964.

47. *The Spark,* April 3, 1964.

*Charles F. Andrain: Guinea and Senegal*

1. For an analysis of social strains and the nationalist stress on common symbols of solidarity, see S. N. Eisenstadt, "Sociological Aspects of Political Development in Underdeveloped Countries," in Seymour Martin Lipset and Neil J. Smelser, eds., *Sociology: The Progress of a Decade* (Englewood Cliffs, N.J.: Prentice-Hall, 1961), pp. 608–23; Mary Matossian, "Ideologies of Delayed Industrialization: Some Tensions and Ambiguities," in John H. Kautsky, ed., *Political Change in Underdeveloped Countries* (New York: Wiley, 1962), pp. 252–64.

2. Léopold Sédar Senghor, *Constituent Congress of the PFA: Report on the Principles and Programme of the Party* (Paris: Présence Africaine, 1959), p. 80.

3. Mamadou Dia, closing speech at the Dakar Colloquium, as quoted in *Africa Report,* VIII (May 1963), p. 18.

4. Sékou Touré, *Expérience guinéenne et unité africaine* (2d ed.; Paris: Présence Africaine, 1961), p. 438.

5. Touré, *Texte des interviews accordées aux représentants de la presse* (Conakry: Imprimerie Nationale, 1959), p. 107.

6. Senghor, "Eléments constructifs d'une civilisation d'inspiration négro-africaine," *Présence Africaine,* February–May 1959, p. 278.

7. Touré, *La Planification économique* (Conakry: Imprimerie Nationale, 1960), p. 292.

8. *Ibid.,* p. 104; Touré, *La Guinée et l'émancipation africaine* (Paris: Présence Africaine, 1959), p. 211.

9. Touré, *La Planification économique*, p. 95; also p. 311.

10. Mamadou Dia, *L'Economie africaine: Etudes et problèmes nouveaux* (Paris: Presses Universitaires de France, 1957), p. 72.

11. Dia, *The African Nations and World Solidarity*, trans. Mercer Cook (New York: Praeger, 1961), p. 91.

12. Dia, *Réflexions sur l'économie de l'Afrique noire* (new ed.; Paris: Présence Africaine, 1960), pp. 36–41.

13. Touré, *La Planification économique*, pp. 293–96.

14. Dia, *L'Economie africaine*, p. 80; Senghor, *Constituent Congress of the PFA*, p. 64.

15. Touré, *La Guinée et l'émancipation africaine*, pp. 17, 52.

16. Senghor, "L'Avenir de la France dans l'Outre-Mer," *Politique Etrangère*, XIX (August–October 1954), 421; Senghor, *Nation et voie africaine du socialisme* (Paris: Présence Africaine, 1961), pp. 94, 106.

17. Senghor, *Nation et voie africaine du socialisme*, pp. 116, 124.

18. Senghor, *Constituent Congress of the PFA*, pp. 83–84.

19. Senghor, "Eléments constructifs d'une civilisation d'inspiration négro-africaine," p. 277; Senghor, "Ce que l'homme noir apporte," *L'Homme de Couleur* (Paris: Librairie Plon, 1939), p. 304.

20. Dia, *The African Nations and World Solidarity*, p. 51.

21. Dia, "Proposition pour l'Afrique noire," *Présence Africaine*, April–May 1957, p. 46.

22. Touré, *La Guinée et l'émancipation africaine*, pp. 68, 122.

23. Touré, *La Planification économique*, p. 423.

24. Dia, *L'Economie africaine*, p. 79.

25. Senghor, *Constituent Congress of the PFA*, pp. 46, 64.

26. Touré, *Texte des interviews*, p. 108.

27. Touré, *La Planification économique*, p. 428.

28. Touré, *La Planification économique*, pp. 84–88.

29. Touré, *The Political Action of the Democratic Party of Guinea for the Emancipation of Guinean Youth* (Cairo: Société Orientale de Publicité Presse, 1961), pp. 12–15; *Africa Report*, VIII (May 1963), 26.

30. Touré, *La Planification économique*, p. 81.

31. Quoted in *Africa Report*, VIII (May 1963), 15.

32. Senghor, "African-Style Socialism," Appendix VI, p. 264; Senghor, *Nation et voie africaine du socialisme*, p. 106.

33. Dia, *Réflexions sur l'économie*, p. 70; Dia, "Economie et culture devant les élites africaines," *Présence Africaine*, June–September 1957, p. 64.

34. Dia, *L'Economie africaine*, pp. 36–37.

35. *Ibid.*, p. 37. See also Senghor, *Nation et voie africaine du socialisme*, p. 96.

36. Senghor, *African Socialism*, trans. Mercer Cook (New York: American Society for African Culture, 1959), p. 32.

37. Senghor, *Nation et voie africaine du socialisme*, pp. 123–24.

38. Dia, *Contribution à l'étude du mouvement coopératif en Afrique noire* (Paris: Présence Africaine, 1958), pp. 11–12, 17; Dia, *Réflexions sur l'économie*, p. 27.

39. Senghor, "Ce que l'homme noir apporte," pp. 302, 304.

40. Senghor, "Eléments constructifs d'une civilisation d'inspiration négro-africaine," p. 269.

41. Dia, "Economie et culture devant les élites africaines," pp. 66–67.

42. Touré, *The Political Action for the Emancipation of Guinean Youth*, p. 108.

43. Touré, *La Planification économique*, p. 87.

44. Touré, *Texte des interviews*, pp. 149–51.

45. See L. Gray Cowan, "Guinea," in Gwendolen M. Carter, ed., *African One-Party States* (Ithaca, N.Y.: Cornell University Press, 1962), pp. 217–25.

46. See *West Africa*, April 14, 1962, p. 403.

47. *West Africa*, May 4, 1963, p. 491.

48. Senghor, "L'Esprit de la civilisation ou les lois de la culture négro-africaine," *Présence Africaine*, June–November 1956, p. 51.

49. See Michael Crowder, *Senegal: A Study in French Assimilation Policy* (London: Oxford University Press, 1962), pp. 70–74.

50. *West Africa*, May 4, 1963, p. 491.

51. Touré, *Guinée: Prélude à l'indépendance* (Paris: Présence Africaine, 1958), p. 174.

52. Dia, *Réflexions sur l'économie*, p. 137.

53. Dia, *L'Economie africaine*, pp. 78, 82. For a description of *animation rurale*, see Crowder, *Senegal*, p. 100.

54. Touré, *La Guinée et l'émancipation africaine*, p. 233.

55. Senghor, *Nation et voie africaine du socialisme*, p. 97; Senghor, *Constituent Congress of the PFA*, p. 63.

56. Senghor, "Some Thoughts on Africa: A Continent in Development," *International Affairs*, XXXVIII (April 1962), 191. See also Senghor, "Ce que l'homme noir apporte," pp. 301–2.

57. Dia, *Réflexions sur l'économie*, p. 66.

*Kenneth W. Grundy: Mali*

1. See Kenneth W. Grundy, "Marxism-Leninism and African Underdevelopment: The Mali Approach," *International Journal*, XVII, No. 3 (Summer 1962), 300–304.

2. "Malian Planner," *West Africa*, No. 2271 (December 10, 1960), p. 1389. Since October 1962, Dr. Kouyate has been Minister of Development under Jean-Marie Koné, Minister of State in Charge of Planning and Economic and Financial Affairs.

3. "Ce qu'est le Plan Quinquennal du Mali: Une interview exclusive du Dr. Seydou Badian Kouyate," *Afrique* (Paris), No. 9, February 1962, p. 20.

4. As quoted in *Afrique Nouvelle*, No. 754, January 17, 1962, p. 4.

5. Modibo Keita, "The Foreign Policy of Mali," *International Affairs* (London), XXXVII, No. 4 (October 1961), 436–37.

6. The author is indebted to Professor Vernon Aspaturian for many of the ideas treated in the following paragraphs. See his "Revolutionary Change in Underdeveloped Countries and the Strategy of the Status Quo," in Laurence W. Martin, ed., *Neutralism and Nonalignment* (New York: Praeger, 1962).

7. République du Mali, *Congrès extraordinaire de l'U.S. RDA, 22 Septembre 1960: Le Mali continue* . . . (n.p., Imprimerie du Gouvernement du Mali, n.d.), p. 7. Italics added.

8. *Ibid.,* pp. 36–37.

9. *Ibid.,* pp. 42–43.

10. République du Mali, Ministère du Plan et de l'Economie Rurale, *Rapport sur le Plan Quinquennal de Développement Economique et Social de la République du Mali: 1961–1965* (n.p., n.d.), p. 7. A great deal of information on the Plan can be found in a special issue of the party's weekly organ, *L'Essor,* No. 136, January 15, 1962.

11. U.S. Department of Commerce, *Economic Developments in the Republic of Mali, 1961* (World Trade Information Service, Economic Reports, Part 1, No. 62–58 [Washington, D.C.: G.P.O., June 1962]), p. 3.

12. *New York Times,* January 16, 1961, p. 2.

13. Kouyate interview, *Afrique,* February 1962, p. 22.

14. Ambassade de la République du Mali aux U.S.A., "L'Essor du Mali: A Brief View of the Republic of Mali" (mimeo., Washington, D.C., n.d.), pp. 8–11. The most comprehensive statement of the newly planned rural organization appears in a special edition of *Action Rurale,* issued by the Ministère du Plan et de l'Economie Rurale (n.p., n.d.). See also U.N. Economic and Social Council, Economic Commission for Africa, *The Cooperative Movement in Africa.* E/CN.14/133 (January 15, 1962), pp. 41–42.

15. *Rapport sur le Plan,* p. 27.

16. *Economic Developments in Mali,* p. 4.

17. Approximately $3,330,000 was due Mali; *Africa Report,* March 1963, p. 23.

18. *Economic Developments in Mali,* p. 4.

19. Extracts from President Keita's speech before the National Assembly proposing his new currency measure are reprinted in *L'Essor* (Bamako), No. 160, July 9, 1962, pp. 1, 11–12.

20. U.N. General Assembly, *Official Records,* 15th session, A/PV. 901, October 12, 1960, p. 658.

21. Modibo Keita, "The Foreign Policy of Mali," p. 434.

22. Mali's imports during 1961, for example, indicate that 60.8 per cent came from the franc zone; 15.0 per cent from the Common Market countries, excluding France; 3.0 per cent from the United States; and 13.0 per cent from the Eastern bloc, excluding Communist China (*Economic Developments in Mali,* pp. 5–6). Another set of figures for 1961 indicates an even lower percentage of trade with the Communist countries. See "New Paths for Mali and Guinea," *West Africa,* No. 2366, October 6, 1962, p. 1109.

23. *L'Essor,* No. 164, August 6, 1962, p. 5.


*Fred G. Burke: Tanganyika*

In conducting research for this article, the writer obtained considerable assistance from many Tanganyikans, who were kind enough to cooperate in conducting and responding in interviews. Shortage of space precludes mentioning all of the people who contributed, but I would like to express my deep appreciation to the many Tanganyikans who facilitated this research. The offices of various people given in the text were held at the time of writing (April 1963) and may have changed since that time.

1. Julius K. Nyerere, "Ujamaa: The Basis of African Socialism," *Tanganyika Standard* (Dar es Salaam), July 26, 1962, p. 1. See Appendix II, p. 238.

2. *Daily Nation* (Kenya), January 25, 1963.

3. Opening Address by the Honorable J. S. Kasambala, Pan-African Cooperative Conference, Moshi, Tanganyika, November 14, 1962 (mimeo.).

4. *Ibid.*

5. Issa Athumani, *Mwenge: The Journal of Kivukoni College,* December 1962, p. 18.

6. *Uhuru,* September 7, 1963.

7. *Ibid.*

8. *Mwafrika,* September 7, 1963.

9. "Scramble for Africa," *Spearhead* (Dar es Salaam), I, No. 4 (February 1962), 14–15; "One Party System," *Spearhead,* II, No. 1 (January 1963), 1, 12–23. The latter also appeared as "Democracy and the Party System," in the *Tanganyika Standard,* January 16, 17, 18, 21, 22, 1963. There is some difference of opinion on whether or not TANU did print a limited number of copies of "Ujamaa" in Swahili. If so, none seem to be available at the present time.

10. A TBC official stated that to the best of his knowledge the only special reference to Ujamaa over the radio was in April 1962, when Dr. Nyerere's speech was relayed from Kivukoni College, and possibly on one other occasion in a general speech.

11. G. J. Chembe, "Unity the Requisite of All Sons and Daughters of Africa," *Mwenge: The Journal of Kivukoni College,* December 1962, p. 8.

12. See, for example, Dr. Kwame Nkrumah, "The Basic Needs of African Socialism," *Pan-Africa,* April 19, 1963. Appears as Appendix V, "Some Aspects of Socialism in Africa," in this volume, pp. 259–66.

13. Nyerere, "Ujamaa," Appendix II, p. 242.

14. *Ibid.,* pp. 240–42.

15. *Ibid.,* p. 246.

16. Tom Mboya, "African Socialism," *Transition,* VIII (March 1963), 17. Appendix IV of this volume, p. 251.

17. Mukyiddis Kimario, "Tanganyikan Neutrality," *Mwenge: The Journal of Kivukoni College,* December 1962, p. 32.

18. Robert MacIver, *The Web of Government* (New York: Macmillan, 1947), chap. I.

19. *Daily Nation,* January 25, 1963.

20. Nyerere, "Ujamaa," Appendix II, pp. 242–43.

21. *Proposals of the Tanganyika Government for Land Tenure Reform* (Government Paper No. 2, 1962. Dar es Salaam: Government Printer). The proposals were translated into legislation in April 1963.

# A Selected Bibliography

In preparing the Bibliography, the editors sought to include as many sources as possible dealing with primary statements on the content and meaning of African Socialism as well as criticism and analysis. If African Socialism continues to emerge as a predominating ideology in Africa, we believe it will be useful to future analysts to return to the sources which will have contributed to formation of this ideology.

Abraham, Willie E. *The Mind of Africa*. Chicago: University of Chicago Press, 1962.

*Africa Report*. "Special Issue on African Socialism," VIII (May 1963). Articles by Ruth S. Morgenthau, "African Socialism: Declaration of Ideological Independence"; William H. Friedland, "Four Sociological Trends in African Socialism"; Walter H. Drew, "How Socialist Are African Economies?"; plus a summary of the Dakar Colloquium on African Socialism and excerpts of statements by African leaders.

"African Unity: Ghana-Guinea-Mali Workers Meet," *The Party* (Accra), No. 15, November 1961, pp. 3–4.

Alexandre, Pierre. "Marxism and African Cultural Traditions," *Survey*, No. 43, August 1962, pp. 65–78.

"Au sommaire: Le Socialisme africain," *Documents pour l'Action*, No. 12, November–December 1962. Articles on "Elites africaines à la recherche d'une doctrine," by René Beeckmans; "Le Socialisme africain," by Jean-Marie van Hille; "L'Animation rurale au Sénégal"; "Textes choisis de L. S. Senghor et de Mamadou Dia"; "Un Congrès d'étudiants à Bukavu." Also reviews of L. S. Senghor, *Nation et voie africaine du socialisme*, and Mamadou Dia, *Réflexions sur l'économie de l'Afrique noire*.

Baako, Kofi. "African Socialism," series of articles published in *The Ghanaian Times*, January 24, 25, 26, 28, 29, 1963.

Balandier, Georges. "De la Négritude au socialisme," *Jeune Afrique* (Tunis), No. 111, December 3–9, 1962, pp. 28–29.

Beauchamp, Kay. "African Socialism in Ghana," *Spearhead* (Dar es Salaam), I, No. 4 (February 1962), 21–25.

Beeckmans, René. Article in *Perspectives de Catholicité*, No. 4, pp. 279–95.

Blanchet, André. *L'Itinéraire des partis africains depuis Bamako*. Paris: Librairie Plon, 1958.

Bomani, Paul. "The Cooperative Way," *Spearhead*, I, No. 2 (December 1961), 13–14.

———. "Uhuru na Ujamaa," *Spearhead*, I, No. 6 (April 1962), 1–2.

Brockway, A. Fenner. *African Socialism*. London: Bodley Head, 1963.

Calvez, J. Y. "Socialismes africains," *Revue de l'Action Populaire*, No. 159, June 1962, pp. 657–72.

Césaire, Aimé. *Discours sur le colonialisme*. 2d ed., rev. and augmented. Paris: Présence Africaine, 1955.

———. "Sékou Touré—His Political Thought," *Spearhead*, I, No. 8 (July/August 1962), 9–13.

Chisiza, D. K. *Africa—What Lies Ahead*. New York: African-American Institute Occasional Paper No. 1, 1962.

Colloque de Dakar. A series of mimeographed transcripts of speeches at the Colloque sur les Politiques de Développement et les Voies Africaines du Socialisme, Dakar, Senegal, December 3–8, 1962. Presentations of S. O. Biobaku, Delegate from Nigeria; Akira Eger, Delegate from Israel; Gabriel d'Arboussier, Minister of Justice, Senegal; A. Kithima, Delegate from the Congo (Trade Union Secretary); Mr. Chaker, Delegate from Tunisia; Mr. Otabela, Delegate from the Cameroons; Chabi Mama, Delegate from Dahomey; the Delegate from Ethiopia; Maurice Adoum, Delegate from Chad; and Kiro Hadzi Vasiley, Delegate from Yugoslavia.

Cowan, L. Gray. "Guinea," in Gwendolen M. Carter, ed., *African One-Party States*. Ithaca, N.Y.: Cornell University Press, 1962, pp. 149–236.

Cox, Idris. "Socialist Ideas in Africa. A Review of the Periodical *Spark*," *Narody Azii i Afriki* (Moscow), No. 4, 1963, pp. 179–83.

Dia, Mamadou. *The African Nations and World Solidarity*. Translated from the French by Mercer Cook. New York: Praeger, 1961.

———. *Contribution à l'étude du mouvement coopératif en Afrique noire*. Paris: Présence Africaine, 1958.

———. *L'Economie africaine: Etudes et problèmes nouveaux*. Paris: Presses Universitaires de France, 1957.

———. *Réflexions sur l'économie de l'Afrique noire*. New ed. Paris: Présence Africaine, 1960.

Diop, Cheikh Anta. *L'Afrique noire pré-coloniale*. Paris: Présence Africaine, 1960.

———. *Nations nègres et culture*. Paris: Présence Africaine, 1959.

———. *L'Unité culturelle de l'Afrique noire*. Paris: Présence Africaine, 1959.

Diop, Majhemout. *Contribution à l'étude des problèmes politiques en Afrique noire*. Paris: Présence Africaine, 1958.

Dumont, René. "L'Afrique est mal partie," *Jeune Afrique*, No. 106, October 29–November 4, 1962, p. 22–23.

———. *L'Afrique noire est mal partie*. Paris: Seuil, 1962.

Engstad, Paul. "Socialism in Africa," *Socialist International Information*, XII, No. 41–42 (October 13, 1962), 610–12.

Fanon, Frantz. *L'An V de la révolution algérienne*. Paris: F. Maspero, 1960.

———. "Racisme et culture," *Présence Africaine*, June–November 1956, Nos. 8–10, pp. 122–31.

Favrod, Charles-Henri. *L'Afrique seule*. Paris: Seuil, 1961.

Fischer, Georges. "Quelques aspects de la doctrine politique Guinéenne, *Civilisations*, IX, No. 4 (1959), 457–78.

"Forward to Socialism" (editorial), *The Party*, No. 15, November 1961, p. 1.

Ghana, *First Seven Year Development Plan*. Accra: Office of the Planning Commission, 1962.

Ghana University Lecturer. " 'African Socialism'—A Neo-colonialist Ruse," *The Spark*, April 19, 1963.

Goka, F. K. D. "Budget Statement," presented October 8, 1962, to the Ghana Parliament by the Minister of Finance and Trade, in Supplement, *Ghana Today*, October 10, 1962.

Gorce, Paul-Marie de la. "En écoutant ceux qui font l'Afrique," *Jeune Afrique*, No. 127, March 25–31, 1963, pp. 16–17.

Grundy, Kenneth W. "Marxism-Leninism and African Underdevelopment: The Mali Approach," *International Journal*, XVII, No. 3 (Summer 1962), 300–304.

———. "Nkrumah's Theory of Underdevelopment: An Analysis of Recurrent Themes," *World Politics*, XV, No. 3 (April 1963), 438–54.

Halpern, Manfred. *The Politics of Social Change in the Middle East and North Africa*. Princeton, N.J.: Princeton University Press, 1963.

Hinden, Rita. *Principles of Socialism, Africa and Asia*. London: Fabian Commonwealth Bureau, 1961.

"L'Investissement humain dans le développement socialiste." Dakar: Commissariat Général au Plan, 1962.

Kanoute, Pierre. "Le Socialisme africain: Expression de l'humanisme africain," *Afrique Nouvelle* (Dakar), November 30–December 6, 1962.

Kerr, Malcolm. "The Emergence of a Socialist Ideology in Egypt," *Middle East Journal*, XVI, No. 2 (Spring 1962), 127–44.

Kyle, Keith. "This Strange Thing Called African Socialism," *The Reporter*, June 6, 1963, pp. 27–29.

Legum, Colin. *Pan-Africanism—A Short Political Guide*. New York: Praeger, 1962.

Lombard, J. "Le collectivisme africain," *Présence Africaine,* June–July 1959, pp. 22–51.

Ly, Abdoulaye. *La Campagnie du Sénégal.* Paris: Présence Africaine, 1958.

──────. *Les Masses africaines et l'actuelle condition humaine.* Paris: Présence Africaine, 1956.

Marcus, Edward, and Mildred R. Marcus. *Investment and Development Possibilities in Tropical Africa.* New York: Brookman Associates, 1960.

Mende, Tibor. "Si les Africains veulent devenir des partenaires . . ." (Le Colloque de Dakar), *Jeune Afrique,* No. 113, December 1962, pp. 17–23.

Milon, René. *Marxisme, communisme, et socialisme africain.* Paris: Imprimerie Edimpra, 1961.

"Une Nation en voie de se faire: La République de Guinée," *Revue de l'Action Populaire,* No. 129, June 1959, pp. 683–705.

Ng'ang'a, Wanguhu. "Which Way Ahead? The African Road to Socialism," *Pan Africa* (Nairobi), July 26, 1963, pp. 11–12.

Nkrumah, Kwame. "The Basic Needs of African Socialism," *Pan Africa,* April 19, 1963, pp. 13–14.

──────. *Building a Socialist State.* Accra: Government Printer, 1961.

──────. *Consciencism.* London: Heinemann, 1964.

──────. *Dawn Broadcast.* Accra: Government Printer, n.d.

──────. *The Autobiography of Kwame Nkrumah.* New York: Nelson, 1957.

──────. *I Speak of Freedom. A Statement of African Ideology.* New York: Praeger, 1961.

──────. "Sessional Address," delivered to National Assembly, October 2, 1962, in Supplement, *Ghana Today,* October 10, 1962.

Nyerere, Julius K. "Address on the Occasion of Makerere College Degree Ceremony," Kampala, April 9, 1962. Typescript. Dar es Salaam: Tanganyika, Director of Information Services.

──────. "Africa's Place in the World," in *Symposium on Africa.* Wellesley, Mass.: Wellesley College, 1960.

──────. "Communitarian Socialism" (short version of "Ujamaa"), *Liberation,* Summer 1962, pp. 12–13.

──────. "One Party Government," contribution to a seminar on "The Concept of Democracy in Africa," *Spearhead,* I, No. 1 (November 1961), 7–9.

──────. "One Party System," *Spearhead,* II, No. 1 (January 1963), 1, 12–23.

──────. "Scramble for Africa," *Spearhead,* I, No. 4 (February 1962), 14–15.

———. "The Task Ahead of Our African Trade Unions," *Labour* (Ghana TUC), June 1961, pp. 12–13, 28–29.

———. "Will Democracy Work in Africa?" *Africa Special Report,* February 1960, p. 4.

Ouzegane, Amar. "Le Marxisme et l'Islam," *Jeune Afrique,* No. 100, September 17–23, 1962, pp. 26–27.

Padmore, George. *Pan-Africanism or Communism? The Coming Struggle for Africa.* London: Dobson, 1956.

Panikkar, Kavalam Madhusudan. *Revolution in Africa.* London: Asia Publishing House, 1961.

Potekhin, I. *Afrika smotrit v budushchee.* Moscow: Oriental Languages Publishing House, 1960. Translated as I. Potechin, *Afrika blickt in die Zukunft* (Berlin: Verlag Tribune, 1961), and I. Potekhine, *L'Afrique regarde vers l'avenir* (Moscow, 1962).

———. "On African Socialism," *International Affairs* (Moscow), January 1963.

Program of the Convention People's Party, *For Work and Happiness.* Accra, 1962, p. 7.

Rabemananjara, Jacques. *Nationalisme et problèmes malgaches.* Paris: Présence Africaine, 1959.

Sago, Julius. "The Ideological Battle in Africa," *The Spark,* April 19, 1963.

Schachter, Ruth. "Single-Party Systems in West Africa," *American Political Science Review,* LV (1961), 294–307.

Seminar. "The Concept of Democracy in Africa," *Spearhead,* I, No. 1 (November 1961), 9–18. Includes Julius K. Nyerere, "One-Party Government"; Masinde Muliro, "Free Association"; Sékou Touré, "The Party and Democracy"; D. F. Heath, "Democratic Developments"; and N. J. J. Olivier, "Separate Development."

Senghor, Léopold Sédar. *African Socialism.* Translated and edited by Mercer Cook. New York: American Society for African Culture, 1959. (Abridged version of one of two essays in *Nation et voie.*)

———. "Eléments constructifs d'une civilisation d'inspiration négro-africaine, *Présence Africaine,* February–May 1959, pp. 249–79.

———. *Nation et voie africaine du socialisme.* Paris: Présence Africaine, 1961.

———. "Negritude and African Socialism," in Kenneth Kirkwood, ed., *African Affairs: Number Two.* St. Antony's Papers, No. 15. London: Chatto & Windus, 1963, pp. 9–22.

———. *Pierre Teilhard de Chardin et la politique africaine.* Paris: Seuil, 1960.

———. "Théorie et pratique du socialisme sénégalais," texte présenté au Seminar des Cadres Politiques, November–December 1962.

————. "La Voie sénégalaise," *Jeune Afrique*, No. 109, November 19–25, 1962, 26–27.

————. Article in *Afrique Action* (Tunisia), January 30, 1961.

————. Article in *Revue de Politique Internationale* (Yugoslavia), No. 258, January 5, 1961.

Serrilien, Sebasoni. Review of L. S. Senghor, *Pierre Teilhard de Chardin et la politique africaine,* in *Documents pour l'Action,* September–October 1962, pp. 314–17.

Shepherd, G. W., Jr. "The Price of Progress," *Africa Today,* December 1962.

Teilhard de Chardin, Pierre. *Le Phénomène humain.* Paris: Editions du Seuil, 1955. Translated by Bernard Wall, *The Phenomenon of Man.* New York: Harper, 1959.

Tevoedjre, Albert. *L'Afrique révoltée.* Paris: Présence Africaine, 1958.

Thomas, L. "Le Socialisme selon L. S. Senghor et l'âme africaine." Unpublished article (mimeo.) circulated at the Dakar Colloquium.

Touré, Sékou. *L'Action du Parti Démocratique de Guinée et lutte pour l'émancipation africaine.* Paris: Editions Présence Africaine, 1959.

————. "African Elite and the People's Struggle," *Spearhead,* I, No. 8 (July/August 1962), 13–17.

————. "Africa's Future and the World," *Foreign Affairs,* October 1962, pp. 1–12.

————. *Le Cinquième Congrès National du Parti Démocratique de Guinée.* Conakry: Republic de Guinée, 1959.

————. *Expérience guinéenne et unité africaine,* 2d ed. Paris: Présence Africaine, 1961.

————. "Road to Economic Unity," *Spearhead,* I, No. 8 (July/August 1962), 19–24.

————. "Speech of March 3, 1961" (mimeo.). Conakry: Chambre Economique de Guinée, Bulletin Mensual, No. 3, March 1961.

————. *Texte des interviews accordées aux représentants de la presse.* Conakry: République de Guinée, 1959.

————. *Toward Full Reafricanization.* Paris: Présence Africaine, 1959.

"Trade Unions and Political Parties," *Petro* (journal of the International Federation of Petroleum Workers), March 1962, pp. 8–10.

Wallerstein, Immanuel. "The Political Ideology of the PDG," *Présence Africaine,* XII (First Quarter, 1962), 30–41.

"What Is Socialism?" *Drum,* September 1962.

# Index

*Superscript numbers are used to indicate quotations by persons identified in the Notes but not in the text. Thus "Biobaku, Dr., 120³⁸" means that the quotation on p. 120 ending with ³⁸ is from Dr. Biobaku.*